D0848825

DIVINE COMMANDS AND
MORALITY

Also published in this series

The Philosophy of Law, edited by Ronald M. Dworkin
Moral Concepts, edited by Joel Feinberg
Theories of Ethics, edited by Philippa Foot
The Philosophy of History, edited by Patrick Gardiner
Knowledge and Belief, edited by A. Philips Griffiths
Philosophy and Economic Theory, edited by Frank Hahn and Martin
    Hollis
Reference and Modality, edited by Leonard Linsky
The Philosophy of Religion, edited by Basil Mitchell
The Philosophy of Science, edited by P. H. Nidditch
Aesthetics, edited by Harold Osborne
The Theory of Meaning, edited by G. H. R. Parkinson
The Philosophy of Education, edited by R. S. Peters
Political Philosophy, edited by Anthony Quinton
Practical Reasoning, edited by Joseph Raz
The Philosophy of Social Explanation, edited by Alan Ryan
The Philosophy of Language, edited by J. R. Searle
Semantic Syntax, edited by Pieter A. M. Seuren
Causation and Conditionals, edited by Ernest Sosa
Philosophical Logic, edited by P. F. Strawson
The Justification of Induction, edited by Richard Swinburne
Locke on Human Understanding, edited by I. C. Tipton
The Philosophy of Perception, edited by G. J. Warnock
The Philosophy of Action, edited by Alan R. White

Other volumes are in preparation

DIVINE COMMANDS AND MORALITY

Edited by
PAUL HELM

OXFORD UNIVERSITY PRESS
1981

Oxford University Press, Walton Street, Oxford OX2 6DP

OXFORD LONDON GLASGOW
NEW YORK TORONTO MELBOURNE WELLINGTON
KUALA LUMPUR SINGAPORE HONG KONG TOKYO
DELHI BOMBAY CALCUTTA MADRAS KARACHI
NAIROBI DAR ES SALAAM CAPE TOWN

Published in the United States by Oxford University Press, New York

British Library Cataloguing in Publication Data

Divine commands and morality. — (Oxford readings
in philosophy).
1. Religion and ethics — Addresses, essays, lectures
I. Helm, Paul   II. Series
200'.8   BJ47   80-41066

ISBN 0-19-875049-8

*Set in IBM Press Roman by Graphic Services, Oxford
Printed in Great Britain by
Butler & Tanner Ltd. Frome and London*

CONTENTS

INTRODUCTION

THE connections between morality and religion are numerous, close, and controversial. For example it has been claimed that the will of God can be known through conscience, that justice requires that sin can be pardoned only through an atonement, that one goal of religious belief and worship is the moral renovation of the individual, and even that the existence of God can be established by reference to the requirements of morality. Some of these connections, like alleged moral proofs of God's existence, imply that religion is logically subordinate to morality. The claim that only religious believers are thrifty, would on the other hand amount to the claim that religion is necessary for the fostering of acceptable social behaviour, and imply a reverse subordination of morality to religion of a weaker, purely factual kind.

If it turned out that morality logically required religion (in the conventional sense of 'religion' which includes belief in the existence of God) then it is all up with morality unless would-be moral agents are also believers. For what this would mean is that the moral judgement 'One ought not to steal' could not *be* a moral judgement unless the one uttering it was a religious believer. But perhaps by 'morality depends upon religion' is meant the idea that unless God exists there are no moral values, 'everything is permitted'. Or that only religion affords properly moral motives for action, that only religious people are capable of acting unselfishly or for the glory of God. As Professor Frankena shows, in the paper with which the selection begins, in order to be philosophically interesting the claim that morality is dependent upon religion must mean logically dependent and by 'religion' must be meant something into which no ethical component has been smuggled. Even so understood, the claim that morality is logically dependent upon religion harbours many different ideas. Is the claimed logical relationship that of logical necessity or sufficiency? Are all moral principles supposedly dependent upon religion, or only some? Is the claim really a camouflaged version of the view that morality ought to be dependent upon religion? Or that only religious people are moral, or that all religious people are moral? It is the great merit of Professor Frankena's paper that it provides a careful exploration of many of the most important of these alleged connections. But even if Frankena is correct and it is false that all morality depends logically upon religion it by no means follows that no morality does. It may be that to attempt to derive moral conclusions from theological premisses is to try to deduce evaluative conclusions from purely factual premisses, and thus to commit the naturalistic fallacy. Or it may be that attempts to define 'ought' in terms of the will of God founder on the shoals of vacuity. But it does not follow from either of these things that God's *commands*, together with additional premisses acceptable to a theist, would carry no moral implications for a theist. And were it the case that we all ought to believe in the existence of God, they ought to carry moral implications for all of us.

To suppose, however, that God does issue commands and that these commands are to form the basis of the believer's morality raises difficulties of its own, three in particular. One, on the side of man, has to do with the possibility that such an idea infringes human autonomy. The second, on the side of God, has to do with the relationship of morality to the power and character of God. A third has to do with reasons for the moral relevance of God's commands.

I

Before we glance at each of these in turn it is important to recognize that although the relation of morality to God's commands has sparked off a good deal of discussion recently among contemporary professional philosophers the issue is almost as old as philosophy itself. In the opinion of many philosophers, when in the *Euthyphro* Plato asked the question 'whether the pious or holy is beloved by the gods' he was in effect raising one crucial difficulty for any Divine Command Theory of ethics. (If he was, he was also raising a difficulty for the relation of morality to any authority whatsoever.) For if the moral is approved or commanded by God because it is moral this appears to make God depend upon morality and so to infringe his sovereignty. If on the other hand God's command is sufficient for the morality of what is commanded then anything that God were to command would be *ipso facto* good. If 'God's command is good' is analytic then anything that God commands will be good. If it is synthetic then it is contingent and if it is true then it depends for its truth upon God's command being dependent upon some prior standard of goodness.

But in fact matters have turned out to be a little more complicated than having the stark choice of being impaled on one or other of the horns of a dilemma. Among those who have favoured the view that a command is morally good because God commands it at least two views can be discerned. What can be labelled an Ockhamist Divine Command Theory holds that morality is founded upon a free divine choice. If God commands fornication then fornication is obligatory, and it is within God's power to do so. He could establish another moral order than the one he has in fact established and he could at any time order what he has actually forbidden. From this position Ockham could consistently only regard ethics as a matter of special divine revelation in Scripture or elsewhere, and not a matter of natural law discerned through reason or conscience. This striking view provides him with a quick answer to the charge that in decreeing the moral evils of the world God is the author of sin. How could that be, since as Creator God could do no evil whateever he did, whereas the creature commits evil every time he disobeys the command of his sovereign creator.[1] For Ockham, then, 'God's command is good' is straightforwardly analytic.

None of the extracts reprinted here adopt this extreme view. Yet it is interesting that in his book *Divine Commands and Moral Requirements* Professor Quinn develops a Divine Command Theory against a theological background that, like Ockham's, makes no assumptions about God's actual moral character but rather assumes that God is free to choose anything he cares to command.[2] And something like the distinction between divine *potentia absoluta* and *potentia normata* is behind Professor Pike's conclusion (in the paper reprinted below) that the individual 'who occupies the position or has the value-status marked by the term "God"' cannot sin, not because it is logically impossible for him to sin but because he steadfastly refuses to do so even though he has the requisite ability to do so. That is, on Pike's view there are possible worlds in which God exists in which he commands what would be at variance with what he has commanded in the actual world, and therefore sinful by the standards that obtain in the actual world. Pike's reasons for taking this view are that thereby one ascribes strength, not limitation, to God and makes him a proper object of praise. But it is at least possible, on this view, that God's strength of character will give out.

Such a thought would have been abhorrent to Augustine, because unacceptably anthropomorphic. For him God is by definition supremely good; indeed, for Augustine God does not merely essentially exemplify

---

[1] *Philosophy in the Middle Ages*, ed. A. Hyman and J. J. Walsh (1973), p. 651. The parallel question of whether or not the atonement of Christ is absolutely required by divine justice for the pardon of sin has also been debated by Christian theologians, e.g. Anselm, *Cur Deus Homo?*. Compare the controversy between Willian Twisse and John Owen to which Owen's *A Dissertation on Divine Justice* (1653) is a contribution.

[2] *Divine Commands and Moral Requirements* (1978), p. 31.

supreme goodness, his goodness is identical with supreme goodness. Thus the question of whether or not God could will evil could not arise. There is no possible world in which God exists in which he commands what fails to be supremely good and hence no possible world in which he exists in which his commands are inconsistent with his commands in this, the actual world. God could not have commanded anything that contradicted what he had in fact commanded.[3] If it is asked what is the goodness that is exemplified essentially in God the answer must be, the goodness instanced in the commands he has in fact issued. Under Augustine's scheme the moral law 'Thou shalt not kill' has exceptions, for example killing in combat in a just war, and particular divine commands to individuals, such as God's command to Abraham to kill Isaac. Presumably one necessary condition for recognizing such exceptions is that there are good non-moral grounds for believing God to have issued the law or command in question, such as the occurrence of a revelation. Unfortunately there does not appear to be a good contemporary presentation of the Augustinian position.

How the *Euthyphro* dilemma is to be faced has on occasion been thought to depend upon what sort of thing is commanded by God. Duns Scotus appears to have held that while God could not command any differently from what is to be found in the natural law, since the natural law is necessarily true, yet God could 'grant dispensations' from some of the actions he has commanded. In particular, although God could not override the first group of the Ten Commandments since these commands belong strictly to the law of nature and are intrinsically necessary, he could override the commands of the second group just as he overrode the commandments he made to the nation of Israel at the coming of Christ.[4] This idea of a two-tier system, with a set of necessary natural laws and a set of contingent exemplifications of them, is akin to the position taken up by Professor Swinburne in 'Duty and the Will of God', though there are important differences between the positions.

There have been those who have held that the obligatoriness of a divine command depends on who is commanded. Aquinas appears to have held the view that, given that God has created men with the powers and nature that he has, it is logically impossible for him consistently with his supremely good nature to have commanded a different morality from

---

[3] Augustine's position is to be found, for example, in *The City of God*, Book I, ch. 20. Similar views can be found expressed by Anselm (*Monologion*, ch. 80), Bradwardine (*De Causa Dei*, i. 21), and Calvin, who says 'We do not advocate the fiction of "absolute might"; because this is profane it ought rightly to be hateful to us' (*Institutes of the Christian Religion*, III. xxiii. 2).

[4] See the selection from Duns Scotus reprinted in Hyman and Walsh, op. cit., pp. 601–4.

that which he has in fact commanded and the morality he has in fact commanded is exceptionless.[5] This seems to leave open the idea of a possible world in which there are intelligent creatures whose nature is such that it would be right for God to command fornication or theft, or at least to regard such actions as permissible. Or is Aquinas's position that in every possible world in which there is private property and marriage God could not fail to forbid theft and fornication? It would not follow from this position that special revelation is unnecessary to reveal God's command, that it can simply be 'read off' from an understanding of human nature, for revelation might be necessary to disclose to man his true nature.

The other horn of the dilemma has also been firmly gripped by those who have taken a broadly Platonist position in morality. To take one example, Ralph Cudworth's *Treatise Concerning Eternal and Immutable Morality* (1731) is an attack on the Divine Command Theory in general and on Thomas Hobbes in particular. That God could not command what was immoral has in Cudworth's view less to do with God than it has to do with the nature of morality. Just as God could not construct a four-sided triangle so he could not change the immutable nature of morality. Even in the case of morally indifferent matters it is not God's command that makes them moral but the moral necessity of keeping faith and covenants. This horn has also been grasped by those who, like Immanuel Kant, have taken up an essentially human command theory of morality, regarding any identification of morality with the will of God as an infringement of human autonomy. This broadly Kantian line of argument, that a Divine Command Theory of ethics is heteronomous, has been pervasively thought to constitute a crucial difficulty for that theory.

II

When certain views are alleged to infringe human autonomy what exactly is meant? One or more of at least the following four things. First, that they infringe the proper, adult decision-making process in accordance with which people make up their minds in the light of what seems to them to be a cogent argument, or the best evidence available, or some combination of the two. Autonomy is here being contrasted with intellectual coercion. Belief in the command of God as the source of moral authority has been alleged to require at least the suspension of such rational processes. Second, a person acts autonomously when he acts in

[5] Aquinas, *Summa Theologiae*, Ia, IIae, 91, 93, 94, 100 art. 8 resp. For a defence of Aquinas see Hugo Meynell, 'The Euthyphro Dilemma' *Proceedings of the Aristotelian Society*, Supplementary volume, 1972.

a purely moral, i.e. altruistic or at least non-self-centred, way. Here 'autonomy' is used in a sense nearer to that of Kant's according to which it is contrasted with heteronomy; morality is contrasted with prudence. Third, by autonomy can be meant conscientiousness, approximating to what existentialists have called 'authenticity'. The autonomous individual holds himself responsible for what he does, not abdicating his responsibility in favour of some superior authority, for in his eyes there are no superior authorities. The non-autonomous individual does what he does simply because he is under orders or is acting in a purely habitual or routine way. Fourth, 'autonomous' can refer to motives. The autonomous agent is one who does things from certain appropriate motives, namely for their own sake and not in subjection to some ulterior end such as pleasure or the avoidance of pain or fear. These senses, though clearly connected and all arising out of the rather complex Kantian notion of autonomy, can be clearly distinguished.

Someone who is faced with the charge that his position is unacceptable because it infringes human autonomy has, in general, two moves open to him. He can argue that the idea that human beings are or ought to be regarded as morally autonomous rests upon too sanguine a view of human moral competence. This is the position taken by J. R. Lucas in a reply to the charge of Professor P. H. Nowell-Smith that religious morality is infantile.[6] The other move is to argue that, to the extent that one or all of the various senses of 'autonomy' make sense, a Divine Command Theory of ethics is not incompatible with them.

Professor Rachels's article presents the objection from human autonomy in a pointed way by means of a moral *dis*proof of God's existence, arguing that though it is a necessary truth that if God exists he is worthy of worship, no being ever could be worthy of worship. Even if Rachels's disproof of God's existence is unsound, as Quinn claims, he has nevertheless succeeded in raising in an acute way the problem that to judge as an autonomous moral agent that something is, or is not, morally good and so is, or is not, a command of God invokes a moral criterion superior to God and so causes the collapse of the Divine Command Theory. Quinn accepts that if one is autonomous (in the first sense discussed) he will test the putative commands of God for their authenticity (and he indicates that there is a strong and complex religious tradition of 'trying the spirits'). Accepting God's commands does not require that the agent suspends his critical faculties. What it does require is that if and when something is accepted as an authentic command of God it ought to be obeyed *ipso facto* if one is a divine command theorist. And when moral dilemmas arise, as they do for the divine command theorist (classically in the biblical story of the divine command to Abraham to offer up Isaac), it is quite compatible with a Divine Command Theory that a person should agonize over the decision of what is the right thing to do, i.e. what in these circumstances represents the authentic command of God. For Quinn the problem is about how the command of God can be known, not about whether, if it is known, it is morally acceptable. All ethical positions have such a problem, and thus its existence is no more an argument against a Divine Command Theory than any other theory of ethics that requires a knowledge of the facts of the case. Quinn seems to be assuming that moral judgements do not enter into an investigation of whether or not a particular moral authority has given a command or not, but this does not seem plausible. One of the things that might have concerned Abraham (though there is no evidence that it did) in deciding on the authenticity of the command was whether or not it accorded with the moral character of God. Quinn may be correct in saying that this is a problem that all moral views share but what this would show is that the idea of 'pure autonomy' is a myth, not that the problem is epistemic and *therefore* not moral. But, supposing Quinn is correct, one major hurdle to establishing a Divine Command Theory has been cleared.

In developing what is one of the most fully worked-out Divine Command Theories of ethics in recent years Professor Adams eschews the idea that to say that an action is forbidden *means* that it is wrong. Instead it means 'wrong' as that word is used in Judaeo-Christian discourse. But does this mean that when an atheist says that stealing is wrong he means something different than when a theist says this? And does this mean that theistic ethics is a *different subject* from atheistic ethics? In the second contribution from Adams reprinted here he makes the suggestion that the difference between the two is like the difference between a child's and a chemist's understanding of the term 'water'.

Adams's theory is modified in a second way. His theory allows that it is logically possible that, say, God should command cruelty for its own sake. The acceptance of the divine command is conditional upon having certain ethical beliefs about God's character, chiefly the belief that he loves human beings. Should these beliefs turn out to be false and God really commands cruelty for its own sake then according to Adams the concept of what was ethically wrong would 'break down' since its criterion, the command of a divine being who is benevolent, would be untrue while at the same time the customary use of 'wrong' as meaning 'commanded by God' would prevail.

To say that this theory is modified is to say that an Ockham-type Divine Command Theory according to which God might command absolutely anything is modified. But Professor Adams is not moving to a fully Augustinian position according to which supreme moral goodness is part of the nature of God since he is allowing the possibility that God might really command cruelty for its own sake. What would cause the breakdown, according to Adams, would be the falsifying of his beliefs about the goodness of God.

It might be useful to dwell for a moment on the contrast between this position and that of Augustine. Since for Augustine God is essentially good it follows that God cannot command evil. Faced with a putative evil command, one of two things is the case: either this is not a command of God or there are reasons (unknown to us) that provide a moral justification or vindication of this command of God. If one supposes that the putative command is cruelty for its own sake then there is no conceivable justification for this and the putative command would be rejected as not authentically divine. If on the other hand the putative command was to inflict pain on another person then it *may be* the case (perhaps more would have to be known before it could be concluded that it *was* the case) that there are reasons for this that are consistent with the divine character. It may be that certain kinds of Divine Command Theory (as certain kinds of theodicy) presuppose consequentialism, an ethic which makes the rightness or wrongness of an action depend solely on the consequences which that action has, or presuppose at least a consequentialist divine ethic along with a human ethic of law or principle.[7] And this in turn would seem to require some version of the distinction between the secret and the revealed will of God. Part of the revealed will of God would consist of commands to be obeyed no matter what the consequences, while the secret will of God would consist of the outcome known to God but unknown or unknowable to human beings. By contrast both a full-blown Ockham-type Divine Command Theory and the view that what was right and wrong was expressible in necessary truths knowable independently of any divine command would have no need for such a distinction because in neither case would a divine command need any further vindication or justification, though a related distinction, between what God commanded or endorsed and what he actually decreed to come to pass, or allowed to come to pass, would still be necessary.

To surrender the unconditional character of one's acceptance of

[7] But see C. Dore, 'God, "Soul-making" and apparently useless suffering', *American Philosophical Quarterly*, 1970, and R. M. Adams, 'Must God Create the Best?', *Philosophical Review*, 1972.

divine commands as providing the standard of ethical rightness and wrongness is an important modification of an Ockham-type theory. Taken with the other modifications that Adams proposes, the question naturally arises as to whether what is left is recognizable as a Divine Command Theory. In summary, the modified position is something like the following: the divine command is not necessary for an action's being either right or wrong nor is it sufficient to cover all ethical situations. The believer values some things independently of the will of God and has favourable and unfavourable attitudes to things independently of the will of God, though these values and attitudes do not amount to judgements of right or wrong. On Adams's theory, for the believer who is a divine command theorist the divine command is a sufficient condition of the rightness of certain ethical principles. At one point (000) Adams comes close to regarding God's will as having a purely functional or pragmatic justification in religious ethics when he says that beliefs about what God does in fact will act as a fuse for one's motives in devotion to God.

It is of less interest to decide if this is a recognizable Divine Command Theory than to determine whether or not it is consistent as it stands. Among several other criticisms of Adams, Robert Young asks whether it is possible, consistent with a Divine Command Theory, to suppose that a believer has a set of values that are independent of the will of God. Where do these values come from, and what is their justification?

The other horn of the *Euthyphro* dilemma, that to suppose that God commands something because it is good is to infringe God's sovereignty, is an obscure claim, to say the least. It makes sense to speak of the infringement of God's sovereignty in circumstances where, say, God is unable to do what he wants to do. But that sort of question does not arise here. In his paper 'Duty and the Will of God' Professor Swinburne attempts some elucidation of this idea by drawing (though not in explicit terms) on what might be called the Platonist stream in ethics. He recognizes moral truths and distinguishes between moral truths that are necessary and those that are contingent. Using this distinction he holds that God's conformity to necessary moral truths would be no infringement of his dignity or power since, being necessary, they could not be otherwise and God could not fail to adhere to them any more than he could fail to assent to the proposition that the internal angles of a plane triangle add up to 180 degrees. But as far as contingent moral truths are concerned, since these depend upon the way the world happens to be, God could have ordained the world differently and thus ordained that a different set of contingent moral truths holds.

By a contingent moral truth Swinburne means the application of a necessary moral truth to a particular set of circumstances. If the necessary moral truth is 'One ought never to steal' then a corresponding contingent moral truth would be 'I ought not to steal Smith's watch' and another would be 'Smith ought not to steal my pen'. These are contingent in the sense that Smith's existence, my existence, the fact that Smith has a watch and I have a pen are all contingent circumstances.

If we suppose that the essence of the *Euthyphro* dilemma can be expressed as 'Is something good because God commands it, or does God command it because it is good?' then Swinburne's apparently neat solution avoids rather than solves the dilemma by changing its terms. For now the idea of a *command* of God has all but disappeared from the solution. A command to do a certain action presupposes the idea of a command not to do some alternative action. But according to Swinburne the action is either a necessary moral truth or the application of that necessary moral truth in a contingent set of circumstances. It is either 'Debts ought to be paid' or 'I ought to pay Smith what I owe him'. If I ask why it is that I ought to pay Smith, the answer is in terms of a necessary truth. God may, as Swinburne emphasizes, *ordain* my existence, Smith's existence and my indebtedness to Smith, but he does not command this. Yet the idea of a divine command has not totally disappeared, for Swinburne does say that God's command could make an action obligatory which would not otherwise be, and that God's command always strengthens the obligatoriness of an action. Presumably the action which God's command makes obligatory are actions which would otherwise be morally indifferent, for God could not override what is already obligatory.

But if Swinburne is correct about his main contention then the objection that God's commanding something because it is good makes God's goodness depend upon an independent moral principle, and so infringes his sovereignty, is empty. God's acceptance of necessary truths, moral or other, could be no infringement of his power.

As noted earlier, Swinburne's distinction is reminiscent of that drawn by Duns Scotus between necessary moral truths, obligatory under all circumstances, and certain divine commandments with respect to which God is able to grant dispensations.

So according to Swinburne the commands of God are, for the most part, exemplifications of necessary moral truths. For every necessary truth there are a large, perhaps infinite, number of possible exemplifications, some of which God actually ordains. But what of the commands of God that are not exemplifications of necessary moral truths but which constitute contingent moral truths? What about, say, the putative divine command that no Israelite ought to seethe a kid in its mother's milk

(Deuteronomy 14:21)? What would make this a moral truth is the divine command. So Swinburne's view emerges as something of a hybrid: a core of necessary moral truths, which the command of God exemplifies, and a fringe of contingent moral truths for which the divine command is necessary and sufficient.

III

At the end of his paper Swinburne discusses the last of the three main questions regarding the relation between morality and the will of God, namely, in virtue of what feature or features of God are his commands obligatory? Earlier, various strands in the notion of autonomy were mentioned and here the second strand is relevant. On this view a person acts autonomously only if he acts out of a purely moral, as opposed to a merely prudential motive. It was with this sort of point in mind that Kant condemned fear of divine punishment as being a heteronomous motive and thus immoral or at best amoral. But, as Bernard Williams argues in 'God, Morality and Prudence', it may be that the moral and the prudential are not exclusive, provided that we distinguish between what we might call competitive self-regarding and non-competitive self-regarding motives. A competitively self-regarding policy is one that pursues selfish aims at the expense of others while a non-competitive self-regarding policy does not. This being so there are clearly numerous non-self-regarding reasons why a person might obey the commands of God. Swinburne instances the obligation to please one's benefactors, and Adams instances gratitude. One crucial question here is: are the qualification or powers that entitle God to claim obedience *moral* qualifications?

Professor Brody argues that the basis of the obligation to recognize God's commands as our duties lies in the fact that he is our sole Creator and hence our owner. Since we are his property we have certain obligations to him, in particular we are obliged to do what he wants us to do.[8] Brody thinks that the idea of God having rights in virtue of his being the Creator can be made plausible by the idea of property rights and that the idea that we and everything else are God's property might entitle God to place restrictions on how we are to treat people and things, ourselves included, but also provide a reason against vegetarianism. Brody may seem to have the support of the Apostle Paul when he said, 'Who art thou that repliest against God? Shall the thing formed say to him that formed it, Why hast thou made me thus?' (Romans 9 :20.) Paul is certainly here appealing to the absolute rights of the owner or Creator.

---

[8] Augustine made the same point in terms of God's rights: as Creator God is entitled to command anyone to take the lives of any of his creatures (*City of God*, i. 25).

Yet Paul is dealing with a rather different question, not of God's right to command and permit in virtue of his Creatorship, but of his right to dispose of his property as he sees fit.

But do the analogies between God and ourselves and the owner and his property stand up? Robert Young does not think so. There may be situations in which a steward is justified in using his master's property for a purpose that is not decreed by his master. But then, the analogy is only an analogy. Yet Brody could hardly take refuge in analogies, for presumably the point of drawing the analogy in the first place is to make the point that theological facts have moral implications (just as facts about families do).

In 'God and Ought' Professor Phillips explores the relation between human and divine fatherhood, in particular the idea that the moral role of fatherhood depends upon what the father *is* and not upon what he does, and that to ask whether 'He is my father' is a factual or an evaluative expression, blurs rather than clarifies the concept. For Phillips the point about morality and religion is that they are separate: religious duty is not moral duty, and to ask 'Is God's will good?' is to signal the invasion of religion by morality. There are points of connection, yet the meaning of religious discourse is to be found within religion.

Most of the papers and articles collected here are contributions to the question of whether, for the theist or religious believer, morality is to be understood solely or at all in terms of the command of God. The problem is a problem that only makes sense given certain premises about God's existence, his moral character, a person's relationship to him, and the like. By contrast Professor Geach's paper is an argument in natural theology, an attempt to show that certain constituents of morality are unjustifiable apart from belief in a God with power to punish. Geach interprets the *Euthyphro* dilemma as a piece of sophistry intended to befuddle the one for whom God's command was morally sufficient.

Geach allows that a knowledge of the difference between right and wrong does not depend upon revelation, and even that acceptance of that revelation depends upon the view that lying is an evil, since otherwise any alleged revelation is incredible. But he claims that the knowledge of God's will is necessary in order consistently to see that we must not do evil that good may come. To someone who says 'Why shouldn't I commit adultery?' the answer is not to invoke a Kant-inspired Sense of Duty but to show that the matters that are thought to be generally undesirable, such as adultery, are in fact absolutely forbidden. To know that adultery is generally undesirable is to know that God absolutely forbids it, according to Geach. Even though this might not be recognized by the person in question, nevertheless by his reason alone he might establish this. And the question 'Why should I obey God's law?' is insane because it is insane to pit oneself against Supreme Power. But what of a situation in which someone is faced with a conflict of divine prohibitions? Geach assures us not that such conflicts will never arise but that by God's providence they will not arise where such a conflict would be no fault of the person concerned.

Two matters at least need to be questioned about this argument. If the question is, What will effectively restrain men from making exceptions in their own cases?, then that can surely only be answered empirically, just as it could only be discovered empirically what, if anything, has been thought by everyone at all times to be generally undesirable. Why should it be thought, apparently *a priori*, that only the fear of God's power to punish could provide such effective restraint? (The fear of God may be the only proper or acceptable motive for action, but that is a rather different question.) And why should it be thought that the only candidates for divine commands are absolute or exception-less moral principles? Many have thought that they owe a duty of obedience to the state arising from a divine command, but they have also recognized that this duty might conflict with others.

IV

Despite the variety and interest of the papers reprinted here, they only begin to scratch the surface of the relation between theology and morality. Partly owing to lack of space, and partly owing to the need to keep the present selection fairly unified, nothing has been included on epistemology, on how God's command might be discerned, nor for that matter on how necessary moral truths might be. Answers to such questions would, in any case, be neutral as regards the Divine Command Theory since it could be that divine commands (or necessary moral truths) are known by reason, or conscience, or Scripture. For the same reason no material has been included on the question of whether there are matters which are morally good though not commanded by God, so-called works of supererogation, nor on the relation of the command of God to morally indifferent matters, nor on the question of the relation of God's creative will to the goodness or otherwise of the creation.[9]

[9] Thanks are due to Robert Young for much advice and criticism.

IS MORALITY LOGICALLY DEPENDENT ON RELIGION?

WILLIAM K. FRANKENA

I

ONE of the central issues in our cultural crisis, on any view, is that of the relation of morality to religion. That morality is dependent on religion is widely maintained by theologians arguing for the need of a return to religion, by moralists seeking to promote virtue, civic or personal, by educators advocating the teaching of religion in the public schools, and, of course, by many laymen and parents, not to mention politicians trying to impose an oath on teachers and other state employees, and political theorists trying to re-establish democracy and Western culture on their 'true basis'. And, indeed, if morality (and hence politics) is dependent on religion, then we must look to religion as a basis for any answer to any personal or social problem of any importance; but, if not, we may answer at least some of these problems on an 'independent bottom', as people used to say; for example, on the basis of history, science, and practical experience. If morality is dependent on religion, then we cannot hope to solve our problems, or resolve our differences of opinion about them, unless and in so far as we can achieve agreement and certainty in religion (not a lively hope); but, if it is not entirely dependent on religion, then we can expect to solve at least some of them by the use of empirical and historical inquiries of a publicly available and testable kind (inquiries that are improving in quality and scope).

Nevertheless, although the thesis that morality is dependent on religion is of such crucial importance, and is so often asserted, assumed, or clung to, it is rarely, if ever, very carefully formulated or argued for

From *Religion and Morality: A Collection of Essays*, edited by Gene Outka and John P. Reeder, Jr. Copyright ©1973 by G. Outka and J. P. Reeder, Jr. Reprinted by permission of Doubleday & Company, Inc.

by those who believe it.[1] The thesis itself is both vague and ambiguous, and the arguments for it are often such as might inspire a modern Celsus to complain again of the lack of intellectual seriousness of the Christians. In this paper, therefore, I shall try to make a contribution to contemporary philosophical thinking by discussing with some care the claim that morality is dependent on religion. But I cannot try to deal with this claim in all of its forms, and so will concentrate on just one of them—the claim that morality is *logically* dependent on religion—and on some of the arguments that are or might be used to support it. My discussion will be almost entirely critical and negative, but this is not due to any desire to disparage religion. It is due rather to a conviction that even religious thinkers should think clearly and rigorously when they speak or write about the relations of morality to religion.

Those who think that morality is dependent on religion need not and do not always mean that it is logically dependent on religion. They may mean only that it is *causally* or *historically* dependent on religion, or that it is *motivationally* or *psychologically* dependent on religion. However, they generally do not make clear in just what sense they hold morality to be dependent on religion (or, for that matter, just what they mean by morality, and how much of it or what form of it is dependent on religion, or what they mean by religion); and they do often seem to say or at least suggest that morality is logically dependent on religion or theology. Thus, Reinhold Niebuhr writes that the ethic of Jesus 'proceeds logically from the presuppositions of prophetic religion', and that 'The justification for these demands [of the ethic of Jesus] is put in purely religious and not in socio-moral terms. We are to forgive because God is impartial in his love'.[2] Hence he seems to be thinking that these demands depend on prophetic religion, not just causally or motivationally, but also logically. This is the question I wish to discuss, though not merely with respect to Niebuhr or to the ethics of Jesus.[3]

[1] There have been some good discussions of it by philosophers. See especially Hywel D. Lewis, *Morals and the New Theology* (New York: Harper, 1947); and *Morals and Revelation* (London: G. Allen, 1951); Arthur C. Garnett, *Religion and the Moral Life* (New York: Ronald, 1955); and *Can Ideals and Norms be Justified?* (Stockton, Calif.: College of the Pacific 1955); W. G. Maclagan, *The Theological Frontier of Ethics* (London: G. Allen, 1961); Richard B. Brandt, *Ethical Theory* (Englewood Cliffs, N.J.: Prentice-Hall, 1959), ch. 4. Also papers by Kai Nielsen and others in *Christian Ethics and Contemporary Philosophy*, ed. Ian Ramsey (London: SCM Press, 1966).

[2] Reinhold Niebuhr, *An Interpretation of Christian Ethics* (New York and London: Harper, 1935), pp. 37, 46. See also Joseph Fletcher, *Situation Ethics* (Philadelphia: Westminster Press, 1966; SCM Press, 1966), p. 49; and Karl Barth, *Community, State and Church* (Garden City, N.Y.: Doubleday, 1960), p. 78.

[3] I discuss it and other forms of the thesis that morality is dependent on religion, though rather briefly, in William K. Frankena, 'Public Education and the Good Life', *Harvard Educational Review*, 31 (1961), pp. 413–26.

II

The claim that morality is logically dependent on religion is still not very clear, however. Let us distinguish between terms or concepts on the one hand and judgments or propositions on the other, and then let us distinguish two groups under each heading:

A. Ethical terms or concepts like 'good', 'bad', 'right', 'wrong', 'ought', 'obligation', 'virtue', etc.

B. Religious or theological terms or concepts like 'God', 'immortal', 'the Atonement', 'the will of God', 'divine forgiveness', etc.

C. Ethical judgments like
   'We ought to love and worship God'
   'We ought to love our neighbor as ourselves'
   'The good is communion with God'
   'Suffering is evil'
   'It is wrong to kill'
   'It is right to keep promises'
   Etc.

D. Religious or theological beliefs or propositions like
   'There is a God'
   'Jesus of Nazareth is the Son of God'
   'Jesus of Nazareth atoned for our sins'
   'God loves and forgives us'
   'Our souls are immortal'
   'God commands us not to kill'
   Etc.

Here some may interpose and say that the terms and judgments I call 'ethical' seem to them to be just as 'religious' as the others. In a sense they are, for we do ordinarily conceive of a religion as including a moral code. If we speak in this way, then of course we must regard ethics as inseparable from religion, for it will be a part of religion. But it does not follow that we *must* conceive of ethics as a part of religion. Nor does it follow that the terms and judgments listed under A and C depend in any way on the terms and judgments listed under B and D. And these are the interesting questions for our purposes.

To continue, then, we may take the thesis that morality is logically dependent on religion as including one or more of the following four claims:

1. The terms and concepts of ethics (A) are to be defined by reference to (derived from or analyzed into) those of religion (B); i.e., the judgments of ethics can be translated into theological ones.

2. The judgments of ethics (C) can be logically inferred, deduced, or derived from those of theology (D).
3. Ethical judgments can be justified by being derived logically from theological ones.
4. Ethical judgments can be justified only by being logically inferred from theological ones, that is, they depend logically on religious beliefs for their justification.

Here (3) entails (2). Taken together, they say that religious or theological premises are *sufficient* to justify logically some or all ethical principles. On the other hand, (4) says that they are *necessary* for the justification of all ethical judgments. Again, if (1) is true, then (2) and (4) are true, and (3) will be true *if* theological propositions can themselves be justified. However, for our purposes, (2), (3), and (4) are the really interesting claims, and (1) is of interest only in so far as it is used to support (2), (3), or (4). It is hard to see how (2), (3), or (4) can be maintained without at least implying (1) or something like it, but some theologians, like Niebuhr, do seem to maintain them without explicitly asserting (1) and without thinking they presuppose (1). Hence we shall discuss (2), (3), and (4), and deal with (1), not for its own sake, but only as a support for (2), (3), or (4). In any case, of them all, (4) is the most crucial claim.

III

Let us now take up claim (2). It asserts that certain religious beliefs logically entail certain ethical beliefs, and that the latter can be logically inferred from the former. The view that ethics depends logically on religion does include making this claim. But it should be noted that, when a theologian says 'C, because D' or 'D, therefore C', where D is a theological proposition and C is an ethical one, he may not mean strictly to assert that C follows logically from D by itself. He may not be making his whole argument explicit. There are such things as enthymemes, and he may be presenting an enthymematic argument, as we often do. Thus, when he says, following I John 4:11, 'God loves us, therefore we ought to love one another', what he may be thinking is this:

    (a) God loves us.
    (b) We ought to love those whom God loves.
    (c) Therefore we ought to love one another.

But then he is thinking that (c) follows logically, not from (a) alone but from (a) together with (b). And (b), it should be observed, is an ethical premise, not a theological one; it is assumed in the argument, and may not itself rest on any theological premise. Now, it may be that when a theologian presents arguments of the form '(a), therefore (c)', in which he appears to reason from a theological premise to an ethical conclusion, he *always* means to be understood as giving an enthymematic argument in this fashion. However, if this is so, then he is always assuming some ethical premise or other, and he cannot claim that any ethical conclusion can be derived from theological premises alone. In short, since he presupposes certain ethical premises like (b), he is not really holding that ethics rests logically on religion. To hold this he must believe that his '(a), therefore (c)' is, sometimes at least, the whole story—that certain theological propositions by themselves logically entail certain ethical conclusions.

That this can be so has, however, often been categorically denied, even by some theologians. 'No Ought from an Is', 'No ethical conclusion from non-ethical premises'—from Hume on this has been a familiar dictum, its neglect being generally castigated nowadays as 'the naturalistic fallacy'. And, properly construed, it is a perfectly correct dictum. By the ordinary cannons of logic a conclusion containing the term 'ought' or 'right' cannot be logically derived from premises which do not contain this term, except in such cases as 'It is raining, therefore either it is raining or we ought to be kind to animals,' which can hardly afford aid and comfort to theologians who make claim (2) or even to those who advocate kindness to animals. In this sense any theologian who offers us an argument of the form

(a) God loves us,
(b) Therefore we ought to love one another,

thinking that (c) follows logically from (a) alone without the help of any (b) which introduces the term 'ought', is making a logical mistake. So far, then, it does look as if claim (2) cannot possibly be correct.[4]

It might be argued in reply that the canons just appealed to are those of deductive logic, and that in inductive reasoning one may, at least sometimes, affirm a conclusion containing a word, W, on the basis of premises which do not contain it, without violating any of the appropriate logical rules. This line of thought is worth exploring in connection with the 'No Ought from an Is' dictum, since this dictum is usually pronounced with deductive reasoning in mind, but to explore it now would carry us too far afield. But whatever might come of it, it does not seem likely to give much solace to our theologians, since the inferences they are interested in making can hardly be classified as inductive ones.[5]

[4] With this paragraph cf. remarks by M. Black, 'The Gap Between "Is" and "Should"', *Philosophical Review*, 73 (1964), pp. 167 ff.; G. I. Mavrodes, 'On Deriving the Normative from the Nonnormative', *Papers of the Michigan Academy of Science, Arts and Letters*, 53 (1968), pp. 353–65.

[5] Julius Kovesi has interesting things to say in this connection. See his *Moral Notions* (New York: Humanities Press, 1967; London: Routledge, 1967), ch. I.

It has also been suggested that there is a 'third logic', in addition to those of induction and deduction, whose canons warrant such inferences from factual premises to ethical conclusions as 'I have promised to do X', or 'Doing Y will injure someone, therefore it is wrong to do Y'. But this suggestion has not been very convincingly worked out, and it is hard to see how the canons of this third logic would differ from what are usually regarded as the moral principles that we ought to keep promises and not to injure anyone. In any case, the suggestion has not been taken up by theologians in support of claim (2), and, even if there is something in it, it is by no means clear that it will help them to justify the inferences they are concerned to make.[6]

There is another move that would be more likely to appeal to them. This is to question the sharpness of the distinction between factual judgements and ethical ones, and particularly the distinction between judgments of the sort listed under D above and those listed under C. Thus it might be contended that the so-called religious or theological beliefs included in D are not really so purely factual as we have been assuming, and that if we dig into them we in fact find that they themselves include an ethical commitment or 'ought' in such a way that ethical conclusions *can* be *logically* inferred from them (without any special canons). There is a good bit to be said for this line of thought. Still, it seems to me that, if it is correct, then it simply turns out that the beliefs listed under D are complex, each consisting of an ethical belief conjoined with a non-ethical one (which could theoretically be expressed in value-neutral terms). And then the interesting question is whether any ethical conclusions follow logically from these more carefully stated non-ethical propositions alone. The answer to this question still may, and it looks as if it must, be negative. In any case, however, it is hard to see what is gained by saying that ethical beliefs rest on religious ones if these religious ones themselves turn out to be in some sense or in part ethical. Hence I do not see that this move does anything to support claim (2), except in a verbal way, even if it is otherwise well taken.[7]

---

[6] See Brandt, *Ethical Theory*, pp. 71–6.

[7] This move is made by Dorothy Emmet, *Facts and Obligations* (London: Dr. Williams Trust, 1958); and Patterson Brown, 'Religious Morality', *Mind*, NS 72 (1963), pp. 235–44. It is discussed by Kai Nielsen, D. Z. Phillips, and Ian Ramsey in Ramsey, ed., *Christian Ethics and Contemporary Philosophy*, pp. 134 ff., 157 ff., 143. See also R. M. Hare 'Descriptivism', reprinted in W. D. Hudson, ed., *The Is-Ought Question* (New York: St. Martins, 1969; London: Macmillan).

IV

So far, it appears that the 'No Ought from an Is' dictum is substantially correct and that claim (2), if understood in any interesting sense, is mistaken. However, the theologians who assert claim (2) are not yet vanquished. It is not usual for them to offer explicit definitions of ethical terms like 'good', 'right', 'ought', etc., but they sometimes do. At any rate, at the present point in the discussion, a theologian might contend that ethical conclusions can be logically inferred from religious or theological propositions (even if these are purely 'factual' in some sense), because ethical terms can be defined by reference to religious or theological ones, i.e., because claim (1) is true. For example, he might say that 'We ought to love one another' follows logically from 'God commands us to love one another', because 'ought' *means* 'commanded by God'. One might reply that he is then using the definitional statement '"Ought" means "commanded by God"' as a kind of premise of his argument; but he might rejoin that, while this is true, the additional premise is a definition and so is not an ethical statement proper but rather a logical or semantical one, and that therefore he is still deriving an ethical conclusion logically from premises that are not ethical. And yet, he might add, since my premises contain a definition of 'ought', I am not sinning against the rule that the term 'ought' cannot appear in the conclusion of an argument if it is not present in its premises.

The point is that one can go logically from Is to Ought, from 'nonethical' premises to 'ethical' conclusions, as claim (2) requires, *if* 'ought' and other ethical concepts can be satisfactorily defined in terms of theological or metaphysical ones. The question, then, is whether any such theological definitions are satisfactory. One cannot answer it, as is sometimes done, by arguing that such definitions cannot be satisfactory, since one cannot get an Ought out of an Is, for to argue thus is to beg the question. Now, theological definitions have been rebutted ever since Plato wrote *Euthyphro* by a variety of arguments, the chief of which was expressed as follows by Richard Price in the eighteenth century:

Right and wrong when applied to actions . . . do not signify merely that such actions are commanded or forbidden [by God] . . . [If they did] it would be palpably absurd in any case to ask whether it is *right* to obey a command [of God], or *wrong* to disobey it, and the proposition, *obeying a command* [of God] *is right* . . . would be most trifling, as expressing no more than that obeying a command [of God] is obeying a command [of God]. . . .[8]

[8] Richard Price, *A Review of the Principal Questions in Morals*, ed. David Raphael (Oxford: Clarendon Press, 1948), p. 16; see also p. 41.

Such criticisms of theological definitions do not seem to me to be as immediately fatal as they are usually thought to be, but I cannot discuss them here. In fact, I shall not now examine the various theological definitions of 'right' and other ethical terms that may be offered.[9] Whatever they are, if they are not merely arbitrary, they must be offered either as reportive elucidations of what we *do* mean by these terms or as recommendations about what we *should* mean by them. I am inclined to think that the criticisms just referred to do show that theological definitions will not do simply as reports of what we do mean. But, even if they did correctly report what we do mean, one could still ask if we should go on using them in this sense. *A fortiori*, if they are proposals about our future use of ethical terms, we may ask for reasons why we should adopt them. Either way, it seems to me that accepting the definition offered as a basis for our future speech, thought, and action is tantamount to accepting a moral principle. I do not mean that a definition is a moral principle. What I mean is that, when one accepts a definition of any term that can be called ethical, one has already in effect accepted an ethical standard. For example, when one agrees to take 'right' to mean 'commanded by God', and at the same time to use it as a key term in one's speech, thought, and action, this is tantamount to acepting the moral principle 'We ought to do what God commands' as a guide in life.[10]

If this is so, then, when a theological definition is offered us, we may always ask why we should adopt this definition, and to answer us the theologian in question must provide us with a justification of the corresponding moral principle. And the point is that he cannot claim that either it or the definition follows logically from any religious or theological belief (which is not itself a disguised ethical judgment). He may, of course, still offer such beliefs as part of the justification of his definition and principle but he cannot argue that they *suffice* to establish them *logically*. And if he asserts that they are *necessary* to establish them he is shifting to claim (4).

A persistent theologian may reply that his proposed definition is not tantamount to a normative principle in disguise—that it is not itself a moral judgment assigning the predicates 'good', 'right', or 'ought' to a certain object or kind of object but rather a semantical rule for assigning

[9] For such an examination, see Brandt, *Ethical Theory*, pp. 71–6. L. Bergstrom has attacked the view that one can go logically from Ises to Oughts *if* ethical concepts are defined in terms of non-ethical ones, in 'Meaning and Morals', in a volume on *Contemporary Philosophy in Scandinavia*. Even if he is right, his point will not rescue claim (2).

[10] My point may not hold for definitions of the kind that have been proposed by F. C. Sharp or R. Firth (see Brandt, *Ethical Theory*, pp. 173 ff.), but these are not theological definitions.

them. This may be. But even then the definition needs justification, and one cannot claim to justify it by arguing that it follows *logically* from certain theological beliefs. What J. S. Mill calls 'considerations capable of determining the intellect to give its assent' must be provided, but they must not be regarded as establishing the definition in a strict logical sense. However, as I have indicated, it seems to me that they will have to be the same considerations that would determine the intellect to give its assent to the corresponding moral principle, no more and no less—in other words that, in the case of an ethical term, a 'definition' is an expression of an accepted or proposed moral principle.

If all this is so, then ethical judgments and principles cannot be said in any very important sense to follow logically from religious or theological beliefs. That they do is only really plausible if the inference is said to be warranted by a definition, but then we may ask about the status of the definition. Whether it is simply the expression of an assumed ethical principle or a semantical rule for the use of ethical terms, it can hardly be thought to be logically deducible from religious or theological premises. I conclude therefore that the theologian must give up or not make claim (2). If he wishes to maintain that an ethics does follow from his theology, he must hold that this is so, not in a strict logical sense, but in some other. About the possibility of such a view I shall say a little at the end of this paper.

V

So much for claim (2). Putting aside claim (3) for the moment, let us now take up claim (4), which alleges that religious or theological premises are *logically necessary* for the justification or vindication of ethical judgments and principles. It may take at least two forms: (a) the claim that certain religious or theological premises are logically required for the justification of a certain ethics, e.g., that of the Judeo-Christian tradition or that of Western democratic culture, and (b) the claim that some religious or theological premises or other are logically required for the justification of any and every ethical judgment or principle whatsoever. Of these two, the second is for our purposes the more important.

That theistic premises are logically necessary for the justification of certain ethical principles seems unquestionable. To justify the duty of keeping the sacraments some such argument as the following is necessary, if the justification is to be logically cogent:

(a) We ought to obey and worship God.
(b) He commands us to worship him by keeping the sacraments.
(c) Therefore, we ought to keep the sacraments.

Here (b) is a theological belief, and something of the kind is needed to yield the conclusion. Again, the justification of any duties toward God or toward Jesus does seem logically to require premises to the effect that there is a God, that Jesus is his Son, etc. This is hardly surprising— the justification of ethical principles that involve religious or theological terms seems bound to presuppose religious or theological premises. The important question is whether the justification of ethical principles that do not contain such terms, e.g., 'We ought to love one another' or 'It is wrong to kill', logically requires an appeal to such premises.

Here the theologian may bring in claim (1) again and reply that the justification of all such principles must involve an appeal to theistic premises of some kind since 'ought', 'wrong', etc., are to be defined in theistic terms. For example, he may say, the justification of 'It is wrong to kill' logically depends on the premise 'God commands us not to kill' because 'X is wrong' *means* 'X is forbidden by God'. But, of course, if this is the line taken in defense of claim (4) then again everything depends on the status and justifiability of the definitions offered. We may ask why we should accept them at this crucial point in our thinking, and again it seems clear that the answer to this question does not *logically* require an appeal to any religious or theological beliefs. If what was said before is correct, then justifying a definition at this point is equivalent to justifying the corresponding ethical standard, and one cannot claim that this justification logically depends on certain theistic premises without in effect begging the question. Even if the definition is just a semantic rule and not an expression of an ethical principle, accepted or proposed, it still cannot be said logically to presuppose any religious beliefs.

It appears, therefore, that if one wishes to maintain that the justification of any and every ethical principle depends on an appeal to premises of a theistic kind, then one must hold that this is so, not in a strict logical sense, but in some other.

VI

So far, however, we have been considering only definitions of ethical terms like 'right' and 'ought' as steps in making out the logical dependence of ethics on religion. But for the theologian who has been following recent developments in moral philosophy two rather more sophisticated ways of defending claim (4) are open. (a) When it is asked if the methods of inductive reasoning are justified, the answer is sometimes given, 'Of course they are! What we *mean* (in certain kinds of cases) by saying that a conclusion is "justified" is precisely that it is reached by the methods of inductive reasoning.' A theologian might, then, say in a similar vein that religious or theological beliefs are logically required for the justification of ethical ones because what we mean by saying that a belief is 'justified' is that it is shown to be based on a set of religious or theological presuppositions about man and the universe. However, to say that this is what we do mean by 'justified' as applied to beliefs seems clearly mistaken; we do not regard theistic premises as required for the justification of scientific or historical beliefs, and I doubt we would regard a belief as justified merely by the fact that it is based on theistic presuppositions unless we regarded these presuppositions as themselves justified by considerations other than their being theistic. But, if it is replied that at any rate this is what we ought to mean by 'justified' then we may ask for reasons—that is, for a justification of this proposal— and it is not obvious that such a justification could be given or that it would have to include an appeal to religious presuppositions. To assume that it would have to include such an appeal, moreover, would simply beg the question.

It would be more plausible to contend that we do or should regard belief as justified if and only if we can show that it is logically entailed by some basic view of man and the universe, whether this is theistic or not.[11] To such a contention some of the remarks just made would also apply, but in any event it would not help to support claim (4) unless it is unfairly assumed that all ultimate views about the universe are *ipso facto* religious even when they are non-theistic—an assumption we shall deal with shortly.

(b) S. E. Toulmin has suggested that the justification of *moral* or *ethical* rules logically entails an appeal to considerations of the general welfare because what we mean by calling a rule 'moral' or 'ethical' is precisely that its justification rests on such an appeal.[12] Similarly our sophisticated theologian might hold that what makes it necessary (logically) to bring religious or theological considerations into the justification of actions or rules of action is not the meaning of 'right', 'ought' or even the meaning of 'justified', but the meaning of 'moral' itself— that we mean or should mean by a *moral* justification of an action or principle of action only one which relates it to a set of religious views about the world, perhaps by showing that it is commanded by God perhaps in some other way. He would then be arguing that claim (4) is true because of the very meaning of 'morality'. Now, if he offers his

[11] William Lillie seems to hold this, in *An Introduction to Ethics* (London: Methuen, 1961), p. 10. Cf. Sir Sarvepalli Radhakrishnan, *Eastern Religions and Western Thought*, 2nd ed. (London: Oxford University Press, 1940), p. 80.

[12] Stephen Toulmin, *An Examination of the Place of Reason in Ethics* (Cambridge: Cambridge University Press, 1950), Pt. III. Here, too, one can find the notion of a 'third logic' referred to earlier.

definition of 'moral' and 'morality' as an elucidation of what we ordinarily mean, he is not only not imitating Toulmin, he is contradicting him. And I am inclined to think that many people do so closely associate morality and religion that he may be right as far as their usage is concerned. In the first paragraph of his preface to *The Scope and Nature of University Education*, for example, Cardinal Newman is clearly using 'moral' and 'religious' as synonyms. To this extent Toulmin may be wrong. But the fact that Toulmin's view is as plausible as it is shows that our theologian is probably also wrong; many people certainly do not use the term 'moral' as he holds they do. Atheists and secularists do not so use it, and neither does Niebuhr when, in the passage quoted earlier, he contrasts 'socio-moral terms' with 'religious' ones. Here Niebuhr is, in fact, speaking good Toulminese, if not good English.[13]

If, on the other hand, our theologian offers his definition of 'moral' and 'morality' as a recommendation about what we should mean—and I see no reason why he should not—then again we may ask him to provide reasons why our intellects should give their assent. Perhaps he can, but until he does, it must suffice to point out that he cannot make use here of the claim that morality *is* logically dependent on religion, and that he has in effect changed claim (4) into a proposal that we *ought* so to conceive morality as to make it dependent on religion, which is by no means obvious.

Thus the two moves envisaged here do not serve effectively to rescue claim (4), and we may hold to the conclusion stated at the end of the previous section.

VII

Before we take up claim (3), it will be well for us to consider a few arguments and contentions put forward by writers who hold that morality is dependent on religion and to see what they come to in the present context. One is the familiar contention that a 'natural' ethics based on reason and experience cannot suffice, and that therefore a special divine revelation is necessary for an adequate morality. This I have no wish to deny; the question is what it proves. It does not prove that all moral principles depend on revelation, for it allows that some may be based on reason and experience. In fact, it does not prove that revelation provides us with any basic *ethical* principles not otherwise known to us. It may be that revelation only provides new sources of motivation, a point not relevant to our problem. Or it may be that revelation also provides us with additional theological insights about the universe and our place

[13] In connection with this paragraph see Brandt, *Ethical Theory*, pp. 71 f., 355 ff.

in it, which enable us to infer new derivative duties from basic ones already known to us. For instance, if we learn from revelation that Jesus has atoned for our sins, we can then deduce the new obligation to show gratitude to him from the already known principle that we ought to be grateful to benefactors. But this fact would only show that these particular derivative ethical judgments depend on revealed theological premises for their justification, not that any of our basic ethical principles do. But suppose we allow that by revelation we learn new *basic* principles we could not know otherwise. It does not follow that these new ethical principles logically require any theological premises for their justification. Though revealed, they may still be logically independent of all non-ethical propositions, even theological ones. They may even be incapable of being justified at all.[14] Being known only by divine revelation does not entail being logically dependent on theology, paradoxical as this may seem. Even the dialectical theologians, so fond of paradoxes, have missed this point.

A second contention, insisted on by Catholic writers in particular, is put by Dietrich von Hildebrand in these words, 'morality as such essentially presupposes God's existence'.[15] His point is that nothing can exist if there is no God—no world, no human society, no morality, no moral truth. This again I have no wish to deny, though I do not believe it can be proved by rational argument, as St. Thomas and his followers do. But to say that something depends on God for its existence is not to say that it rests logically on any theological propositions. To put it poetically, 'Only God can make a tree,' but it does not follow that a tree is somehow rooted in theology. Its 'hungry mouth' may still need to be pressed 'against the earth's sweet-flowing breast'. Similarly, even if morality objectively presupposes God's existence in the sense indicated, its basic principles may still be self-evident, or they may even depend logically on 'the earth's sweet-flowing breast' of experience, as the conclusions of physics do. Von Hildebrand sees this, and even insists on it, when he immediately adds that his contention does not mean 'that we must have a knowledge of God's existence . . . in order to grasp [moral values] together with their call and obligation'. But this means that it does not entail claim (4), as one might be tempted to think.

Some writers who hold that ethics depends on theology appear to reason as follows. To say that we ought to live in a certain way is to say that it is required for the completion or fulfillment of our being or

---

[14] e.g., they may be self-evident to God, though not to us, and so not dependent in his sight on any non-ethical premises, not even on theological ones.
[15] Dietrich von Hildebrand, *Christian Ethics* (New York: McKay, 1953), p. 455. See also p. 457.

nature. But love of and communion with God and this alone will complete or fulfill our being or nature. Therefore God is our good and we ought to love him and do what will bring us into communion with him. Thus we arrive at an ethics, and hence our ethics depends on theology. Tillich and the two Niebuhrs, for example, seem to reason in this way, at least at times.[16] Tillich does so in arguing that ethics is, or should be, neither 'autonomous' nor 'hereronomous', but rather 'theonomous'. This sounds grand, but let us look closer. The ethical conclusion does seem to presuppose certain theological premises, e.g., that God exists and that we stand in certain relations to him. But the first and basic step in the argument is not a theological proposition in any proper sense. It is simply a basic definition or principle of obligation and it does not seem to depend on theology for its justification. Moreover, if it is taken as basic, it will yield an ethics even without the help of theological premises. For all that it says, biology, psychology, and sociology might suffice to tell us how to live in order to complete our natures or fulfill our beings, and, if this were so, nothing more would be needed to give us an ethics. A theonomous ethics follows only if theological premises are required for us to know how to realize the tendencies of our nature, but this is not obvious and must be shown. However, even if it is true, there is still the question whether or not the basic presupposition that we ought to do what will fulfill our natural tendencies is itself acceptable. As I say, *it* does not seem to depend logically on any religious or theological beliefs. What is more, it would be disputed by all those who refuse to take 'nature' as a norm.

A fourth line of thought, which one hears over and over in recent discussions, and which has already been referred to, goes like this: Every ethical system or moral code depends on some set of ultimate beliefs about man, the meaning of the universe, and his place in it; therefore every ethical code or system depends on a religion of some kind. Thus Reinhold Niebuhr writes,

In any case both the foundation and the pinnacle of any cultural structure are religious; for any scheme of values is finally determined by the ultimate answer which is given to the ultimate question about the meaning of life.[17]

It is easy to be taken in by this kind of argument. The trouble with it is

---

[16] Here, see Paul Tillich, *Love, Power and Justice* (New York: Oxford University Press, 1960), pp. 76 ff.; Reinhold Niebuhr, *The Nature and Destiny of Man* (New York: Scribner, 1941), I, ch. X; H. Richard Niebuhr, 'The Center of Value,' in *Moral Principles of Action*, ed. Ruth Anshen (New York: Harper, 1952), pp. 162–75.

[17] Reinhold Niebuhr, *The Children of Light and the Children of Darkness* (New York: Scribner, 1960), p.125.

not so much in its assertion that every ethics rests on a set of ultimate metaphysical beliefs, though some would quarrel with this too, as in its use of the term 'religion'. It uses this term so widely that all ultimate views about the world, and not only theistic ones, are religions, even atheism and naturalism. One can do this, of course, and if one does, then claim (4) becomes true by virtue of the definition of 'religion'. But it does not follow—though the unwary reader of such an argument, and even its unwary author, may well draw this conclusion—that an ethics always must depend on a *theistic* view of the world. But this is the interesting question, the question we are concerned with here. The argument being discussed may win a victory but it is a hollow and verbal one.

There is a similar ploy—I do not know a better word for it—which one sometimes encounters. This consists in admitting or insisting that our basic ethical principles and value judgments are simply fundamental commitments or postulates which we make or adopt for the guidance of our lives, and then claiming that any such basic commitment or postulate is *ipso facto* an act of religious faith, concluding that therefore every ethics rests on religion.[18] Again, this ploy makes claim (4) verbally true by defining 'religion' in a very wide sense—in such a wide sense that any basic ethical or value commitment is by definition an act of religious faith. Then, of course, every ethics rests on an act of 'religious' faith, but this does not mean that ethics necessarily rests on a *theistic* faith. For in this wide sense even the ethics of an atheist or of a naturalist would be religious, as John Dewey makes clear in *A Common Faith*. It seems to me to be simply misleading to use the term 'religion' in this way. In any event, however, the ploy in question does nothing to show that basic ethical principles and value judgments depend logically on beliefs of a theological nature. For all it shows, they may rest on nothing at all. In fact, in taking them to be essentially postulates of faith, its employers seem to be regarding them as logically autonomous and as *not* logically deducible even from theology.[19]

The sixth and last contention I want to say something about here is very similar, only it depends on the meaning of 'morality' as well as that of 'religion'. A. C. Garnett comes very close to stating it in his *Religion and the Moral Life*, otherwise a careful and sensible book[20] It runs as follows: morality by its very nature involves an attitude of supreme devotion to some cause or object, a state of what Tillich calls 'ultimate concern'; but this is precisely what is meant by 'religion' or by

---

[18] See, e.g., John A. Hutchison, *The Two Cities* (Garden City, N.Y.: Doubleday, 1957).
[19] Cf. Fletcher, *Situation Ethics*, pp. 47–9.
[20] Garnett, *Religion and the Moral Life*, pp. 5 ff.

'religious faith'; hence morality is necessarily religious. That morality calls for ultimate commitment in quite this way might be disputed; the theologians who contrast 'mere morality' with religious ethos apparently would deny it. But let us grant this point; any moralist is bound to call for a very high devotion to his ideal. The criticisms just expressed in dealing with the fourth and fifth lines of thought apply here again. In any case, however, the sixth line would only show that morality requires an agent to be ultimately devoted to an ideal, it would not show that this ideal depends for its justification on any religious beliefs of a theistic sort.[21] It may be that no man can be or remain ultimately concerned unless he has such beliefs, or that he is hopelessly deluded if he is ultimately concerned without having such beliefs, but these are further points and do not bear on our question.

VIII

It has appeared that most, if not all, of the actual and possible methods of supporting claims (2) and (4), or, in other words, of showing that morality is logically dependent on religion, involve explicit or implicit definitions either of ethical terms like 'right' or 'ought', or of more epistemic terms like 'justified', or of the terms 'morality' and 'religion' themselves. It has also appeared, I think, that all of them fall short on one count or another, I conclude that neither claim (2) nor claim (4) has been or can be established. This brings us at long last to claim (3), which says that ethical judgments can be justified by being derived logically from theological ones, and which can now be dealt with rather briefly. In part, claim (3) simply repeats claim (2), viz., that ethical judgments are logically deducible from religious ones, and so has already been covered. But claim (3) also says that ethical judgments would in fact be justified if they were shown to be based on certain theological beliefs. Now this part of claim (3) could be held to be true by virtue of the meaning of 'justified', but we have already seen that this view is not plausible. In fact, I believe, we would not and should not think that our ethical beliefs were justified by being shown to rest on and follow from certain religious or theological beliefs unless we thought that these were themselves in some way rationally justifiable. Hence claim (3) can only be true, it seems to me, if religious beliefs of a theistic kind can be justified.

I have no wish to deny that the essential beliefs of theism are in some sense justifiable, though I doubt that they can be proved by argument

---

[21] Garnett sees this, and does not believe ethics is logically dependent on theistic beliefs. See ibid., pp. 13 ff. For him the dependence of morality on theism is psychological, not logical.

in any rationally conclusive way. But this raises a large and age-old issue that cannot be discussed here. It does seem to me however, that the outcome of this debate is by no means clear and that, to this extent, the truth of claim (3) is uncertain. In fact, the conviction that this is so is part of what motivates me in writing this paper. However deep and sincere one's own religious beliefs may be, if one reviews the religious scene, contemporary and historical, one cannot help but wonder if there is any rational and objective method of establishing any religious belief against the proponents of other religions or of irreligion. But then one is impelled to wonder also if there is anything to be gained by insisting that all ethical principles are or must be logically grounded on religious beliefs. For to insist on this is to introduce into the foundations of any morality whatsoever all of the difficulties involved in the adjudication of religious controversies, and to do so is hardly to encourage hope that mankind can reach, by peaceful and rational means, some desirable kind of agreement on moral and political principles. It also encourages ethical and political skepticism in those who do not or cannot accept the required religious beliefs. That is why it strikes me as important to reject the view that all morality is logically dependent on religion and to leave open the possibility that at least some important ethical judgements can be justified independently of religion and theology—a possibility which, fortunately, many theologians already accept. Of course, one cannot simply reject the view that morality is dependent on religion for this reason; if it rests on good grounds, we must still espouse it. But, as we have seen it does not rest on good grounds.

Motives for rejecting a view may be countered by motives for accepting it. No doubt one motive for arguing that morality is dependent on religion is a desire to establish the importance of religious faith. One must, however, be careful here. For one can hardly at the same time contend that morality has no sound basis unless it rests on religion and admit that there is no good argument for religion except that it is necessary as a basis for morality. This is neither good logic nor good religion. If one is honestly to hold that morality can be established if and only if it is grounded in religion, then one must also believe that religion has adequate grounds of its own to stand on.

IX

Thus none of the claims involved in the thesis that morality is logically dependent on religion can be regarded as established, and the thesis itself, in particular claim (4), which is its really crucial part, is only doubtfully salutary either to morality or to religion. In thus attacking *that* thesis, however, I have said nothing about other claims that have been made about the relation of morality to religion. I have not contended that morality is in no way dependent on religion for dynamics, motivation, inspiration, or vision. Nor have I contended that religion adds nothing to morality—it may add motivation, an additional obligation to do what is right, new duties, a new spirit in which to do them, a new dimension to already existing duties, or a sense of sin. All this may be true for anything that has been said here. But none of it entails the thesis that morality is *logically* dependent on religion of a theistic kind, and I am here concerned only to dispute *this*. I am not even arguing that 'natural law', 'natural morality', and 'moral philosophy' are sufficient, certainly not that they are omnicompetent. For all that I have said, it may still be that no adequate ethics can be developed without the help of religious beliefs as premises in addition to certain basic ethical ones, and, if this is so, ethics does still rest on religion in a sense—not for its basic principles but for the development of its working rules and conclusions, or at least some of them. This too I have not been concerned to deny (or to affirm).

I cannot end, however, without pointing out a direction for further inquiry. To what has been said the following reply is apt to be made. 'If or in so far as morality does not depend on religion for its justification, how is it to be justified? Must we not choose between saying that ethical principles rest on religion and saying that they have no justification whatever?' This may be the real conviction behind the thesis we have been discussing. But from our conclusion that ethical principles are not all logically dependent on theology, it does not follow that they cannot be justified in any objective and rational sense. Some of them may still be provable on non-theological grounds, or they may be self-evident and hence self-justifying. Many theologians have, in fact, admitted one or another of these alternatives. I doubt both that basic ethical judgments are self-evident and that they can be proved logically by derivation from other propositions, whether these are religious ones or not. But, even if this is so, it does not follow that they cannot be justified in any objective and rational way. It seems to me that Mill was right when, having said that a basic ethical principle is neither intuited nor amenable to strict proof, he added (in a passage already borrowed from):

We are not, however, to infer that its acceptance or rejection must depend on blind impulse, or arbitrary choice. There is a larger meaning of the word 'proof' [I would rather say 'justification'], in which this question is as amenable to it as any other of the disputed questions of philosophy. The subject is within the cognizance of the rational faculty. . . .

Considerations may be presented capable of determining the intellect either to give or withhold its assent. . . . [22]

I think that it is in this 'larger meaning' of justification that Mill thought he could justify the doctrine that pleasure is the good by showing that pleasure is the ultimate object of all desire. At any rate, suppose that it could be conclusively shown that pleasure is the basic object of desire. This would not prove logically that pleasure alone is desirable or good, but would it not be in some sense 'reasonable' to draw this conclusion and 'absurd' to offer something other than pleasure as the *summum bonum*? [23] If so, then there is after all a sense, though not a strictly logical one, in which factual considerations may serve to justify ethical conclusions. Moreover, if this example is at all a fair one, it also shows that theological premises are not necessarily required in justifications of this sort.

Of course, it may be replied that religious considerations are among those capable of thus determining the intellect to give its assent to a certain ethical principle. In fact, I am inclined to think that they are. Suppose again that one has a sincere belief in or convincing experience of God as love and vividly realizes what this means, as Bergson's mystics do. Must he not take the 'law of love' as his guiding principle in life, and regard it as entirely reasonable that he should do so? It seems to me plausible to claim that religious beliefs and experiences do *suffice* to justify this, and perhaps other ethical principles in this wider sense of the word 'justify', at least for those who have them. [24] It does not follow, however, that they are *necessary* to justify those ethical principles even in this larger sense, for it may be that certain non-religious considerations are also capable of determining the intellect to give them its assent. *A fortiori*, it does not follow that religious considerations are necessary to determine it to give its assent to *any* ethical principle *whatsoever*.

There are also other lines along which philosophers, including analytical philosophers, have sought or are seeking to develop the possibility suggested by Mill's sentences. I mention the one just described because it involves a kind of justification theologians are bound to take seriously. In any case, however, until they show that no objective and rational kind of justification of ethical judgments can be given if we reject the claim that morality is logically dependent on religion, we may relinquish this claim without fear. If they admit that such a larger kind of objective and rational justification of ethics is possible, but insist that it requires

[22] John Stuart Mill, *Utilitarianism*, from *Mill's Ethical Writings*, ed. J. B. Schneewind (New York: Collier, 1965), p. 279.

[23] Cf. Aristotle, *Nicomachean Ethics*, bk. X, ch. 2: 'Those who object that that at which all things aim is not necessarily good are talking nonsense.'

[24] See Lillie, *An Introduction to Ethics*, p. 328.

religious premises, though not in a logical sense of 'requires', they may be right for all that I have shown here.[25] Indeed, I believe that this is the line to be taken by theologians who wish to hold that religion is required to justify the principles of morality (and not merely to motivate people to act according to them). I myself think that even this weaker claim about the dependence of morality on religion is at best true only if it is carefully qualified. But that is another story.

[25] My point about Mill does, however, throw doubt on such a view.

II
GOD AND HUMAN ATTITUDES

JAMES RACHELS

Kneeling down or grovelling on the ground, even to express your reverence for heavenly things, is contrary to human dignity.

Kant

I

IT is necessarily true that God (if He exists) is worthy of worship.[1] Any being who is not worthy of worship cannot be God, just as any being who is not omnipotent, or who is not perfectly good, cannot be God. This is reflected in the attitudes of religious believers who recognize that, whatever else God may be, He is a being before whom men should bow down. Moreover, He is unique in this; to worship anyone or anything else is blasphemy. In this paper I shall present an *a priori* argument against the existence of God which is based on the conception of God as a fitting object of worship. The argument is that God cannot exist, because no being could ever *be* a fitting object of worship.

However, before I can present this argument, there are several preliminary matters that require attention. The chief of these, which will hopefully have some independent interest of its own, is an examination of the concept of worship. In spite of its great importance this concept has received remarkably little attention from philosophers of religion; and when it has been treated, the usual approach is by way of referring to God's awesomeness or mysteriousness: to worship is to 'bow down in silent awe' when confronted with a being that is 'terrifyingly mysterious'.[2] But neither of these notions is of much help in understanding worship. Awe is certainly not the same thing as worship; one can be awed by a performance of *King Lear*, or by witnessing an eclipse of the sun or an earthquake, or by meeting one's favourite film-star, without

From *Religious Studies*, Vol. 7, 1971, pp. 325–37. Reprinted by permission of Cambridge University Press and the author.

[1] Hartshorne and Pike suggest that the formula 'that than which none greater can be conceived' should be interpreted as 'that than which none more worthy of worship can be conceived'. Charles Hartshorne, *Anselm's Discovery* (LaSalle, Illinois, 1966), pp. 25–6; and Nelson Pike, *God and Timelessness* (London, 1970), pp. 149–60.

[2] These phrases are from John Hick, *Philosophy of Religion* (Englewood Cliffs, New Jersey, 1963), pp. 13–14.

worshipping any of these things. And a great many things are both terrifying and mysterious that we have not the slightest inclination to worship—I suppose the Black Plague fits that description for many people. The account of worship that I will give will be an alternative to those which rely on such notions as awesomeness and mysteriousness.

II

Consider McBlank, who worked against his country's entry into the Second World War, refused induction into the army, and was sent to jail. He was active in the 'ban the bomb' movements of the fifties; he made speeches, wrote pamphlets, led demonstrations, and went back to jail. And finally, he has been active in opposing the war in Vietnam. In all of this he has acted out of principle; he thinks that all war is evil and that no war is ever justified. I want to make three observations about McBlank's pacifist commitments. (*a*) One thing that is involved is simply his recognition that certain facts are the case. History is full of wars; war causes the massive destruction of life and property; in war men suffer on a scale hardly matched in any other way; the large nations now have weapons which, if used, could destroy the human race; and so on. These are just facts which any normally informed man will admit without argument. (*b*) But of course they are not *merely* facts, which people recognise to be the case in some indifferent manner. They are facts that have special importance to human beings. They form an ominous and threatening backdrop to people's lives—even though for most people they are a backdrop only. But not so for McBlank. He sees the accumulation of these facts as having radical implications for his conduct; he behaves in a very different way from the way he would behave were it not for these facts. His whole style of life is different; his conduct is altered, not just in its details, but in its pattern. (*c*) Not only is his overt behaviour affected; so are his ways of thinking about the world and his place in it. His *self-image* is different. He sees himself as a member of a race with an insane history of self-destruction, and his self-image becomes that of an active opponent of the forces that lead to this self-destruction. He *is* an opponent of militarism just as he is a father or a musician. When some existentialists say that we 'create ourselves' by our choices, they may have something like this in mind.

Thus, there are at least three things that determine McBlank's role as an opponent of war: first, his recognition that certain facts are the case; second his taking these facts as having important implications for his conduct; and third, his self-image as living his life (at least in part) in response to these facts. My first thesis about worship is that the worshipper has a set of beliefs about God[3] which function in the same way as McBlank's beliefs about war.

First, the worshipper believes that certain things are the case: that the world was created by an all-powerful, all-wise being who knows our every thought and action; that this being, called God, cares for us and regards us as his children; that we are made by him in order to return his love and live in accordance with his laws; and that, if we do not live in a way pleasing to him, we may be severely punished. Now these beliefs are certainly not shared by all reasonable people; on the contrary, many thoughtful persons regard them as nothing more than mere fantasy. But these beliefs are accepted by religious people, and that is what is important here. I do not say that this particular set of beliefs is definitive of religion in general, or of Judaism or Christianity in particular; it is meant only as a sample of the sorts of belief typically held by religious people in the West. They are, however, the sort of beliefs about God that are required for the business of worshipping God to make any sense.

Second, like the facts about warfare, these are not merely facts which one notes with an air of indifference; they have important implications for one's conduct. An effort must be made to discover God's will both for people generally and for oneself in particular; and to this end, the believer consults the church authorities and the theologians, reads the scripture, and prays. The degree to which this will alter his overt behaviour will depend, first, on exactly what he decides God would have him do, and second, on the extent to which his behaviour would have followed the prescribed pattern in any case.[4]

Finally, the believer's recognition of these 'facts' will influence his self-image and his way of thinking about the world and his place in it. The world will be regarded as made for the fulfilment of divine purposes; the hardships that befall men will be regarded either as 'tests' in some sense or as punishments for sin; and most important, the believer will think of himself as a 'Child of God' and of his conduct as reflecting either honour or dishonour upon his Heavenly Father.

What will be most controversial in what I have said so far (to some philosophers, though perhaps not to most religious believers) is the treatment of claims such as 'God regards us as his children' as in some

---

[3] In speaking of 'beliefs about God' I have in mind those typical of Western religions. I shall construct my account of worship in these terms, although the account will be adaptable to other forms of worship such as Satan-worship (see footnote 10, below).

[4] For example, one religious believer who thinks that his conduct must be very different on account of his belief is P. T. Geach: see his essay 'The Moral Law and the Law of God', in *God and the Soul* (London, 1969). [Reading XI in the present volume.]

sense factual. Wittgenstein[5] is reported to have thought this a total mis-understanding of religious belief; and others have followed him in this.[6] Religious utterances, it is said, do not report putative facts; instead, we should understand such utterances as revealing the speaker's *form of life*. To have a form of life is to accept a language-game; the religious believer accepts a language-game in which there is talk of God, creation, Heaven and Hell, a Last Judgment, and so forth, which the sceptic does not accept. Such language-games can only be understood on their own terms; we must not try to assimilate them to other sorts of games. To see how this particular game works we need only to examine the way the language of religion is used by actual believers—in its proper habitat the language-game will be 'in order' as it is. We find that the religious believer uses such utterances for a number of purposes, e.g. to express reasons for action, to show the significance which he attaches to various things, to express his attitudes, etc.—but not to 'state facts' in the ordinary sense. So when the believer makes a typically religious assertion, and non-believer denies the same, *they are not contradicting one another*; rather, the non-believer is simply refusing to play the believer's (very serious) game. Wittgenstein (as recorded by his pupils) said:

Suppose that someone believed in the Last Judgement, and I don't, does this mean that I believe the opposite to him, just that there won't be such a thing? I would say: "not at all, or not always."

Suppose I say that the body will rot, and another says "No. Particles will rejoin in a thousand years, and there will be a Resurrection of you".

If some said: "Wittgenstein, do you believe in this?" I'd say: "No." "Do you contradict the man?" I'd say: "No."[7]

Wittgenstein goes on to say that the difference between the believer and the sceptic is not that one holds something to be true that the other thinks false, but that the believer takes certain things as 'guidance for life' that the sceptic does not, e.g. that there will be a Last Judgment. He illustrates this by reference to a person who 'thinks of retribution' when he plans his conduct or assesses his condition:

Suppose you had two people, and one of them, when he had to decide which course to take, thought of retribution, and the other did not. One person might, for instance, be inclined to take everything that happened to him as a reward or punishment, and another person doesn't think of this at all.

If he is ill, he may think: "What have I done to deserve this?" This is

[5] Ludwig Wittgenstein, *Lectures and Conversations on Aesthetics, Psychology, and Religious Belief* (Berkeley, 1967). Edited by Cyril Barrett, from notes taken by Yorick Smythies, Rush Rhees, and James Taylor.
[6] For example, Rush Rhees, in *Without Answers* (London, 1969), ch. 13.
[7] Wittgenstein, p. 53.

one way of thinking of retribution. Another way is, he thinks in a general way whenever he is ashamed of himself: "This will be punished."

Take two people, one of whom talks of his behaviour and of what happens to him in terms of retribution, the other does not. These people think entirely differently. Yet, so far, you can't say they believe different things.

Suppose someone is ill and he says: "This is punishment," and I say: "If I'm ill, I don't think of punishment at all." If you say: "Do you believe the opposite?"—you can call it believing the opposite, but it is entirely different from what we would normally call believing the opposite.

I think differently, in a different way. I say different things to myself. I have different pictures.'[8]

I will limit myself to three remarks about this very difficult view.[9] First it is not at all clear that this account is true to the intentions of those who actually engage in religious discourse. If a believer (at least, the great majority of those whom I have known or read about) says that there will be a Last Judgment, and a sceptic says that there will not, the believer certainly will think that he has been contradicted. Of course, the sceptic might not think of denying such a thing except for the fact that the believer asserts it; and in this trivial sense the sceptic might 'think differently' from the believer—but this is completely beside the point. Moreover, former believers who become sceptics frequently do so because they come to believe that religious assertions are *false*; and then, they consider themselves to be denying exactly what they previously asserted. Second, a belief does not lose its ordinary factual import simply because it occupies a central place in one's way of life. McBlank takes the facts about war as 'guidance for life' in a perfectly straightforward sense; but they remain facts. I take it that just as the man in Wittgenstein's example 'thinks of retribution' often, McBlank thinks of war often. So, we do not need to assign religious utterances a special status in order to explain their importance for one's way of life. Finally, while I realise that my account is very simple and mundane, whereas Wittgenstein's is 'deep' and difficult, nonetheless this may be an advantage, not a handicap, of my view. If the impact of religious belief on one's conduct and thinking can be explained by appeal to nothing more mysterious than putative facts and their impact on conduct and thinking, then the need for a more obscure theory will be obviated. And if a man believes that, *as a matter of fact*, his actions are subject to review by a just God who will mete out rewards and punish

    [8] Wittgenstein, pp. 54–5.
    [9] The whole subject is explored in detail in Kai Nielsen, 'Wittgensteinian Fideism' *Philosophy,* 42 (1967), pp. 191–209.

ments on a day of final reckoning, that will explain very nicely why he 'thinks of retribution' when he reflects on his conduct.

III

Worship is something that is *done*; but it is not clear just *what* is done when one worships. Other actions, such as throwing a ball or insulting one's neighbour, seem transparent enough. But not so with worship: when we celebrate Mass in the Roman Catholic Church, for example, what are we doing (apart from eating a wafer and drinking wine)? Or when we sing hymns in a protestant church, what are we doing (other than merely singing songs)? What is it that makes these acts acts of *worship*? One obvious point is that these actions, and others like them, are ritualistic in character; so, before we can make any progress in understanding worship, perhaps it will help to ask about the nature of ritual.

First we need to distinguish the ceremonial form of a ritual from what is supposed to be accomplished by it. Consider, for example, the ritual of investiture for an English Prince. The Prince kneels; the Queen (or King) places a crown on his head; and he takes an oath: 'I do become your liege man of life and limb and of earthly worship, and faith and trust I will bear unto thee to live and die against all manner of folks.' By this ceremony the Prince is elevated to his new station; and by this oath he acknowledges the commitments which, as Prince, he will owe the Queen. In one sense the ceremonial form of the ritual is quite unimportant: it is possible that some other procedure might have been laid down, without the point of the ritual being affected in any way. Rather than placing a crown on his head, the Queen might break an egg into his palm (that could symbolise all sorts of things). Once this was established as the procedure to be followed, it would do as well as the other. It would still be the ritual of investiture, so long as it was understood that by the ceremony a Prince is created. The performance of a ritual, then, is in certain respects like the use of language: in speaking, sounds are uttered and, thanks to the conventions of the language, something is said, or affirmed, or done, etc.: and in a ritual performance, a ceremony is enacted and, thanks to the conventions associated with the ceremony, something is done, or affirmed, or celebrated, etc.

How are we to explain the point of the ritual of investiture? We might explain that certain parts of the ritual symbolise specific things, for example that the Prince kneeling before the Queen symbolises his subordination to her (it is not, for example, merely to make it easier for her to place the crown on his head). But it is essential that, in explaining the point of the ritual as a whole, we include that a Prince is being created, that he is henceforth to have certain rights in virtue of having been made

a Prince, and that he is to have certain duties which he is now acknowledging, among which are complete loyalty and faithfulness to the Queen,
and so on. If the listener already knows about the complex relations
between Queens, Princes, and subjects, then all we need to tell him is
that a Prince is being installed in office; but if he is unfamiliar with this
social system, we must tell him a great deal if he is to understand what
is going on.

So, once we understand the social system in which there are Queens,
Princes, and subjects, and therefore understand the role assigned to each
within that system, we can sum up what is happening in the ritual of
investiture in this way: someone is being made a Prince, and he is accepting that role with all that it involves. (Exactly the same explanation
could be given, *mutatis mutandis*, for the marriage ceremony.)

The question to be asked about the ritual of worship is what analogous
explanation can be given of it. The ceremonial form of the ritual may
vary according to the customs of the religious community; it may involve singing, drinking wine, counting beads, sitting with a solemn expression on one's face, dancing, making a sacrifice, or what-have-you.
But what is the point of it?

As I have already said, the worshipper thinks of himself as inhabiting
a world created by an infinitely wise, infinitely powerful, perfectly good
God; and it is a world in which he, along with other men, occupies a
special place in virtue of God's intentions. This gives him a certain role
to play: the role of a 'Child of God'. My second thesis about worship is
that in worshipping God one is acknowledging and accepting this role,
and that this is the primary function of the ritual of worship. Just as
the ritual of investiture derives its significance from its place within the
social system of Queens, Princes, and subjects, the ritual of worship gets
its significance from an assumed system of relationships between God
and men. In the ceremony of investiture, the Prince assumes a role with
respect to the Queen and the citizenry; and in worship, a man affirms
his role with respect to God.

Worship presumes the superior status of the one worshipped. This is
reflected in the logical point that there can be no such things as mutual
or reciprocal worship, unless one or the other of the parties is mistaken
as to his own status. We can very well comprehend people loving one
another or respecting one another, but not (unless they are misled)
worshipping one another. This is because the worshipper necessarily
assumes his own inferiority; and since inferiority is an asymmetrical
relation, so is worship. (The nature of the 'superiority' and 'inferiority'
involved here is of course problematic; but on the account I am presenting it may be understood on the model of superior and inferior

positions within a social system. More on this later.) This is also why *humility* is necessary on the part of the worshipper. The role to which he commits himself is that of the humble servant, 'not worthy to touch the hem of His garment'. Compared to God's gloriousness, 'all our righteousnesses are as filthy rags' (Isaiah 64:6). So, in committing one-self to this role, one is acknowledging God's greatness and one's own relative worthlessness. This humble attitude is not a mere embellish-ment of the ritual: on the contrary, worship, unlike love or respect, *requires* humility. Pride is a sin, and pride before God is incompatible with worshipping him.

On the view that I am suggesting, the function of worship as 'glorify-ing' or 'praising' God, which is usually taken to be its primary function, may be regarded as derivative from the more fundamental nature of worship as commitment to the role of God's Child. 'Praising' God is giving him the honour and respect due to one in his position of eminence, just as one shows respect and honour in giving fealty to a King.

In short, the worshipper is in this position: He believes that there is a being, God, who is the perfectly good, perfectly powerful, perfectly wise Creator of the Universe; and he views himself as the 'Child of God,' made for God's purposes and responsible to God for his conduct. And the ritual of worship, which may have any number of ceremonial forms according to the customs of the religious community, has as its point the acceptance of, and commitment to, one's role as God's Child, with all that this involves. If this account is accepted, then there is no mystery as to the relation between the act of worship and the worshipper's other activity. Worship will be regarded not as an isolated act taking place on Sunday morning, with no necessary connection to one's behaviour the rest of the week, but as a ritualistic expression of and commitment to a role which dominates one's whole way of life.[10]

IV

An important feature of roles is that they can be violated; we can act and think consistently with a role, or we can act and think inconsistently with it. The Prince can, for example, act inconsistently with his role as Prince by giving greater importance to his own interests and welfare than to the Queen's; in this case, he is no longer her 'liege man'. And a father

[10] This account of worship, specified here in terms of what it means to worship God, may easily be adapted to the worship of other beings such as Satan. The only changes required are (a) that we substitute for beliefs about God analogous beliefs about Satan, and (b) that we understand the ritual of worship as committing the Satan-worshipper to a role as Satan's servant in the same way that worshipping God commits theists to the role of His servant.

who does not attend to the welfare of his children is not acting consistently with his role as a father (at least as that role is defined in our society), and so on. The question that I want to raise now is, What would count as violating the role to which one is pledged in virtue of worshipping God?

In Genesis there are two familiar stories, both concerning Abraham, that are relevant here. The first is the story of the near-sacrifice of Isaac. We are told that Abraham was 'tempted' by God, who commanded him to offer Isaac as a human sacrifice. Abraham obeyed without hesitation: he prepared an altar, bound Isaac to it, and was about to kill him until God intervened at the last moment, saying 'Lay not thine hand upon the lad, neither do thou any thing unto him: for now I know that thou fearest God, seeing thou hast not withheld thy son, thine only son from me' (Genesis 22:12). So Abraham passed the test. But how could he have failed? What was his 'temptation'? Obviously, his temptation was to disobey God; God had ordered him to do something contrary to both his wishes and his sense of what would otherwise be right and wrong. He could have defied God; but he did not—he subordinated himself, his own desires and judgments, to God's command, even when the temptation to do otherwise was strongest.

It is interesting that Abraham's record in this respect was not perfect. We also have the story of him bargaining with God over the conditions for saving Sodom and Gomorrah from destruction. God had said that he would destroy those cities because they were so wicked; but Abraham gets God to agree that if fifty righteous men can be found there, then the cities will be spared. Then he persuades God to lower the number to forty-five, then forty, then thirty, then twenty, and finally ten. Here we have a different Abraham, not servile and obedient, but willing to challenge God and bargain with him. However, even as he bargains with God, Abraham realises that there is something radically inappropriate about it: he says, 'Behold now, I have taken upon me to speak unto the Lord, which am but dust and ashes . . . Oh let not the Lord be angry...' (Genesis 18:27, 30).

The fact is that Abraham could not, consistently with his role as God's subject, set his own judgment and will against God's. The author of Genesis was certainly right about this. We cannot recognise any being *as God*, and at the same time set ourselves against him. The point is not merely that it would be imprudent to defy God, since we certainly can't get away with it; rather, there is a stronger, logical point involved—namely, that if we recognise any being *as God*, then we are committed, in virtue of that recognition, to obeying him.

To see why this is so, we must first notice that 'God' is not a proper name like 'Richard Nixon' but a title like 'President of the United States' or 'King'.[11] Thus, 'Jehovah is God' is a nontautological statement in which the title 'God' is assigned to Jehovah, a particular being—just as 'Richard Nixon is President of the United States' assigns the title 'President of the United States' to a particular man. This permits us to understand how statements like 'God is perfectly wise' can be logical truths, which is highly problematic if 'God' is regarded as a proper name. Although it is not a logical truth that any particular being is perfectly wise, it nevertheless is a logical truth that if any being is God (i.e. if any being properly holds that title) then that being is perfectly wise. This is exactly analogous to saying: although it is not a logical truth that Richard Nixon has the authority to veto congressional legislation, nevertheless it is a logical truth that if Richard Nixon is President of the United States then he has that authority.

To bear the title 'God', then, a being must have certain qualifications. He must, for example, be all-powerful and perfectly good in additon to being perfectly wise. And in the same vein, to apply the title 'God' to a being is to recognise him as one to be obeyed. The same is true, to a lesser extent, of 'King'—to recognise anyone as King is to acknowledge that he occupies a place of authority and has a claim on one's allegiance as his subject. And to recognise any being as God is to acknowledge that he has *unlimited* authority, and an unlimited claim on one's allegiance.[12] Thus, we might regard Abraham's reluctance to defy Jehovah as grounded not only in his fear of Jehovah's wrath, but as a logical consequence of his acceptance of Jehovah *as God*. Camus was right to think that 'From the moment that man submits God to moral judgment, he kills Him his own heart'.[13] What a man can 'kill' by defying or even questioning God

[11] Cf. Nelson Pike, 'Omnipotence and God's Ability to Sin', *American Philosophical Quarterly*, (1969), pp. 208-9 [Reading IV in the present volume], and C. B. Martin, *Religious Belief* (Ithaca, 1964), ch. 4.

[12] This suggestion might also throw some light on the much-discussed problem of how we could, even in principle, *verify* the existence of God. Sceptics have argued that, even though we might be able to confirm the existence of an all-powerful cosmic superbeing (if one existed), we still wouldn't know what it means to verify that this being is *divine*. And this, it is said, casts doubt on whether the notion of divinity, and related notions such as 'Christ' and 'God', are intelligible. (Cf. Kai Nielsen, 'Eschatological Verification', *The Canadian Journal of Theology*, 9, 1963.) Perhaps this is because, in designating a being as God, we are not only describing him as having certain factual properties (such as omnipotence), but also *ascribing* to him a certain place in our devotions, and taking him as one to be obeyed, worshipped, praised, etc. If this is part of the logic of 'God', then we shouldn't be surprised if God's existence, in so far as that includes the existence of divinity, is not entirely confirmable—for only the 'factual properties' such as omnipotence will be verifiable in the usual way. But once the reason for this is understood, it no longer seems such a serious matter.

[13] Albert Camus, *The Rebel*, translated by Anthony Bower (New York, 1956), p. 62.

is not the being that (supposedly) *is* God, but *his own conception of that being as God.* That God is not to be judged, challenged, defied, or disobeyed, is at bottom a truth of logic; to do any of these things is incompatible with taking him as One to be worshipped.

V

So the idea that any being could be *worthy* of worship is much more problematical than we might have at first imagined. For in admitting that a being is worthy of worship we would be recognising him as having an unqualified claim on our obedience. The question, then, is whether there could be such an unqualified claim. It should be noted that the description of a being as all-powerful, all-wise, etc., would not automatically settle the issue; for even while admitting the existence of such an awesome being we might still question whether we should recognise him as having an unlimited claim on our obedience.

In fact, there is a long tradition in moral philosophy, from Plato to Kant, according to which such a recognition could never be made by a moral agent. According to this tradition, to be a moral agent is to be an autonomous or self-directed agent; unlike the precepts of law or social custom, moral precepts are imposed by the agent upon himself, and the penalty for their violation is, in Kant's words, 'self-contempt and inner abhorrence'.[14] The virtuous man is therefore identified with the man of integrity, i.e. the man who acts according to precepts which he can, on reflection, conscientiously approve in his own heart. Although this is a highly individualistic approach to morals, it is not thought to invite anarchy because men are regarded as more or less reasonable and as desiring what we would normally think of as a decent life lived in the company of other men.

On this view, to deliver oneself over to a moral authority for directions about what to do is simply incompatible with being a moral agent. To say 'I will follow so-and-so's directions no matter what they are and no matter what my own conscience would otherwise direct me to do' is to opt out of moral thinking altogether; it is to abandon one's role as a moral agent. And it does not matter whether 'so-and-so' is the law, the customs of one's society, or God. This does not, of course, preclude one from seeking advice on moral matters, and even on occasion following that advice blindly, trusting in the good judgment of the adviser. But this is to be justified by the details of the particular case, e.g. that you cannot in that case form any reasonable judgment of your own due to ignorance or inexperience in dealing with the types of matters involved.

[14] Immanuel Kant, *Foundations of the Metaphysics of Morals*, translated by Lewis White Beck (New York, 1959), p. 44.

What *is* precluded is that a man should, while in possession of his wits, adopt this style of decision-making (or perhaps we should say this style of *abdicating* decision-making) as a general strategy of living, or abandon his own best judgment in any case where he can form a judgment of which he is reasonably confident.

What we have, then, is a conflict between the role of worshipper, which by its very nature commits one to total subservience to God, and the role of moral agent, which necessarily involves autonomous decision-making. The point is that the role of worshipper takes precedence over every other role which the worshipper has—when there is any conflict, the worshipper's commitment to God has priority over any other commitments which he might have. But the first commitment of a moral agent is to do what in his own heart he thinks is right. Thus the following argument might be constructed:

(*a*) If any being is God, he must be a fitting object of worship.

(*b*) No being could possibly be a fitting object of worship, since worship requires the abandonment of one's role as an autonomous moral agent.

(*c*) Therefore, there cannot be any being who is God.

VI

The concept of moral agency underlying this argument is complex and controversial; and, although I think it is sound, I cannot give it the detailed treatment here that it requires. Instead, I will conclude by answering some of the most obvious objections to the argument.

(1) What if God lets us go our own way, and issues no commands other than that we should live according to our own consciences? In that case there would be no incompatibility between our commitment to God and our commitments as moral agents, since God would leave us free to direct our own lives. The fact that this supposition is contrary to major religious traditions (such as the Christian tradition) doesn't matter, since these traditions could be mistaken. The answer here is that this is a mere contingency, and that even if God did not require obedience to detailed commands, the worshipper would still be committed to the abandonment of his role as a moral agent, *if* God required it.

(2) It has been admitted as a necessary truth that God is perfectly good; it follows as a corollary that He would never require us to do anything except what is right. Therefore in obeying God we would only be doing what we should do in any case. So there is no incompatibility between obeying him and carrying out our moral commitments. Our primary commitment as moral agents is to do right, and God's commands *are* right, so that's that.

This objection rests on a misunderstanding of the assertion that (necessarily) God is perfectly good. This can be intelligibly asserted only because of the principle that *No being who is not perfectly good may bear the title 'God'.*[15] We cannot determine whether some being is God without first checking on whether he is perfectly good;[16] and we cannot decide whether he is perfectly good without knowing (among other things) whether his commands to us are right. Thus our own judgment that some actions are right, and others wrong, is logically prior to our recognition of any being as God. The upshot of this is that we cannot justify the suspension of our own judgment on the grounds that we are deferring to God's command (which, as a matter of logic, *must* be right); for if, by our own best judgment, the command is wrong, this gives us good reason to withhold the title 'God' from the commander.

(3) The following expresses a view which has always had its advocates among theologians: 'Men are sinful; their very consciences are corrupt and unreliable guides. What is taken for conscientiousness among men is nothing more than self-aggrandisement and arrogance. Therefore, we cannot trust our own judgment; we must trust God and do what he wills. Only then can we be assured of doing right.'

This view suffers from a fundamental inconsistency. It is said that we cannot know for ourselves what is right and what is wrong; and this is because our judgment is corrupt. But how do we know that our judgment is corrupt? Presumably, in order to know that, we would have to know (*a*) that some actions are morally required of us, and (*b*) that our own judgment does not reveal that these actions are required. However, (*a*) is just the sort of thing that we can*not* know, according to this view. Now it may be suggested that while we cannot know (*a*) by our own judgment, we can know it as a result of God's revelation. But even setting aside the practical difficulties of distinguishing genuine from bogus revelation (a generous concession), there is still this problem: if we learn that God (i.e. some being that we take to be God) requires us to do a certain action, and we conclude on this account that the action is morally right, then we have *still* made at least one moral judgment of our own, namely that whatever this being requires is morally right. Therefore, it is impossible to maintain the view that we do have some moral knowledge, and that *all* of it comes from God's revelation.

[15] See above, section 4.

[16] Of course we cannot ever know that such a being is *perfectly* good, since this would require an examination of *all* his actions and commands, etc., which is impossible. However, if we observed many good things about him and no evil ones, we would be justified in putting forth the hypothesis that he is perfectly good and acting accordingly. The hypothesis would be confirmed or disconfirmed by future observations in the usual way.

(4) Many philosophers, including St Thomas, have held that the voice of individual conscience *is* the voice of God speaking to the individual, whether he is a believer of not.[17] This would resolve the alleged conflict because in following one's conscience one would at the same time be discharging his obligation as a worshipper to obey God. However, this manoeuvre is unsatisfying, since if taken seriously it would lead to the conclusion that, in speaking to us through our 'consciences', God is merely tricking us: for he is giving us the illusion of self-governance while all the time he is manipulating our thoughts from without. Moreover, in acting from conscience we are acting under the view that our actions are right and not merely that they are decreed by a higher power. Plato's argument in the *Euthyphro* can be adapted to this point: If, in speaking to us through the voice of conscience, God is informing us of what is right, then there is no reason to think that we could not discover this for ourselves—the notion of 'God informing us' is eliminable. On the other hand, if God is only giving us arbitrary commands, which cannot be thought of as 'right' independently of his promulgating them, then the whole idea of 'conscience', as it is normally understood, is a sham.

(5) Finally, someone might object that the question of whether any being is *worthy* of worship is different from the question of whether we *should* worship him. In general, that X is worthy of our doing Y with respect to X does not entail that we should do Y with respect to X. For example, Mrs Brown, being a fine woman, may be worthy of a marriage proposal, but we ought not to propose to her since she is already married. Or, Seaman Jones may be worthy of a medal for heroism but perhaps there are reasons why we should not award it. Similarly, it may be that there is a being who is worthy of worship and yet we should not worship him since it would interfere with our lives as moral agents. Thus God, who is worthy of worship, may exist; and we should love, respect, and honour him, but not worship him in the full sense of the word. If this is correct, then the argument of section 5 is fallacious.

This rebuttal will not work because of an important disanalogy between the cases of proposing marriage and awarding the medal, on the one hand, and the case of worship on the other. It may be that Mrs Brown is worthy of a proposal, yet there are circumstances in which it would be wrong to propose to her. However, these circumstances are contrasted with others in which it would be perfectly all right. The same

---

[17] Cf. Geach, [Reading XI, pp. 165–74, below]: 'The rational recognition that a practice is generally undesirable and that it is best for people on the whole not even to think of resorting to it is thus *in fact* a promulgation to a man of the Divine law forbidding the practice, even if he does not realise that this is a promulgation of the Divine law, even if he does not believe there is a God.'

goes for Seaman Jones's medal: there are *some* circumstances in which awarding it would be proper. But in the case of worship—if the foregoing arguments have been sound—there are *no* circumstances under which anyone should worship God. And if one should *never* worship, then the concept of a fitting object of worship is an empty one.

The above argument will probably not persuade anyone to abandon belief in God—arguments rarely do—and there are certainly many more points which need to be worked out before it can be known whether this argument is even viable. Yet it does raise an issue which is clear enough. Theologians are already accustomed to speaking of theistic belief and commitment as taking the believer 'beyond morality', and I think they are right. The question is whether this should not be regarded as a severe embarrassment.[18]

[18] A number of people read earlier versions of this paper and made helpful comments. I have to thank especially Kai Nielsen, William Ruddick, Jack Glickman, and Steven Cahn.

RELIGIOUS OBEDIENCE AND MORAL AUTONOMY

PHILIP L. QUINN

IT has become fashionable to try to prove the impossibility of there being a God. Findlay's celebrated ontological disproof has in the past quarter century given rise to vigorous controversy.[1] More recently James Rachels has offered a moral argument intended to show that there could not be a being worthy of worship.[2] In this paper I shall examine the position Rachels is arguing for in some detail. I shall endeavor to show that his argument is unsound and, more interestingly, that the genuine philosophical perplexity which motivates it can be dispelled without too much difficulty.

I

Rachels summarizes his position in the form of the following argument:[3]

(1) If any being is God, he must be a fitting object of worship.

(2) No being could possibly be a fitting object of worship, since worship requires the abandonment of one's role as an autonomous moral agent.

(3) Therefore, there cannot be any being who is God.

In order to test this argument for validity some uniform interpretation of its English modal auxiliaries in terms of a philosophically well understood set of modalities must be found. It seems clear that Rachels intends (1) to be read as a proposition of *de dicto* logical or conceptual necessity. He claims that 'it is necessarily true that God (if he exists) is worthy of worship. Any being who is not worthy of worship cannot

From *Religious Studies*, Vol. 11, 1975, pp. 265–81. Reprinted by permission of Cambridge University Press and the author.

[1] J. N. Findlay, 'Can God's Existence Be Disproved?' in *New Essays in Philosophical Theology* (ed. A. Flew and A. MacIntyre), New York, 1964. See discussion in the replies to Findlay by G. E. Hughes and A. C. Rainer in *New Essays in Philosophical Theology* and in P. C. Appleby, 'On Religious Attitudes', *Religious Studies* 6, pp. 359–68.

[2] J. Rachels, 'God and Human Attitudes', *Religious Studies* 7, pp. 325–37. [Reading II in the present volume: page numbers in cross-references have been adjusted accordingly.]

[3] Ibid., p. 45. The argument (1)–(3) is expressed in Rachels' own words.

be God'.[4] Hence, no violence is done to his intentions if we recast the argument in the following canonical form:

(4) Necessarily, if some being is God, then that being is worthy of worship.

(5) It is not possible that some being is worthy of worship.

(6) It is not possible that some being is God.

In the restated argument all the modal operators are to be understood as expressing *de dicto* logical necessity and possibility as explicated in one of the standard systems of alethic modal logic in order to avoid fallacies of quivocation. On this interpretation the argument is valid.[5] Furthermore, on Rachels' view that 'God' is not a proper name but a title,[6] there is no reason to object to (4). The soundness of the argument then hangs, as it should, on whether (5) is true.

Now (5) is certainly not an obvious modal truth, and so it is incumbent upon Rachels to argue for it. That he accepts this onus is evident from the since-clause in (2) which signals the argument that is the most interesting feature of Rachels' paper. Unfortunately, however, Rachels does not make this argument perfectly clear, and so it must be reconstructed for him. The following valid argument would suffice to establish (5) if it were sound:

(7) It is not possible that some being is worthy of worship and there are some moral agents.

(8) Necessarily, there are some moral agents.

(5) It is not possible that some being is worthy of worship.

To evaluate the soundness of this argument something more must be said about the concept of moral agency. Rachels' views on this matter place him squarely within what might be called, speaking loosely, the Kantian tradition. He asserts that 'to be a moral agent is to be an autonomous or self-directed agent . . . The virtuous man is therefore identified with the man of integrity, i.e. the man who acts according to precepts which he can, on reflection, conscientiously approve in his own heart'.[7] Let us suppose, for the sake of argument, that this view of moral agency is correct. Rachels admits that it is controversial and requires a detailed treatment which is beyond the scope of his paper. But he thinks it is sound, and since I agree with him on this point, I shall grant him this conception without objection.

---

[4] Ibid., p. 34.

[5] My strategy is to reconstruct Rachels' arguments so that they turn out to be valid in order to focus my criticism on the truth value of their premises. I have, therefore, checked to be sure that the reconstructed arguments are formally valid at least in the Feys system T and the Lewis systems $S4$ and $S5$.

[6] Rachels, op. cit., p. 43.

[7] Ibid., p. 44.

Unfortunately, on this view (8) seems to be false. Far from always being self-directed agents who act on principles they can conscientiously and reflectively approve, most people in fact often enough act in unprincipled and unreflective ways such that they cannot conscientiously approve all of their own conduct in their own hearts. And even if each of us is sometimes a moral agent in the requisite sense, this is a contingent truth and not a necessary one. It would be slightly unfair, however, to challenge what is intended as an *a priori* argument on empirical grounds, and so I propose to resort to the somwhat drastic expedient of stipulating that (8) is a necessary truth about the possibility of moral agency. A more formal paraphrase of (8) can then be expressed as follows:

(9) Necessarily, it is possible that there are moral agents.

One must as a consequence of this stipulation accept the conclusion that most of us most of the time are not in fact full-fledged moral agents, but this is not, I think, an intolerable perversion of at least some of the evaluative uses of 'moral agent'. And we can now reformulate the argument in a more perspicuous way:

(10) It is not possible that some being is worthy of worship and that it is possible that there are moral agents.

(9) Necessarily, it is possible that there are moral agents.

(5) It is not possible that some being is worthy of worship.

This argument is also valid, and only the acceptability of (10) remains to be examined. Here we reach what is for Rachels' argument the heart of the matter; it also seems to be the heart of darkness.

Why should anyone be tempted to accept (10)? Rachels thinks he has found grounds for accepting it in certain features of the concept of worship. On his view, 'That God is not to be judged, challenged, defied, or disobeyed, is at bottom a *truth of logic*; to do any of these things is incompatible with taking him as one to be worshipped.'[8] He also says: 'The point is not merely that it would be imprudent to defy God, since we certainly can't get away with it; rather, there is a stronger, *logical point* involved—namely, that if we recognise any being *as God*, then we are committed, in virtue of that recognition, to obeying him'.[9] Hence, 'in admitting that a being is worthy of worship we would be recognizing him as having an unqualified claim on our obedience'.[10] We are then faced, according to Rachels, with 'a conflict between the role of worshipper, which by its very nature commits one to total subservience to God, and the role of moral agent, which necessarily involves autonomous decision making'.[11] In other words, there is, roughly speaking,

[8] Rachels, op. cit., p. 44.
[9] Ibid., p. 42.
[10] Ibid., p. 44.
[11] Ibid. p. 45.

supposed to be a conflict between regarding some being as worthy of worship and being a moral agent.

But, after all, role-conflict is not logical contradiction, and it is not clear just how the alleged conflict is supposed to enhance the plausibility of (10). For consider what someone who accepts Rachels' views on the logic of worship would be committed to. He would accept, I suppose, the following argument:

(11) Necessarily, God is worthy of worship.

(12) Necessarily, if God is worthy of worship, then for all persons p and all actions a if God commands a person p to do an action a, then p ought to do a.

(13) Necessarily, for all persons p and all actions a if God commands a person p to do an action a, then p ought to do a.

This argument is valid with the modal operators taken, as before, to express *de dicto* logical necessity, 'a' and 'p' taken to be bound variables. and 'ought' in (12) and (13) taken to express a moral ought. Since 'God' is not taken to be a proper name, (11)–(13) should be understood as not implying the existence of God, parallel to our construal of (1) and (4). Hence, (13) does not imply by itself any existential claims about God, or for that matter about persons or actions, but merely expresses the logical connection between the concept of God and the concept of unqualified obedience. Let us also suppose, for the sake of argument, that (11)–(13) are true. The question which remains is how (13) is supposed to support (10). After all, since (13) is consistent with there being no divine commands, it hardly seems to conflict logically with the autonomy of any moral agent.

Rachels has anticipated an objection of this sort. His response is to claim that 'even if God did not require obedience to detailed commands, the worshipper would still be committed to the abandonment of his role as a moral agent *if* God required it'.[12] It is clear that, if God issues commands, then the worshipper is committed to obeying them; what is not so obvious is just how this is supposed to commit the worshipper to abandoning his role as a moral agent. In order to see whether this latter commitment is involved in worship, let us suppose that God does issue a command:

(14) God commands P to do A.

where 'P' and 'A' are constants substituted for the variables 'p' and 'a'. From (13) and (14) it follows:

(15) P ought to do A.

It should be noted that (14) is not a necessary truth but that it does

[12] Rachels, op. cit., p. 45.

imply the existence of God and at least one person. That (14) is not a necessary truth should be obvious from the fact that, even if God exists necessarily, it is not necessary that he ever issues any commands. Does the supposition expressed by (14) conflict with the autonomy of a moral agent?

Presumably a moral agent might, on reflection, conclude that (15) was unacceptable. He might assert:

(16) It is not the case that P ought to do A.

On the assumption that ought-statements can be incompatible, he would then be driven to denying (15) and, to preserve consistency, to denying either (13) or (14). Since (13) is a necessary truth, his only consistent option would be to deny (14). But denying (14) does not by itself compel him to deny the existence of God, for (14) is an internally complex proposition which can be partially analysed as follows:

(17) There is something which is God and which commands P to do A.

The denial of (17) is equivalent to the following:

(18) Everything is such that either it is not God or it does not command P to do A.

And a moral agent can assert (18) without denying the existence of God by asserting its second disjunct and claiming:

(19) God exists but God does not command P to do A.

In other words, an autonomous moral agent can admit the existence of God if he is prepared to deny that any putative divine command which is inconsistent with his hard-core reflective moral judgments really is a divine command. He can resolve the supposed role-conflict by acknowledging that genuine divine commands ought to be obeyed unconditionally but maintaining that no directive which he does not accept on moral grounds is a genuine divine command. For the following three propositions are logically compatible:

(20) God exists.

(21) God sometimes commands agents to do certain things.

(22) God never commands anything an autonomous and well-informed moral agent would, on reflection, disapprove.

Hence, since (13) does not entail or otherwise support (10) and because Rachels has given no other reason for accepting (10), it is rational to reject (10). Indeed, (10) seems to be demonstrably false. After all, Rachels would admit, as was noted above, the following claim:

(23) It is possible that some being is worthy of worship and that this being issues no commands and that it is possible that there are moral agents.

Furthermore, an obvious truth is the following:

(24) That some being is worthy of worship and that this being issues no commands and that it is possible that there are moral agents entails that some being is worthy of worship.

And, using the logical truth,

(25) (Possibly (p and q) and (p and q entail r)) entail possibly (p and r)

it can be validly inferred:

(26) It is possible that some being is worthy of worship and that it is possible that there are moral agents.

which is the negation of (10). Therefore, the argument for (6) from (4), (5), (9) and (10) is unsound. Rachels has failed to provide what he promised—a valid and sound 'a priori argument against the existence of God which is based on the conception of God as a fitting object of worship'.[13]

II

At this point the reader may suspect that, although Rachels' modal argument fails to show that there could not be anything worthy of worship, it does raise some philosophical issues which have not yet been dealt with adequately. This suspicion seems to me essentially correct, and so I shall press on in the attempt to get at the underlying perplexity which might have led Rachels to construct his argument.

One begins to appreciate what may be troubling Rachels when one asks whether someone who proposes to accept (18) is justified in all cases in asserting the second disjunct and denying the first. At first blush it would seem that the theist has a good reason for supposing that God would not, indeed could not, command anything which a well-informed autonomous moral agent should be unable to accept. After all, Rachels explicitly allows that 'it has been admitted as a necessary truth that God is perfectly good; it follows as a corollary that He would never require us to do anything except what is right'.[14] In other words, the theist is committed to the following claim:

(27) Necessarily, God is perfectly good.

with (27) interpreted in the same way as (11). Hence, it seems open to him to argue that, because (27) is true, any command which is not acceptable to a well-informed and autonomous moral agent could not be a divine command. So the theist seems driven logically, for reasons which Rachels acknowledges, to accept the second disjunct of (18) and to deny that wicked commands could come from God.

[13] Rachels, op. cit., p. 34.   [14] Ibid., p. 45.

It comes as a surprise, therefore, to find Rachels contending that this line of argument rests on a misunderstanding of (27). What he offers in support of this contention are the following remarks:

'We cannot determine whether some being is God without first checking on whether he is perfectly good; and we cannot decide whether he is perfectly good without knowing (among other things) whether his commands to us are right. Thus our own judgment that some actions are right, and others wrong, is logically prior to our recognition of any being as God. The upshot of this is that we cannot justify the suspension of our own judgment on the grounds that we are deferring to God's commands (which, as a matter of logic, *must* be right); for if, by our own best judgment, the command is wrong, this gives us good reason to withhold the title "God" from the commander.'[15]

Now these remarks seem to be correct; one need only note that the situation being described involves epistemic rather than logical priority. What is puzzling is why Rachels thinks this description of the theistic moral agent's epistemic situation shows up a misunderstanding of (27). Surely the theist need only be committed to obeying God's commands because they are necessarily morally legitimate themselves; he need not be committed to obeying such commands simply because they are the decrees of a superior power.[16] What could be more natural, then, than using his reflective moral judgments as a touchstone for determining which claims to moral authority might plausibly be regarded as divine? Doubtless, many theists do in fact surrender their moral autonomy to human institutions and authorities, but then so do many nontheists. What seems clear is that the theist is not required by logic to suspend his moral judgment in the face of any human authority. Of course, the theist is committed to the view that if God commands then he should obey, but he may not be able to justify the belief that God has commanded a certain action without first having good moral reasons to think that he ought to do what has been commanded.

Why should Rachels be inclined to suppose that the theist should find this situation unsatisfactory? I suspect that it is because he imagines that a theist who uses his own moral judgments as a basis for deciding whether or not to obey commands cannot be yielding the appropriate sort of unqualified obedience which is owed to a being which is worthy of worship. To put the point crudely: if a moral agent sits in judgment on God's commands, accepting some and rejecting others, then he is not totally subservient to God.

[15] Ibid., p. 46.
[16] However, some theists, the socalled divine command theorists, among whom Descartes and perhaps Ockham are to be numbered, come perilously close to such a commitment.

If this is what Rachels supposes, then it is clear that he has misunderstood the position of the theist who is also an autonomous moral agent. This misunderstanding can be traced, I think, to a failure to make an important distinction between unqualified obedience to a command which is of divine origin and unqualified acceptance of the claim that a command is of divine origin. This distinction can be made clearer by examining the contrast between the following propositions:

(28) If God commands P to do A, then P ought to do A only if conditions C are satisfied.

(29) P ought to assent to the claim that God commands P to do A only if conditions C′ are satisfied.

Presumably, since the theist accepts (13) and (27), he is committed to rejecting (28) for any nonvacuous specification of conditions C. This is what unqualified obedience amounts to. But the theist can accept (29) with rather strong nonvacuous specifications of the epistemic conditions C′ which qualify his assent to the claim that a command is of divine origin. Since many theists believe that there are powerful evil spirits trying to deceive them, they ought to, and do, require that particularly stringent epistemic conditions be satisfied before they accept the claim that God has promulgated a certain decree. Frequently such conditions are formulated in terms of coherence with scripture and dogma, but there is no logical reason why coherence with moral judgments about which theist, on reflection, is very certain should not be included in such conditions. It is not as if the theist is sitting in judgment on commands which are known by him to be of divine origin and qualifying his obedience to God. Rather, he is endeavouring to determine whether certain commands are genuinely God's and, hence, ought to be obeyed and is qualifying his assent to claims of moral authority made on religious grounds. This he must do if he is not to become a fanatic or the victim of charismatic religious charlatans. Therefore, it is a mistake to suppose that the theist who is cautious about accepting putative divine commands as genuine is thereby qualifying his obedience to those commands which he does accept with justification as being divine.[17]

But, surely, it may be objected, in support of Rachels, God might command just anything; after all, he is necessarily omnipotent. In particular, it might seem that he could command a person to abandon his role as a moral agent, that is to say, to relinquish his moral autonomy. If so, then by instantiation of (13) it would follow:

(30) Necessarily, if God commands P to relinquish his moral autonomy, then P ought to relinquish his moral autonomy.

[17] A similar critical point has been elaborated in some detail in R. A. Oakes 'Reply to Professor Rachels', *Religious Studies* 8, pp. 165-7.

And if God did so command, it would be correct to assert:

(31) God commands P to relinquish his moral autonomy.

and to infer by *modus ponens*:

(32) P ought to relinquish his moral autonomy.

Surely (32), though not a logical impossibility, seems to be troublesome at least to those theists who wish to subscribe to a Kantian view of moral agency. Except, of course, that such theists would be prepared to assert:

(33) It is not the case that P ought to relinquish his moral autonomy.

and to infer by *modus tollens*:

(34) It is not the case that God commands P to relinquish his moral autonomy.

One person's *modus ponens* is another's *modus tollens*, and our Kantian theist is at no logical disadvantage in this argument. Indeed, since he accepts (27), he might assert the stronger proposition:

(35) It is not possible that God commands P to relinquish his moral autonomy.

and justify this claim in terms of a theory of the divine attributes which has it that God's omnipotence is necessarily limited by his perfect goodness.

In any case, we have found no argument so far, *a priori* or empirical, which would pose a logical threat to the position of the theist who wishes to adopt a Kantian view of moral agency.

III

What does seem to threaten the position of the Kantian theist is not a matter of the logic of the concepts of moral agency or of worthiness of worship but rather of certain possible questions of fact and evidence. For it seems possible that a theist should have both good reasons for believing that God has commanded him to perform a certain action and good reasons for believing that it would be morally wrong for him to perform that action. Thus a theist can be confronted with moral dilemmas of a peculiar sort. The story of Abraham provides an illustration of the kind of moral problem which might arise. This story need not be interpreted in the idiosyncratic Kierkegaardian manner as involving a teleological suspension of the ethical in order for Abraham's dilemma to raise serious moral problems.[18]

[18] For criticism of the Kierkegaardian interpretation see G. Outka, 'Religious and Moral Duty: Notes on *Fear and Trembling*' in *Religion and Morality* (ed. G. Outka and J. P. Reeder), Garden City, 1973.

We may imagine that Abraham accepts (13). He also has good reason to accept the following:

(36) God commands Abraham to kill Isaac.

After all, Abraham had reason to believe that God had made and kept some rather remarkable promises to him in the past, such as giving him a son when he was one hundred years old.[19] Thus Abraham, we may suppose, had what he took to be good inductive evidence to support his assent to (36). Hence, from (13) and (36) he could infer:

(37) Abraham ought to kill Isaac.

But now we may also imagine, anachronistically perhaps, that Abraham is a Kantian moral agent who is inclined to accept, on reflection, the following argument:

(38) One ought not to kill an innocent child.
(39) Isaac is an innocent child.
(40) Abraham ought not to kill Isaac.

Obviously, Abraham cannot consistently accept both (37) and (40). What is he to do? Well, supposing that he does not even consider doubting (39), he must reject either (36) or (38). But he has good reasons to accept both of these propositions. His reasons for accepting (36), being inductive, are admittedly less than logically conclusive. However, since even reflective moral judgments are fallible, his reasons for accepting (38) will also be logically inconclusive; perhaps his reflective moral judgments are slightly askew.

There is, of course, an easy way out of this dilemma. Kant was aware of it, and it is rather surprising that Rachels does not seem to be. In discussing the case of an inquisitor, Kant makes these remarks:

'That it is wrong to deprive a man of his life because of his religious faith is certain, unless (to allow for the most remote possibility) a Divine Will, made known in extraordinary fashion, has ordered it otherwise. But that God has ever uttered this terrible injunction can be asserted only on the basis of historical documents and is never apodictically certain. After all, the revelation has reached the inquisitor only through men and has been interpreted by men, and even did it appear to have come to him from God Himself (like the command delivered to Abraham to slaughter his own son like a sheep) it is at least possible that in this instance a mistake has prevailed. But if this is so, the inquisitor would risk the danger of doing what would be wrong in the highest degree; and in this very act he is behaving unconscientiously. This is the case with respect to all historical and visionary faith; that is, the *possibility* ever remains that an error may be discovered in it. Hence it is unconscientious to follow such a faith with the possibility that perhaps what

[19] *Genesis* 21:1–3.

it commands or permits may be wrong, i.e., with the danger of disobedience to a human duty which is certain in and of itself.'[20]

Kant's claim, which is bound to be attractive to many contemporary
philosophers, is that Abraham is or can be certain of (38) but cannot
have reasons good enough to warrant accepting (36). Needless to say,
this is a very controversial thesis, and one which Abraham, and other
theists, need not accept. For Abraham can reasonably judge that, in
cases of conflict of duties, his actual duty is to obey God's commands
because obedience to God's commands overrides his other *prima facie*
duties in such cases. In so judging he would not abandon his role as an
autonomous moral agent, for, as Rachels himself admits, 'if we learn
that God (i.e. some being that we take to be God) requires us to do a
certain action, and we conclude on this account that the action is
morally right, then we have *still* made at least one moral judgment of
our own, namely that whatever this being requires is morally right'.[21]
Furthermore, Abraham might have very good reasons, at least, it seems,
in terms of the evidential canons of his theistic conceptual framework,
for believing that God has given him a command. Hence, he might be
certain of (36) and dubious about (38).

Now it is fairly clear that this Abraham is no knight of faith; he is a
moral rationalist who disagrees with Kant about the probative force of
various sorts of evidence. His position is at least logically consistent. Is
it utterly irrational? That depends, I suppose, on whether it is possible
to have evidence which makes it certain that God has commanded a
certain action. This question raises the hardest problems of religious
epistemology, but, as far as I know, it is an open question. For I know
of no argument which shows:

(41) It is not possible that there is evidence which makes it certain
that God has commanded someone to kill an innocent child.

with 'God' here taken to have existential import. Here we seem to reach
an impasse at the epistemological chasm which separates theistic from
nontheistic basic assumptions.

Of course, Abraham need not be certain of (36) in any very strong
sense; Kant is surely correct in thinking that it is possible that Abraham
is mistaken. But neither is the duty not to kill an innocent child 'certain
in and of itself' as Kant supposes, or at least there seems to be no good

[20] I. Kant, *Religion Within the Limits of Reason Alone* (tr. T. M. Greene and
H. H. Hudson), New York, 1960, p. 175. Kant also says: 'That I ought not to kill
my good son is certain beyond a shadow of a doubt; that you, as you appear to
be, are God, I am not convinced and will never be even if your voice would resound
from the (visible) heavens'. This remark from *Der Streit der Facultäten* is cited in
G. Outka, *op. cit.*, p. 235.
[21] Rachels, op. cit., p. 46.

reason for the theist to subscribe to this variety of moral dogmatism. In the absence of logically conclusive evidence either way, Abraham can remain reasonable if for him (36) is epistemically preferable to (38). This may seem unlikely given Abraham's total evidence, or ours, but it is not impossible. It is not that Abraham need be thought of as acting unconscientiously; he is running grave risks of doing wrong no matter how he acts. If he kills Isaac and God has not commanded it, he acts wrongly, but equally if he does not kill Isaac and God has commanded it, he acts wrongly. His dilemma is an agonizing one, and ordinary theists should breathe a sigh of relief because it does not confront them. However, if a theist like Abraham confronts such a dilemma, then it does seem unfair to accuse him of being unconscientious simply because he must risk doing wrong and cannot be certain what would be wrong to do in his circumstances. Soldiers who had to decide whether to shoot a Vietnamese, not knowing whether he was a Viet Cong agent armed with grenades or an innocent peasant, also ran serious moral risks, but even if a soldier kills an innocent peasant he need not be regarded as having acted unconscientiously. Risky moral decisions made under uncertainty can have appalling consequences even if they are made in reasonable ways.

If our Abraham is neither conceptually confused nor provably irrational, is he wicked? It is not clear that this is the case. Abraham freely accepts the moral principle:

(42) If God commands someone to kill an innocent person, then he ought to kill that person.

Is this principle a manifestly repugnant one? The theist, arguing on his own ground, need not be driven to agree that it is. From a consequentialist point of view he can maintain that God, since he is omniscient, omnipotent and perfectly good, can appropriately compensate both the killer and his victim in the relevant felicific or beatific respects either here or hereafter. Furthermore, on more formal gounds the theist can successfully apply the universalizability or reciprocity test to (42). He may acknowledge that if God commands someone to kill him then that person ought to kill him, for he may think that he would acquire special merit in the sight of God were he to be a willing sacrifice in such circumstances. He might, of course, consistent with this admission, also believe that no one who claims to have been commanded to sacrifice him has in fact been so commanded by God, and so resist vigorously all sorts of assassination attempts by religious fanatics. The most the theist can be forced to concede, provided he is moderately clever, is that (42) *sounds* harsh and inhumane. But then he will hasten to add that this is merely because we cannot understand why God does what he does, though we may trust that it is all for the best.

If correct, this establishes that our rationalistic Abraham has a way out of the moral dilemma posed by (37) and (40) which does not require him to abandon his role as an autonomous moral agent. Furthermore, this way out allows that he may consistently accept the command to sacrifice Isaac as specifying his actual moral duty and, within his own conceptual framework, correctly claim that he is neither irrational nor wicked. Of course, he may well be mistaken. And, naturally enough, the nontheist, who does not accept many of the assumptions of this framework, will be scandalised. He will, for instance, find the compensations and special merits alluded to above utterly fanciful and quite literally incredible. He may well claim that if the theist can swallow all this then he is a dangerous and undesirable sort of person to have around, and he may devoutly wish that there should be fewer theists so that the moral order should stand a chance of being stable and secure. What this shows is the depth of the differences which can separate some theists from some nontheists. Perhaps Kant's way out of the dilemma is the only exit the nontheist is prepared to tolerate on the part of the theist. This would show, if it were so, something about the limits of the nontheist's tolerance. It would not establish that the theist has confused or inconsistent beliefs. Nor would it prove, as Rachels may think, that theistic belief is bound to take the worshipper 'beyond morality' or that theistic beliefs should, in this respect, be regarded as a source of 'severe embarrassment'.[22]

IV

Perhaps some embarrassment for the theist could be generated by means of a more careful scrutiny of some of the central concepts used in the argument so far. The terms 'obedience' and 'autonomy' have been used rather loosely, and artfully contrived definitions of these or related terms might produce a result that would bother the theist. In any case, this possibility seems interesting enough to warrant some further exploration.

Let us consider first the notion of obedience. When would it be appropriate to say that someone is actually obeying a command rather than merely doing what has, in fact, been commanded? A suggestion as to how this question might be answered is found in the following remarks by Max Weber:

'"Obedience" will be taken to mean that the action of the person obeying follows in essentials such a course that the content of the command

[22] Rachels, op. cit., p. 48.

may be taken to have become the basis of action for its own sake. Furthermore, the fact that it is so taken is referable only to the formal obligation, without regard to the actor's own attitude to the value or lack of value of the content of the command as such.[23]

As it stands, the suggestion is a bit nebulous; moreover, it seems stipulative rather than lexicographically descriptive. However, it does suffice to motivate the introduction of a technical notion of subservience, which may be formulated as follows:

(43) Agent p is subservient in doing action a if and only if p's only reason for doing a is p's belief that a has been commanded.

Now (43) does not quite capture the concept which is relevant to the problem at hand. After all, the theist need not be subservient to earthly commanders in anything he does; he may even consider himself obliged by conscience to engage in civil disobedience from time to time. What is wanted is a notion of religious subservience, which can be explicated as follows:

(44) Agent p is religiously subservient in doing action a if and only if p's only reason for doing a is p's belief that a has the property of being commanded by God.

'Religious subservience' is, of course, a term of art; however, it may express some of what Rachels has in mind when he speaks of the worshipper's 'total subservience to God'.[24] Even if it is not what Rachels intends, the concept of religious subservience has some interest in its own right.

It is a bit harder to see just how the notion of autonomy should be reshaped to suit present purposes. Since at this point no pretense to either lexicographical accuracy or historical fidelity is being made, misunderstanding will be avoided if technical locutions are introduced to pick out the concepts under discussion. A preliminary stab at what is wanted can be made using the following stipulation:

(45) Agent p is correct in doing action a if and only if p's only reason for doing a would, if true, suffice to show that a is what p ought to do.

The intuitive idea encapsulated in this stipulation is that an agent acts correctly provided that his reason for action provides epistemic warrant for the conclusion that he acts as he ought to do. The reason why (45) represents only a preliminary attempt to capture the concept being sought is that a particular agent can be both religiously subservient and

---

[23] M. Weber, *The Theory of Social and Economic Organisation* (tr. A. M. Henderson and T. Parsons), New York, 1964, p. 327.

[24] Rachels, op. cit., p. 45.

correct in doing a particular action. To show that this is the case the theist can deploy the following valid argument:

(46) Necessarily, if God is perfectly good, then for all actions *a* and for all agents *p*, if *a* has the property of being commanded by God, then *a* is what *p* ought to do.

(27) Necessarily, God is perfectly good.

(47) Necessarily, for all actions *a* and for all agents *p*, if *a* has the property of being commanded by God, then *a* is what *p* ought to do.

Let us suppose, no reason to the contrary being obvious, that this argument is sound. Consider now a particular agent P and a particular action A. Assume that P is religiously subservient in doing A. This implies that P's only reason for doing A is his belief that A has the property of being commanded by God. If this belief were true, we could assert:

(48) A has the property of being commanded by God.

But (47) and (48) together entail:

(49) A is what P ought to do.

Hence, P's only reason for doing A would, if true, suffice to show, by a valid and sound deductive argument, that A is what P ought to do, and this implies that P is correct in doing A. Of course, this involves assuming that (47) is true, but that assumption seems unproblematic because (47) follows from (46), which is innocuous enough, and (27), which even Rachels will allow. Therefore, we must cast about for a concept rather different from correctness if we wish to make trouble for the religiously subservient theist.

The term 'moral correctness' will serve to pick out the required concept. It can be introduced using the following locution:

(50) Agent *p* is morally correct in doing action *a* if and only if there is some property *m* such that (i) *m* makes *a* what *p* ought to do, and (ii) *p*'s only reason for doing *a* is *p*'s belief that *a* has *m*.

The idea behind this stipulation is that an agent acts morally correctly provided that his reason for action is the belief that the action in question has a certain property and that the very property he believes the action to have makes it the thing he ought to do. Of course, (50) and (44) are not inconsistent, for the property referred to in (50) might be identical with the property of being commanded by God. Thus, consider again a particular agent P and a particular action A. Suppose both that P's only reason for doing A is P's belief that A has the property of being commanded by God and that being commanded by God makes A what P ought to do. On these suppositions, P is morally correct in doing A, and P is religiously subservient in doing A. But notice that we have, in effect, imported a variant of the divine command theory into this argument in assuming that being commanded by God makes A what P ought to do. This assumption would be objectionable to many theists and to non-theistic moral theorists.

So let us rule out this possibility by means of the following stipulation:

(51) For all agents p, all actions a and all properties m, it is not the case both that m makes a what p ought to do and that m is identical with the property of being commanded by God.

It is easy to see that (44), (50) and (51) are an inconsistent triad. Assuming (51), the proof goes as follows. Consider an arbitrary agent P and an arbitrary action A. Suppose, first, that P is morally correct in doing A. Then, according to (50), some M makes A what P ought to do and P's only reason for doing A is his belief that A has M. But then, by (51), M is not identical with the property of being commanded by God. Hence, it is not the case that P's only reason for doing A is his belief that A has the property of being commanded by God. Therefore, by (44), it is not the case that P is religiously subservient in doing A. Suppose, second, that P is religiously subservient in doing A. Then, according to (44), P's only reason for doing A is his belief that A has the property of being commanded by God. By (51), for arbitrary M, either M is not identical with the property of being commanded by God or M does not make A what P ought to do. If M makes A what P ought to do, then, since M is not identical with the property of being commanded by God, it is not the case that P's only reason for doing A is P's belief that A has M, in which case P is not morally correct in doing A by (50). On the other hand, if M is identical with the property of being commanded by God, M does not make A what P ought to do, in which case P is not morally correct in doing A by (50). In either case, P is not morally correct in doing A. Therefore, given (51), (44) and (50) are inconsistent.

What this shows, roughly speaking, is that, on the assumption that a certain version of the divine command theory is false, in doing an action A and agent P cannot be both religiously subservient and morally correct in the technical senses given to these notions. It is not surprising that, allowed enough latitude for stipulation, one can introduce incompatible terms into a philosophical vocabulary. The interesting question is whether the theist would, or should, be bothered by such contrivances. But it is easy to see that the theist need not be unduly perturbed by this particular set of manoeuvres. After all, he may simply reject (51).[25] Moreover,

[25] There are several variants of the divine command theory which might then be considered. For suggestive discussion see R. M. Adams, 'A Modified Divine Command Theory of Ethical Wrongness' in *Religion and Morality* (ed. G. Outka and J. P. Reeder), Garden City, 1973. [Reading V in the present volume.]

even if he chooses not to reject (51), he can challenge (50) by pointing out that it places such stringent conditions on moral correctness that even secular moral theorists may find it embarrassing. Notice that (50) requires that an agent's only reason for doing an action be his belief that it has the very property which, as it happens, makes that action what he ought to do. But consider two agents P_1, a utilitarian, and P_2, a deontologist, and two actions A_1 and A_2 which are alike in all morally relevant respects. Suppose that P_1 does A_1 because he believes that A_1 has the property of maximizing expected utility and that P_2 does A_2 because he believes that A_2 has the property of being prescribed by a correct moral rule. On the assumption that both these properties would not make similar actions what one ought to do, at least one of these agents, and very possibly both, are not morally correct in doing what they do. But this would seem to be too harsh a judgment. Since most, perhaps all, agents frequently do what they ought to do for mixed reasons or the wrong reasons, when indeed they even manage to do what they ought to do, it would seem that (50) stipulates an unreasonably high standard for moral correctness in action. Perhaps it is a symptom of unhealthy scrupulosity when an agent is much concerned with moral correctness in the sense of (50); an agent might well do what he ought to do more often and with less strain, and lead a happier life to boot, if he aspired only to correctness in action in the sense of (45) and, in addition, took reasonable precautions to include many truths and few falsehoods among his reasons for action. If endorsing (50), or something like it, is the price that must be paid to bother the theist, then moral theorists may be unwilling to pay such a high price for such meagre benefits. And, even if some nontheists are willing to accept (50), there seems to be no compelling reason why a theist should accept it.

I shall conclude with a brief summary of my argument. In Section I I tried to show that Rachels' attempt to prove that no being could be a fitting object of worship rests on a false premiss and is, therefore, unsound. In Section II I contended that two other arguments, which can be constructed from premisses congenial to Rachels in order to embarrass the theist who would hold a Kantian view of moral agency, turn out on close inspection to be inconclusive or to rest on confusions. In Section III I attempted to elucidate how a theist might consistently deal with conflicts between divine commands and ordinary moral duties so as to make sense of the Abraham story without retreating to Kierkegaardian irrationalism. In Section IV I tried to show how with a bit of ingenuity one can construct contextually incompatible concepts of religious subservience and moral correctness, but I argued that there is no reason for the theist to be especially perturbed by such artifices. I have not undertaken to show that the views I attribute to the theist are plausible given the evidence base I share with Rachels; I suspect that I could not hope to succeed at that task. Instead, I have merely tried to defend the theist against some arguments which purport to demonstrate that his beliefs could not possibly be true.[26]

[26] It is a pleasure to thank my colleagues D. W. Brock and J. W. Lenz for helpful comments on an earlier version of this paper.

OMNIPOTENCE AND GOD'S ABILITY TO SIN

NELSON PIKE

IN the first chapter of the *Epistle of James* (verse 13) it is said that 'God cannot be tempted by evil.' This idea recurs in the confessional literature of the Christian tradition,[1] and is stated in its fullest form in the theological doctrine of God's *impeccability*.[2] God is not only free from sin, He is incapable of moral deviation. God not only does not sin, He *cannot* sin. This is generally held to be part of what is communicated in the claim thát God is perfectly good. On the surface, at least, this doctrine appears to be in conflict with the traditional Christian doctrine of divine omnipotence. An omnipotent being is one that can do all things possible. But, surely, it is possible to sin. Men do this sort of thing all the time. It would thus appear that if God is perfectly good (and thus impeccable) He cannot sin; and if God is omnipotent (and thus can do all things possible), He can sin.

This argument appears to be sophistical. We are tempted to dismiss it with a single comment, viz., it involves an equivocation on the modal element in the statement 'God can (cannot) sin.' In the long run, I think (and shall try to show) that this single remark is correct. But that's in the long run; and in the interim there is a complicated and interesting terrain that has not yet been adequately explored. In this paper I shall discuss this matter in detail. After working through what I judge to be a number of conceptual tangles that have accumulated in this literature on this topic, I shall end by making a suggestion as to how the various senses of 'God can (cannot) sin' ought to be sorted out.

I

I shall begin by identifying three assumptions that will work importantly in the discussion to follow.

First, I shall assume that within the discourse of the Christian religion,

From *American Philosophical Quarterly*, Vol. 6, No. 3, July 1969, pp. 208-16. Reprinted by permission of Basil Blackwell Publisher.

[1] See, for example, the *Westminster Confession*, ch. V, sect. IV and the *Longer Catechism of the Eastern Church*, sects. 156-7.
[2] See the *Catholic Encyclopedia* (New York: Robert Appleton Co., 1967).

the term 'God' is a descriptive expression having an identifiable meaning. It is not, e.g., a proper name. As part of this first assumption, I shall suppose, further, that 'God' is a very special type of descriptive expression—what I shall call a *title*. A title is a term used to mark a certain position or value-status as does, e.g., 'Caesar' in the sentence 'Hadrian is Caesar.' To say that Hadrian is Caesar is to say that Hadrian occupies a certain governmental position; more specifically, it is to say that Hadrian is Emperor of Rome. To affirm of some individual that He is God is to affirm that the individual occupies some special position (e.g., that He is Ruler of the Universe) or that that individual has some special value-status (e.g., that He is a being a greater than which cannot be conceived).

Secondly, I shall assume that whatever the particular semantical import of the term 'God' may be (i.e., whether it means, for instance, 'Ruler of the Universe', 'a being than which no greater can be conceived', etc.), the attribute-terms 'perfectly good', 'omnipotent', 'omniscient', and the like, attach to it in such a way as to make the functions 'If x is God, then x is perfectly good', 'If x is God, then x is omnipotent', etc., necessary truths. It is a logically necessary condition of bearing the title 'God', that an individual be perfectly good, omnipotent, omniscient, and so on for all of the standard attributes traditionally assigned to the Christian God. If we could assume that in order to be Emperor (as opposed to Empress) of Rome one had to be male (rather than female), then if 'x is Caesar' means 'x is Emperor of Rome', then 'If x is Caesar, then x is male' would have the same logical status as I am assuming for 'If x is God, then x is perfectly good.' 'If x is God, then x is omniscient', etc.

If there is an individual (e.g., Yahweh) who occupies the position or has the value-status marked by the term 'God', then that individual is perfectly good, omnipotent, omniscient, etc. If He were not, then He could not (logically) occupy the position or have the value-status in question. However, with respect to the predicate 'perfectly good', I shall assume that any individual possessing the attribute named by this phrase might not (logically) have possessed that attribute. This assumption entails that any individual who occupies the position or who has the value-status indicated by the term 'God' might not (logically) have held that position or had that status. It should be noticed that this third assumption covers only a *logical* possibility. I am not assuming that there is any real (i.e., material) possibility that Yahweh (if He exists) is not perfectly good. I am assuming only that the hypothetical function 'If x is *Yahweh*, then x is perfectly good' differs from the hypothetical function 'If x is *God*, then x is perfectly good' in that the former, unlike the latter, does not formulate a necessary truth. With Job, one might at least *entertain* the idea that Yahweh is not perfectly good. This is at least a *consistent* conjecture even though to assert such a thing would be to deny a well-established part of the Faith.[3]

I now want to make two further preliminary comments—one about the predicate 'omnipotent' and one about the concept of moral responsibility.

Pre-analytically, to say that a given individual is omnipotent is to say that that individual has unlimited power. This is usually expressed in religious discourse with the phrase 'infinite power'. St. Thomas explicated the intuitive content of this idea as follows: 'God is called omnipotent because He can do all things that are possible absolutely.'[4] As traditionally understood, St. Thomas' formula must be given a relatively restricted interpretation. The permissive verb 'do' in 'do all things possible' is usually replaced with one of a range of more specific verbs such as 'create', 'bring about', 'effect', 'make-to-be', 'produce', etc.[5] God's omnipotence is thus to be thought of as creative-power only. It is not to be understood as the ability to *do* anything at all, e.g., it is not to be interpreted as including the ability to swim the English Channel or ride a bicycle. God is omnipotent in that He can create, bring about, effect, make-to-be, produce, etc., anything possible absolutely. For St. Thomas, something is 'possible absolutely' when its description is logically consistent. Thus, on the finished analysis, God is omnipotent insofar as He can bring about any consistently describable object or state of affairs. In his article on 'Omnipotence' in the *Catholic Encyclopedia*,[6] J. A. McHugh analyzes the notion in this way. It seems clear from the context of this piece that McHugh meant to be reformulating St. Thomas' view of the matter. I might add that I think this restricted interpretation of the pre-analytical notion of infinite power is an accurate portrayal of the way this concept works in the ordinary as well as in most of the technical (theological) discourse of the Christian religion.

Now, let us suppose that an innocent child suffers a slow and torturous death by starvation. Let it be true that this event was avoidable and that no greater good was served by its occurrence. Let it also be true that neither the child (or its parents) committed an offense for which it (or its parents) could be righteously punished. This is a consistently describable state of affairs (whether or not it ever occurred). I think it is clear that an individual that knowingly brought this state of affairs about would be morally reprehensible.

[3] The truth of this assumption is argued at some length by C. B. Martin in the fourth chapter of his *Religious Belief* (Ithaca: Cornell Press, 1964).
[4] *Summa Theologica*, Pt. I, Q. 25, a 3. This passage taken from *The Basic Writings of St. Thomas Aquinas*, ed. by Anton Pegis, p. 263.
[5] These verbs are sometimes called 'factitive verbs'.
[6] New York: Robert Appleton Co., 1911.

We can now formulate the problem under discussion in this paper more rigorously than above. God is omnipotent. When read hypothetically, this statement formulates a necessary truth. On the analysis of 'omnipotent' with which we are working, it follows that God (if He exists) can bring about any consistently describable state of affairs. However, God is perfectly good. Again, when read hypothetically, this statement formulates a necessary truth. Further, an individual would not qualify as perfectly good if he were to act in a morally reprehensible way. Thus, the statement 'God acts in a morally reprehensible way' is logically incoherent. This is to say that 'God sins' is a logical contradiction.[7] Hence, some consistently describable states of affairs are such that God (being perfectly good) could not bring them about.[8] The problem, then, is this: If God is both omnipotent and perfectly good, there are at least some consistently describable states of affairs that He both can and cannot bring about. There would thus appear to be a logical conflict in the claim that God is both omnipotent and perfectly good.

I think it is worth noting that the problem just exposed is not the same as the classical theological problem of evil. The problem of evil is generally formulated as follows: Evil exists. If God exists and is omnipotent, He could have prevented evil if He had wanted to. If God exists and is perfectly good, He would have wanted to. Since evil in fact exists, it follows that God does not exist. This argument is supposed to point up a conflict between the attribute of perfect goodness and the attribute of omnipotence. But the conflict is not of a rigorous sort. So far as this argument goes, it is logically possible for there to exist a being who is both perfectly good and omnipotent. The argument is supposed to show only that since it is contingently true that evil exists, it is contingently false that omnipotence and perfect goodness are possessed by a single individual. However, the problem we are now discussing has a sharper report than this. The argument generating this latter is supposed to show that there is a direct logical conflict between the attribute of perfect goodness and the attribute of omnipotence. No contingent premiss is employed (such as, e.g., that evil exists) and the conclusion drawn is that it is logically impossible (not just contingently false) that there exists an individual who is both omnipotent and perfectly good.

[7] There is probably some distinction to be made between acting in a morally reprehensible way and sinning. However, for purposes of this discussion, I shall treat these concepts as one.

[8] I am here assuming that if God brings about a given circumstance, He does so *knowingly*. God could not bring about a given circumstance by mistake. I think this follows the idea that God is omniscient.

II

In reply to objection 2, article 3, question 25, Part I of the *Summa Theologica*, St. Thomas Aquinas writes as follows[9]

To sin is to fall short of a perfect action; hence to be able to sin is to be able to fall short in action, which is repugnant to omnipotence. Therefore, it is that God cannot sin, because of his omnipotence. Now, it is true that the philosopher says that *God can deliberately do what is evil.* But this must be understood either on condition, the antecedent of which is impossible—as, for instance, if we were to say that God can do evil things if He will. For there is no reason why a conditional proposition should not be true, though both the antecendent and the consequent are impossible; as if one were to say: *If a man is an ass, he has four feet.* Or, he may be understood to mean that God can do some things which now seem to be evil: which, however, if He did them, would then be good. Or he is, perhaps, speaking after the common manner of the pagans, who thought that men became gods, like Jupiter or Mercury.

In this passage St. Thomas offers three suggestions as to how the problem we are discussing might be solved. (I do not count the suggestion made in the last sentence of this passage because it is clear that St. Thomas is not here talking about *God* but about individuals such as Jupiter or Mercury who are mistakenly thought to be God by certain misguided pagans.) Let us look at these three suggestions:

(A) St. Thomas begins with the claim that 'to sin is to fall short of a perfect action'. He then says that an omnipotent being cannot fall short in action. The conclusion is that God cannot sin because He is omnipotent. Essentially this same reasoning is developed in slightly more detail in the seventh chapter of St. Anselm's *Proslogium.* Anselm says:[10]

But how art Thou omnipotent, if Thou are not capable of all things? or, if Thou canst not be corrupted and canst not lie . . . how art Thou capable of all things? Or else to be capable of these things is not power but impotence. For he who is capable of these things is capable of what is not for his good, and of what he ought not to do and the more capable of them he is, the more power have adversity and perversity against him; and the less has he himself against these.

Anselm concludes that since God is omnipotent, adversity and perversity have no power against Him and He is not capable of anything through impotence. Therefore, since God is omnipotent, He is not capable of performing morally reprehensible actions.

[9] This passage is taken from *The Basic Writings of St. Thomas Aquinas*, p. 264.
[10] This passage is taken from S. N. Deane, *St. Anselm* (LaSalle: Open Court, 1958), p. 14.

This argument is interesting. Both Thomas and Anselm agree that God is unable to sin. Their effort is to show that instead of being in conflict with the claim that God is omnipotent, the assignment of this inability is a direct consequence of this latter claim. However, I think that the reasoning fails. Let us agree that to the extent that an individual is such that 'adversity and perversity' can prevail against him, to that extent is he weak—*morally* weak. He is then capable of 'falling short in action', i.e., of doing 'what he ought not to do'. So far as I can see, an individual that is able to bring about any consistently describable state of affairs might well be morally weak. I can find no conceptual difficulty in the idea of a diabolical omnipotent being. Creative-power and moral strength are readily discernible concepts. If this is right, then it does not follow from the claim that God is omnipotent that He is unable to act in a morally reprehensible way. In fact, as was set out in the original statement of the problem, quite the opposite conclusion seems to be warranted. If a being is able to bring about *any* consistently describable state of affairs, it would seem that he should be able to bring about states of affairs the production of which would be morally reprehensible. St. Thomas' first suggestion thus seems to be ineffective as a solution to the problem we are confronting. (I shall have something more to say on this topic in the fourth section of this paper.)

(B) The Philosopher says that God can deliberately do what is evil. Looking for a way of understanding this remark whereby it can be squared with his own view on the matter, St. Thomas suggests that what Aristotle may have meant is that the individual that is God can do evil *if He wants to*. Thomas adds that this last statement might be true even if it impossible that God should want to do evil and even if it is also impossible that He can do evil. The point seems to be that although the statements 'The individual that is God wants to do evil' and 'The individual that is God can do evil' are false (or impossible), the conditional statement containing the first of these statements as the antecedent and the second of these statements as the consequent, might nonetheless be true.

Consider the statement: 'Jones has an ace in his hand if he wants to play it'. This statement has the surface grammar of a conditional, but it is not a conditional. The item mentioned in the 'if . . .' clause does not condition the item described in the rest of the statement. If Jones has an ace in his hand, he has an ace in his hand whether or not he wants to play it. What, then, does the 'if . . .' clause do in this statement? I think that it serves as a way of recording a certain indeterminacy as to what will be done about (or, with respect to) the unconditional fact described in the rest of the statement. Whether or not this last remark is precisely right, the major point to be seen here is this: the statement 'Jones has an ace in his hand if he wants to play it' is false if the statement 'Jones has an ace in his hand' is false. We are here dealing with a use of 'if . . .' that does not fit the analysis usually given conditional statements such as 'I shall be nourished if I eat'.

Now consider the statement: 'Jones can wiggle his ear if he wants to.' I think that this is another instance in which 'if . . .' operates in a non-conditional capacity. If Jones has the ability to wiggle his ear, he has the ability whether or not he wants to wiggle his ear. The question of whether he wants to wiggle his ear is independent of whether he has the ability to do so. As in the case above, what the 'if . . .' clause adds in this statement is not a condition on the claim that Jones has an ability. It serves as a way of recording the idea that there is some indeterminacy as to whether the ability that Jones has will be exercised. But again, I am less concerned with whether this last remark about the function of the 'if . . .' clause is precisely right than I am with the relation between the truth values of 'Jones can wiggle his ear if he wants to' and 'Jones can wiggle his ear'. In this case, as above, if Jones does not have the ability to wiggle his ear, then the statement 'Jones can wiggle his ear if he wants to' is false. If the second of the above statements is false, then the first is false too.

St. Thomas says that the statement 'God can sin if He wants to' is true. He adds that both the antecedent and the consequent of this conditional are 'impossible'. The trouble here, I think, is that 'God can sin if He wants to' is not a conditional statement; and the most important point to be seen in this connection is that this statement is false if its component 'God can sin' is false. But, St. Thomas clearly holds that 'God can sin' is false (or impossible)—he says that God's inability to sin is a consequence of the fact that He is omnipotent. The conclusion must be that 'God can sin if He wants to' is also false (or impossible). Thomas has not provided a way of understanding The Philosopher's claim that God can deliberately do what is evil. As long as St. Thomas insists that God does not have the ability to sin (which, he says, follows from the claim that God is omnipotent) he must deny that God can sin if He wants to. He must then reject The Philosopher's claim that God can deliberately do what is evil if this latter means that God can sin if He wants to.

(C) Still looking for a way of understanding the idea that God can deliberately do what is evil, St. Thomas' next suggestion is that God can do things which seem evil to us but which are such that if God did them, they would not be evil. I think that there are at least two ways of understanding this comment.

First, Thomas may be suggesting that God has the ability to bring about states of affairs that are, in fact, good, but which seem evil to us due to our limited knowledge, sympathy, moral insight, etc. However, even if we were to agree that this is true, Thomas could draw no conclusion as regards the starving-child situation described earlier. We have specified this situation in such a way that it not only *seems* evil to us, but *is* evil in fact. We have included in our description of this case that the child suffers intensely; that this suffering is not deserved and that it might have been avoided. We have added that the suffering does not contribute to a greater good. Thus, this line of reasoning does not really help with the major problem we are discussing in this paper. We still have a range of consistently describable states of affairs that God (being perfectly good) cannot bring about. We thus still have reason to think that God (being perfectly good) is not omnipotent.

Secondly, St. Thomas may be suggesting that God has the ability to bring about *any* consistently describable states of affairs (including the starving-child situation), but that if *He* were to bring about such a situation), it would no longer count as evil. Let 'evil' cover any situation which is such that if one were to (knowingly) bring it about (though it is avoidable), that individual would be morally reprehensible. The view we are now considering requires that we append a special theory about the meanings of the *other* value-terms involved in our discussion. In particular, it requires that when applied to God, the expressions 'not morally reprehensible' and 'perfectly good' be assigned meanings other than the ones they have when used to characterize individuals other than God. If a man were knowingly to bring about the starving-child situation, he would be morally reprehensible. He could no longer be described as perfectly good. But (so the argument goes) if God were to bring about the same situation, He might still count as perfectly good (not morally reprehensible) in the special sense of 'not morally reprehensible' and 'perfectly good' that apply *only* to God.

I have two comments to make about this second way of understanding St. Thomas' claim that God can do things that seem evil to us but which are such that if He did them, they would not be evil.

First, in my opinion the view we are now entertaining about the theological use of 'perfectly good' and 'not morally reprehensible' is one that was decisively criticized by Duns Scotus, Bishop Berkeley, and John Stuart Mill.[11] If God were to bring about circumstances such as

[11] See Scotus' *Oxford Commentary on the Sentences of Peter Lombard*, Q. II ('Man's Natural Knowledge of God'), second statement, argument IV; Berkeley's *Alciphron*, Dialogue IV, sects. 16–22 (especially sect. 17); and J. S. Mill's *An Examination of Sir William Hamilton's Philosophy*, ch. 6. What follows in this paragraph is what I think constitutes the center of these three discussions.

the starving-child situation, He would be morally reprehensible and thus not perfectly good in the ordinary senses of these phrases. If we now contrive some special phrases (retaining the tabletures 'not morally reprehensible' and 'perfectly good') that might apply to God though He produces the situation in question, this will be of no special interest. Whatever *else* can be said of God, if He were to bring about the starving-child situation, He would not be an appropriate object of the *praise* we ordinarily convey with the phrase 'perfectly good'. He would be an appropriate object of the *blame* we ordinarily convey with the phrase 'morally reprehensible'. We might put this point as follows: If we deny that God is perfectly good in the ordinary sense of 'perfectly good', and if we cover this move by introducing a technical, well-removed, sense of 'perfectly good' that can apply to God though He brings about circumstances such as the starving-child situation, it may appear that we have solved the problem under discussion in this paper, but we haven't. We have eliminated conflict by agreeing that God lacks one of the 'perfections', i.e., one of the qualities the possession of which makes an individual better (more praiseworthy) than he would otherwise be. Unless a being is perfectly good in the *ordinary* sense of 'perfectly good', that being is not as praiseworthy as he might otherwise be. It was the sense of 'perfectly good' that connects with the idea of being morally praiseworthy (in the ordinary sense) that gave rise to the problem in the first place. Surely, it is this sense of 'perfectly good' that religious people have in mind when they characterize God as perfectly good.

The second remark I should like to make about this second interpretation of St. Thomas' third suggestion is that the view assigned to St. Thomas in this interpretation is one that he would most likely reject. I shall need a moment to develop this point.[12]

Consider the word 'triangle' as it occurs in the discourse of geometry. Compare it with 'triangle' as it is used in the discourse of carpentry or wood-working. Within the discourse of geometry, the criteria governing the use of this term are more strict than are the criteria governing its use in the discourse of carpentry. The geometrical figure is an exemplary (i.e., perfect) version of the shape embodied in the triangular block of wood. We reach an understanding of the geometrical shape by correcting imperfections (i.e., irregularities) in the shape of the triangular block. Now, let's ask whether 'triangle' has the same meaning in the two cases. We might answer this question in either way. Once the relation between

[12] The next two paragraphs are taken almost without change from the Introduction to my book *God and Timelessness* (London: Routledge and Kegan-Paul, 1969). What I say here about the relation between 'triangle' as used in the discourse of geometry and 'triangle' as used in the discourse of carpentry is very much like a thesis developed by John Stuart Mill in the text mentioned above.

the criteria governing its use in the two cases is made clear, no one would be confused if we were to say that 'triangle' has the same meaning in the two cases, and no one would be confused if we were to say that 'triangle' has different meaning in the two cases. Regarding the relation between the criteria, the following point seems to me to be of considerable importance: If a block of wood is triangular, it has three angles that add up (roughly) to 180 degrees and its sides are (roughly) straight. *At least this much* is implied with respect to a geometrical figure when one characterizes it as a triangle. By this I mean that if one could find reasons sufficient for rejecting the claim that a given thing is a triangle as 'triangle' is used in the discourse of carpentry (suppose that one of its sides is visibly curved or suppose it has four angles), these same reasons would be sufficient for rejecting the claim that the thing in question is a triangle as 'triangle' is used in the discourse of geometry. In fact, more than this can be said. If one could find slight irregularities in the shape of a thing that would cause some hesitation or prompt some reservation about whether it is a triangle as 'triangle' is used in the discourse of carpentry, such irregularities would be sufficient to establish that the thing in question is not a triangle as 'triangle' is used in the discourse of geometry.

According to St. Thomas, finite things are caused by God. They thus bear a 'likeness' to God. God's attributes are exemplary-versions of the attributes possessed by finite things. We reach whatever understanding we have of God's attributes, by removing 'imperfections' that attend these qualities when possessed by finite things.[13] With respect to the predicate 'good', St. Thomas writes as follows in the *Summa Theologica* (Pt. I, Q. 6, A. 4):[14]

Each being is called good because of the divine goodness, the first exemplar principle as well as the efficient and telic cause of all goodness. Yet it is nonetheless the case that each being is called good because of a likeness of the divine goodness by which it is denominated.

[13] In the *Summa Theologica* (Pt. I, Q. 14, a.1) St. Thomas says:
Because perfections flowing from God to creatures exist in a higher state in God Himself, whenever a name taken from any created perfection is attributed to God, there must be separated from its signification anything that belongs to the imperfect mode proper to creatures. (Quoted from *The Basic Writings of St. Thomas Aquinas*, p. 136.)

[14] Both of the following passages were translated by George P. Klubertanz, S. J., *Thomas Aquinas on Analogy* (Chicago: Loyola Press, 1960), p. 55. For a good analysis of St. Thomas' views on the topic of theological predication, see the whole of Klubertanz' discussion in ch. III. For an enlightening discussion of how poorly St. Thomas has been understood on this topic (even by his most illustrious interpreters) see Klubertanz' remarks in ch. I and Berkeley's discussion of St. Thomas in *Alciphron IV*, sects. 20–22. According to Berkeley, St. Thomas' doctrine of 'analogy by proportionality' is to be regarded as an expression of the view we are now discussing.

Again, in *questiones disputatae de veritate* (XXI, 4), St. Thomas says:

Every agent is found to produce effects which resemble it. Hence, if the first goodness is the efficient cause of all things, it must imprint its like-ness upon things which it produces. Thus each thing is called good because of an intrinsic goodness impressed upon it, and yet is further denominated good because of the first goodness which is the exemplar and efficient cause of all created goodness.

Shall we say that 'good' has the same meaning when applied to God as it has when applied to things other than God (e.g. Socrates)? As above, it seems to me that the answer we give to this question is unimportant once we get this far into the discussion. We might say that 'good' has the same meaning in the two cases, and we might say that it has different meanings in the two cases. We might even say (as St. Thomas sometimes says) that we are here dealing with a case in which 'good' is 'midway between' having the same meaning and having different meanings in the two cases. However, as above, the following point has importance re-gardless of how one answers the question about same or different mean-ings. When St. Thomas affirms that God is good, I think he means to be saying *at least as much* about God as one would say about, e.g., Socrates, if one were to affirm that Socrates is good. A study of 'good' in non-theological contexts reveals at least the minimum implications of the corresponding predication statements relating to God. If we could find reasons sufficient for rejecting the claim that a given thing is good as 'good' is used in discourse about finite agents, these same reasons would be sufficient for rejecting the claim that the thing in question is good as 'good' is used in discourse about the nature of God. In fact, if we could find moral irregularities sufficient to cause hesitations or prompt reservations about whether a thing is good as 'good' is used in discourse about finite agents, these irregularities would be sufficient to establish that the agent under consideration is not good as 'good' is used in the discourse of theology.

So far as I can see, St. Thomas would not endorse a technical, well-removed sense of the phrase 'perfectly good' that could apply to God even if God were to bring about circumstances or states of affairs the production of which would be morally reprehensible (in the ordinary sense of 'morally reprehensible'). When St. Thomas says that God is good, he means to be saying that God possesses the exemplary version of the quality assigned to Socrates in the sentence 'Socrates is good'. This is to say that while Socrates is good, God is *perfectly* good. But on this understanding of the matter, God could not be perfectly good were He to bring about the starving-child situation described earlier. If Socrates were to bring about such a situation, we would probably refuse to describe him as 'good'. At the very least, we would surely have hesitations or reservations concerning his moral goodness. But, if such an action would be sufficient to cause hesitations concerning an application of 'good' in discourse about finite agents, this same action would be sufficient to *defeat* an application of 'good' in discourse about the nature of God. In this latter context, 'good' means '*perfectly* good'. The logic of this phrase will not tolerate even a minor moral irregularity.

III

I want now to discuss an approach to our problem that is very different from any of those suggested by St. Thomas. It is an approach taken by J. A. McHugh in the *Encyclopedia* article mentioned above. I think we can best get at the center of McHugh's thinking if we start with a review of that side of the problem generated by the concept of perfect goodness.

God is perfectly good. This is a necessary statement. If a being is perfectly good, that being does not bring about objects or states of affairs the production of which would be morally reprehensible. This, too, is a necessary truth. Thus, the statement 'God brings about objects or states of affairs the production of which would be morally reprehensible' is logically contradictory. It follows that God cannot bring about such states of affairs. But, McHugh argues, this should not be taken as a reason for denying God's omnipotence. As St. Thomas has pointed out, a being may be omnipotent and yet not be able to do an act whose description is logically contradictory. (A being may be omnipotent though he is not able to make a round-square.) Since the claim that God acts in a morally reprehensible way is logically contradictory, God's inability to perform such acts does not constitute a limitation of power.

Consider the following argument: The term 'Gid' is the title held by the most efficient of those who make only leather sandals. 'Gid makes leather belts' is thus a logical contradiction. It follows that the individual that is Gid cannot make leather belts. But Gid may still be omnipotent. Though He does not have the ability to make leather belts, our analysis of 'omnipotence' requires only that an omnipotent being be able to do an act whose description is logically consistent and 'Gid makes leather belts' is logically inconsistent. Thus, Gid's inability to make leather belts does not constitute a limitation on his power.

I think it is plain that this last argument is deficient since its conclusion is absurd. I think, too, that in this case, two difficulties are forced pretty close to the surface.

First, the description of the kind of object that Gid is (allegedly) unable to make (viz., leather belts) is not logically contradictory. What is contradictory is the claim that *Gid makes them.* But our definition of 'omnipotent' requires only that the *state of affairs* brought about be consistently describable (excluding, therefore, round squares). It does not require that a statement in which it is claimed that a given individual brings it about be consistent. Thus, if Gid does not have the ability to produce leather belts, he is not omnipotent on St. Thomas' definition of 'omnipotent'. If it follows from the definition of 'Gid' that the individual who bears this title cannot make leather belts; and if this entails that the individual in question does not have the creative-ability to make belts, the conclusion must be that, by definition, the individual who bears this title is a limited being. I think the same kind of conclusion must be drawn in the case of God's ability to sin. If it follows from the definition of 'God' that the individual bearing this title cannot bring about objects or states of affairs the production of which would be morally reprehensible; and if it follows from this that the individual bearing this title does not have the creative power necessary to bring about such states of affairs though they are consistently describable; the conclusion is that the individual who is God is not omnipotent on the analysis of 'omnipotent' that we are supposing. The fact (if it is a fact) that this creative limitation is built into the definition of 'God' making 'God sins' a logical contradiction does not disturb this conclusion. The upshot is, simply, that the term 'God' has been so specified that an individual qualifying for this title could not be omnipotent. (Of course, this is awkward because it is also a condition of bearing this title that the individual in question be omnipotent.)

The second difficulty in the argument about Gid is this: The term 'Gid' has been defined in such a way that 'Gid makes leather belts' is logically contradictory. The conclusion drawn is that Gid *cannot* make belts. What this means is that if some individual makes leather belts, this is logically sufficient to assure that the individual in question does not bear the title 'Gid'. But it does not follow from this (as is supposed in the argument) that the individual who is Gid does not have the *ability* to make leather belts. All we can conclude is that if he does have this ability, it is one that he does not *exercise*. Thus, as is affirmed in the argument, the individual who is Gid might be omnipotent though he cannot make leather belts (and be Gid). If we suppose that he is omnipotent, we must conclude that has the ability to make belts; but since, by hypothesis, the individual in question is Gid, we know (analytically) that he does not exercise this ability. Again, I think the same is true with respect to the argument about God's inability to sin. The term 'God' has been so specified that the individual who is God *cannot* sin and be God. But it will not follow from this that the individual who is God does not have the *ability* to sin. He might have the creative power necessary to bring about states of affairs the production of which would be morally reprehensible. He is perfectly good (and thus God) insofar as He does not exercise this power.

IV

If we collect together a number of threads developed in the preceding discussions, I think we shall have enough to provide at least a tentative solution to the problem we have been discussing. I shall proceed by distinguishing three ways in which the statement 'God cannot sin' might be understood.

'God cannot sin' might mean: 'If a given individual sins, it follows logically that the individual does not bear the title "God".' In this case, the 'cannot' in 'cannot sin' expresses logical impossibility. The sentence as a whole might be rewritten as follows: $N(x)$ (If x is God then x does not sin.) On the assumptions we are making in this paper, this statement is true. We have supposed that the meaning of the title term 'God' is such that it is a logically necessary condition of bearing this title that one be perfectly good and thus that one not perform actions that are morally reprehensible.

Secondly, 'God cannot sin' might mean that if a given individual is God, that individual does not have the ability to sin, i.e., He does not have the creative power necessary to bring about states of affairs the production of which would be morally reprehensible, such as, e.g., the starving-child situation described earlier. In this case, the 'cannot' in 'cannot sin' does not express logical impossibility. It expresses a material concept—that of a limitation of creative-power (as in, e.g., 'I cannot make leather sandals'). On St. Thomas' analysis of 'omnipotence' if the individual who is God (Yahweh) cannot sin in this sense, He is not omnipotent. Further, I think there is strong reason to suspect that if the individual that is God (Yahweh) cannot sin in this sense, He is not perfectly good either. Insofar as the phrase 'perfectly good' applies to the individual that is God (Yahweh) as an expression of praise—warranted by the fact that this individual does not sin—God could not be perfectly good if He does not have the ability to sin. If an individual does not have the creative-power necessary to bring about evil states of affairs, he cannot be praised (morally) for failing to bring them about. Insofar as I do not have the physical strength necessary to crush my next door neighbor with my bare hands, it is not to my credit (morally) that I do not perform this heinous act.

Thirdly, 'God cannot sin' might mean that although the individual that is God (Yahweh) has the ability (i.e., the creative power necessary) to bring about states of affairs the production of which would be morally reprehensible, His nature or character is such as to provide material assurance that He will not act in this way. This is the sense in which one might say that Jones, having been reared to regard animals as sensitive and precious friends, just *cannot* be cruel to animals. Here 'cannot' is not to be analyzed in terms of the notion of logical impossibility and it does not mark a limitation on Jones's physical power (he may be physically able to kick the kitten). It is used to express the idea that Jones is *strongly disposed* to be kind to animals or at least to avoid actions that would be cruel. We have a special locution in English that covers this idea. When we say that Jones cannot be cruel to animals, what we mean is that Jones cannot *bring himself* to be cruel to animals. On this third analysis of 'God cannot sin', the claim conveyed in this form of words is that the individual that is God (Yahweh) is of such character that he cannot bring himself to act in a morally reprehensible way. God is strongly disposed to perform only morally acceptable actions.

Look back for a moment over the ground we have covered.

McHugh noticed that the statement 'God sins' is logically incoherent. He thus (rightly) concluded that God cannot sin. He was here affirming that the semantical import of the title term 'God' is such that an individual could not (logically) bear this title and be a sinner. McHugh's conclusion ('God cannot sin') was thus intended in the first sense just mentioned. But McHugh then went on to suppose that God cannot sin in a sense of this phrase that connects with the notion of omnipotence. This is the second sense mentioned above. This conclusion was not warranted. The individual who bears the title 'God' (Yahweh) might have the creative power necessary to bring about objects or states of affairs the production of which would be morally reprehensible even though 'God sins' is logically contradictory. The conclusion is, simply, that if an individual bears the title 'God', He does not exercise this creative-power.

St. Thomas and St. Anselm said that God cannot sin in that 'adversity and pervisity cannot prevail against Him'. This appears to be the claim put forward in the *Epistle of James* 1:13—the claim embodied in the theological doctrine of God's impeccability—viz., 'God cannot be tempted by evil.' The individual that is God has a very special kind of strength—moral strength, or strength of character. He is, as we say, 'above temptation'. Both Thomas and Anselm concluded that God's inability to sin has a direct connection with the notion of omnipotence. It is because God is omnipotent that He is unable to sin. This line of reasoning confuses the second and third senses of the statement 'God cannot sin.' If we say that the individual who is God cannot sin in this second sense (i.e., in the sense that connects with the idea of creative power and thus with the standard notion of omnipotence) this is not to assign that individual strength. It is to assign Him a very definite limitation. The strength-concept in this cluster of ideas is the notion of not being able to *bring oneself* to sin. God has a special strength of character. But this latter concept is expressed in the third sense of 'God cannot sin'. As I argued earlier, this third sense appears to have no logical connection with the idea of having or lacking the creative power to bring about consistently describable states of affairs. It thus appears to have no logical connection to the notion of omnipotence as this latter concept is explicated by St. Thomas.

The individual that is God cannot sin and bear the title 'God'. The individual that is God cannot sin in that sinning would be contrary to a firm and stable feature of His nature. These claims are compatible with the idea that the individual that is God has the ability (i.e., the creative power necessary) to bring about states of affairs the production of which would be morally reprehensible. All we need add is that there is complete assurance that He will not exercise this ability and that if He did exercise this ability (which is logically possible but materially excluded), He would not bear the title 'God'. Further, if God is to be omnipotent in St. Thomas' sense of 'omnipotent', and if God is to be perfectly good in a sense of this phrase that expresses praise for the fact that He refrains from sinful actions, this appears to be the conclusion that *must* be drawn.

A MODIFIED DIVINE COMMAND THEORY OF ETHICAL WRONGNESS

ROBERT MERRIHEW ADAMS

I

IT is widely held that all those theories are indefensible which attempt to explain in terms of the will or commands of God what it is for an act to be ethically right or wrong. In this paper I shall state such a theory, which I believe to be defensible; and I shall try to defend it against what seem to me to be the most important and interesting objections to it. I call my theory a *modified* divine command theory because in it I renounce certain claims that are commonly made in divine command analyses of ethical terms. (I should add that it is *my* theory only in that I shall state it, and that I believe it is defensible—not that I am sure it is correct.) I present it as a theory of ethical *wrongness* partly for convenience. It could also be presented as a theory of the nature of ethical obligatoriness or of ethical permittedness. Indeed, I will have occasion to make some remarks about the concept of ethical permittedness. But as we shall see (in Section IV) I am not prepared to claim that the theory can be extended to all ethical terms; and it is therefore important that it not be presented as a theory about ethical terms in general.

It will be helpful to begin with the statement of a simple, *un*modified divine command theory of ethical wrongness. This is the theory that ethical wrongness *consists in* being contrary to God's commands, or that the word 'wrong' in ethical contexts *means* 'contrary to God's commands'. It implies that the following two statement forms are logically equivalent.

(1) It is wrong (for A) to do X.
(2) It is contrary to God's commands (for A) to do X.

Of course that is not all that the theory implies. It also implies that (2) is conceptually prior to (1), so that the meaning of (1) is to be explained in terms of (2), and not the other way round. It might prove fairly diffi-

From *Religion and Morality: A Collection of Essays*, edited by Gene Outka and John P. Reeder, Jr. Copyright ©1973 by G. Outka and J. P. Reeder, Jr. Reprinted by permission of Doubleday and Company, Inc.

cult to state or explain in what that conceptual priority consists, but I shall not go into that here. I do not wish ultimately to defend the theory in its unmodified form, and I think I have stated it fully enough for my present purposes.

I have stated it as a theory about the meaning of the word 'wrong' in ethical contexts. The most obvious objection to the theory is that the word 'wrong' is used in ethical contexts by many people who cannot mean by it what the theory says they must mean, since they do not believe that there exists a God. This objection seems to me sufficient to refute the theory if it is presented as an analysis of what *everybody* means by 'wrong' in ethical contexts. The theory cannot reasonably be offered except as a theory about what the word 'wrong' means as used by *some but not all* people in ethical contexts. Let us say that the theory offers an analysis of the meaning of 'wrong' in Judeo-Christian religious ethical discourse. This restriction of scope will apply to my modified divine command theory too. This restriction obviously gives rise to a possible objection. Isn't it more plausible to suppose that Judeo-Christian believers use 'wrong' with the same meaning as other people do? This problem will be discussed in Section VI.

In Section II, I will discuss what seems to me the most important objection to the unmodified divine command theory, and suggest how the theory can be modified to meet it. Section III will be devoted to a brief but fairly comprehensive account of the use of 'wrong' in Judeo-Christian ethical discourse, from the point of view of the modified divine command theory. The theory will be further elaborated in dealing with objections in Sections IV to VI. In a seventh and final section, I will note some problems arising from unresolved issues in the general theory of analysis and meaning, and briefly discuss their bearing on the modified divine command theory.

II

The following seems to me to be the gravest objection to the divine command theory of ethical wrongness, in the form in which I have stated it. Suppose God should command me to make it my chief end in life to inflict suffering on other human beings, for no other reason than that He commanded it. (For convenience I shall abbreviate this hypothesis to 'Suppose God should command cruelty for its own sake.') Will it seriously be claimed that in that case it would be wrong for me not to practice cruelty for its own sake? I see three possible answers to this question.

(1) It might be claimed that it is logically impossible for God to command cruelty for its own sake. In that case, of course, we need not

worry about whether it would be wrong to disobey if He did command it. It is senseless to agonize about what one should do in a logically impossible situation. This solution to the problem seems unlikely to be available to the divine command theorist, however. For why would he hold that it is logically impossible for God to command cruelty for its own sake? Some theologians (for instance, Thomas Aquinas) have believed (a) that what is right and wrong is independent of God's will, and (b) that God always does right by the necessity of His nature. Such theologians, if they believe that it would be wrong for God to command cruelty for its own sake, have reason to believe that it is logically impossible for Him to do so. But the divine command theorist, who does not agree that what is right and wrong is independent of God's will, does not seem to have such a reason to deny that it is logically possible for God to command cruelty for its own sake.

(2) Let us assume that it is logically possible for God to command cruelty for its own sake. In that case the divine command theory seems to imply that it would be wrong not to practice cruelty for its own sake. There have been at least a few adherents of divine command ethics who have been prepared to accept this consequence. William Ockham held that those acts which we call 'theft', adultery', and 'hatred of God' would be meritorious if God had commanded them.[1] He would surely have said the same about what I have been calling the practice of 'cruelty for its own sake'.

This position is one which I suspect most of us are likely to find somewhat shocking, even repulsive. We should therefore be particularly careful not to misunderstand it. We need not imagine that Ockham disciplined himself to be ready to practice cruelty for its own sake if God should command it. It was doubtless an article of faith for him that God is unalterably opposed to any such practice. The mere logical possibility that theft, adultery, and cruelty might have been commanded by God (and therefore meritorious) doubtless did not represent in Ockham's view any real possibility.

(3) Nonetheless, the view that if God commanded cruelty for its own sake it would be wrong not to practice it seems unacceptable to me; and I think many, perhaps most, other Jewish and Christian believers would find it unacceptable too. I must make clear the sense in which I find it unsatisfactory. It is not that I find an internal inconsistency in it. And I would not deny that it may reflect, accurately enough, the way

---

[1] Guillelmus de Occam, *Super 4 libros sententiarum*, bk. II, qu. 19, O, in Vol. IV of his *Opera plurima* (Lyon, 1494–6; reimpression en fac-similé, Farnborough, Hants, England: Gregg Press, 1962). I am not claiming that Ockham held a divine command theory of exactly the same sort that I have been discussing.

in which some believers use the word 'wrong'. I might as well frankly avow that I am looking for a divine command theory which at least might possibly be a correct account of how I use the word 'wrong'. I do not use the word 'wrong' in such a way that I would say that it would be wrong not to practice cruelty if God commanded it, and I am sure that many other believers agree with me on this point.

But now have I not rejected the divine command theory? I have assumed that it would be logically possible for God to command cruelty for its own sake. And I have rejected the view that if God commanded cruelty for its own sake, it would be wrong not to obey. It seems to follow that I am committed to the view that in certain logically possible circumstances it would not be wrong to disobey God. This position seems to be inconsistent with the theory that 'wrong' means 'contrary to God's commands'.

I want to argue, however, that it is still open to me to accept a modified form of the divine command theory of ethical wrongness. According to the modified divine command theory, when I say, 'It is wrong to do X', (at least part of) what I *mean* is that it is contrary to God's commands to do X. 'It is wrong to do X' *implies* 'It is contrary to God's commands to do X'. But 'It is contrary to God's commands to do X' implies 'It is wrong to do X' only if certain conditions are assumed—namely, only if it is assumed that God has the character which I believe Him to have, of loving His human creatures. If God were really to command us to make cruelty our goal, then He would not have that character of loving us, and I would not say it would be wrong to disobey Him.

But do I say that it would be wrong to obey Him in such a case? This is the point at which I am in danger of abandoning the divine command theory completely. I do abandon it completely if I say both of the following things.

(A) It would be wrong to obey God if He commanded cruelty for its own sake.

(B) In (A), 'wrong' is used in what is for me its normal ethical sense.

If I assert both (A) and (B), it is clear that I cannot consistently maintain that 'wrong' in its normal ethical sense for me means or implies 'contrary to God's commands'.

But from the fact that I deny that it would be wrong to disobey God if He commanded cruelty for its own sake, it does not follow that I must accept (A) and (B). Of course someone might claim that obedience and disobedience would both be ethically permitted in such a case; but that is not the view that I am suggesting. If I adopt the modified divine command theory as an analysis of my present concept of ethical wrongness (and if I adopt a similar analysis of my concept of ethical permittedness), I will not hold either that it would be wrong to disobey, or that it would be ethically permitted to disobey, or that it would be wrong to obey, or that it would ethically permitted to obey, if God commanded cruelty for its own sake. For I will say that my concept of ethical wrongness (and my concept of ethical permittedness) would 'break down' if I really believed that God commanded cruelty for its own sake. Or to put the matter somewhat more prosaically, I will say that my concepts of ethical wrongness and permittedness could not serve the functions they now serve, because using those concepts I could not call any action ethically wrong or ethically permitted, if I believed that God's will was so unloving. This position can be explained or developed in either of two ways, each of which has its advantages.

I could say that by 'X is ethically wrong' I mean 'X is contrary to the commands of a *loving* God' (i.e., 'There is a *loving* God and X is contrary to His commands') and by 'X is ethically permitted' I mean 'X is in accord with the commands of a *loving* God' (i.e., 'There is a *loving* God and X is not contrary to His commands'). On this analysis we can reason as follows. If there is only one God and He commands cruelty for its own sake, then presumably there is not a *loving* God. If there is not a loving God then neither 'X is ethically wrong' nor 'X is ethically permitted' is true of any X. Using my present concepts of ethical wrongness and permittedness, therefore, I could not (consistently) call any action ethically wrong or permitted if I believed that God commanded cruelty for its own sake. This way of developing the modified divine command theory is the simpler and neater of the two, and that might reasonably lead one to choose it for the construction of a theological ethical theory. On the other hand, I think it is also simpler and neater than ordinary religious ethical discourse, in which (for example) it may be felt that the statement that a certain act is wrong is *about* the will or commands of God in a way in which it is not about His love.

In this essay I shall prefer a second, rather similar, but somewhat untidier, understanding of the modified divine command theory, because I think it may lead us into some insights about the complexities of actual religious ethical discourse. According to this second version of the theory, the statement that something is ethically wrong (or permitted) says something about the will or commands of God, but not about His love. Every such statement, however, *presupposes* that certain conditions for the applicability of the believer's concepts of ethical right and wrong are satisfied. Among these conditions is that God does not command cruelty for its own sake—or, more generally, that God loves His human creatures. It need not be assumed that God's love is the only such condition.

The modified divine command theorist can say that the possibility of God commanding cruelty for its own sake is not provided for in the Judeo-Christian religious ethical system as he understands it. The possibility is not provided for, in the sense that the concepts of right and wrong have not been developed in such a way that actions could be correctly said to be right or wrong if God were believed to command cruelty for its own sake. The modified divine command theorist agrees that it is logically possible[2] that God should command cruelty for its own sake; but he holds that it is unthinkable that God should do so. To have *faith* in God is not just to believe that He exists, but also to trust in His love for mankind. The believer's concepts of ethical wrongness and permittedness are developed within the framework of his (or the religious community's) religious life, and therefore within the framework of the assumption that God loves us. The concept of the will or commands of God has a certain function in the believer's life, and the use of the words 'right' (in the sense of 'ethically permitted') and 'wrong' is tied to that function of that concept. But one of the reasons why the concept of the will of God can function as it does is that the love which God is believed to have toward men arouses in the believer certain attitudes of love toward God and devotion to His will. If the believer thinks about the unthinkable but logically possible situation in which God commands cruelty for its own sake, he finds that in relation to that kind of command of God he cannot take up the same attitude, and that the concept of the will or commands of God could not then have the same function in his life. For this reason he will not say that it would be wrong to disobey God, or right to obey Him, in that situation. At the same time he will not say that it would be wrong to obey God in that situation, because he is accustomed to use the word 'wrong' to say that something is contrary to the will of God, and it does not seem to him to be the right word to use to express his own personal revulsion toward an act against which there would be no divine authority. Similarly, he will not say that it would be 'right', in the sense of 'ethically permitted', to disobey God's command of cruelty; for that does not seem to him to be the right way to express his own personal attitude toward an act which would not be in accord with a divine authority. In this way the believer's concepts of ethical rightness and wrongness would break down

---

[2] Perhaps he will even think it is causally possible, but I do not regard any view on that issue as an integral part of the theory. The question whether it is causally possible for God to act 'out of character' is a difficult one which we need not go into here.

in the situation in which he believed that God commanded cruelty for its own sake—that is, they would not function as they now do, because he would not be prepared to use them to say that any action was right or wrong.

III

It is clear that according to this modified divine command theory, the meaning of the word 'wrong' in Judeo-Christian ethical discourse must be understood in terms of a complex of relations which believers' use of the word has, not only to their beliefs about God's commands, but also to their attitudes toward certain types of action. I think it will help us to understand the theory better if we can give a brief but fairly comprehensive description of the most important features of the Judeo-Christian ethical use of 'wrong', from the point of view of the modified divine command theory. That is what I shall try to do in this section.

(1) 'Wrong' and 'contrary to God's commands' at least contextually imply each other in Judeo-Christian ethical discourse. 'It is wrong to do X' will be assented to by the sincere Jewish or Christian believer if and only if he assents to 'It is contrary to God's commands to do X'. This is a fact sufficiently well known that the known believer who says the one commits himself publicly to the other.

Indeed 'wrong' and such expressions as 'against the will of God' seem to be used interchangeably in religious ethical discourse. If a believer asks his pastor, 'Do you think it's always against the will of God to use contraceptives?' and the pastor replies, 'I don't see anything wrong with the use of contraceptives in many cases', the pastor has answered the same question the inquirer asked.

(2) In ethical contexts, the statement that a certain action is wrong normally expresses certain volitional and emotional attitudes toward that action. In particular it normally expresses an intention, or at least an inclination, not to perform the action, and/or dispositions to feel guilty if one has performed it, to discourage others from performing it, and to react with anger, sorrow, or diminished respect toward others if they have performed it. I think this is true of Judeo-Christian ethical discourse as well as of other ethical discourse.

The interchangeability of 'wrong' and 'against the will of God' applies in full force here. It seems to make no difference to the expressive function of an ethical statement in a Judeo-Christian context which of these expressions is used. So far as I can see, the feelings and dispositions normally expressed by 'It is wrong to commit suicide' in a Judeo-Christian context are exactly the same as those normally expressed by 'It is against

God's will to commit suicide', or by 'Suicide is a violation of the commandments of God.'

I am speaking of attitudes *normally* expressed by statements that it is wrong to do a certain thing, or that it would be against God's will or commands to do that thing. I am not claiming that such attitudes are *always* expressed by statements of those sorts. Neither am I now suggesting any analysis of the *meaning* of the statements in terms of the attitudes they normally express. The relation between the meaning of the statements and the attitudes expressed is a matter about which I shall have somewhat more to say, later in this section and in Section VI. At this point I am simply observing that in fact statements of the forms 'It is wrong to do X', 'It is against God's will to do X', 'X is a violation of the commandments of God', normally do express certain attitudes, and that in Judeo-Christian ethical discourse they all typically express the same attitudes.

Of course these attitudes can be specified only within certain very wide limits of normality. The experience of guilt, for instance, or the feelings that one has about conduct of others of which one disapproves, vary greatly from one individual to another, and in the same individual from one occasion to another.

(3) In a Judeo-Christian context, moreover, the attitudes expressed by a statement that something is wrong are normally quite strongly affected and colored by specifically religious feelings and interests. They are apt to be motivated in various degrees by, and mixed in various proportions with, love, devotion, and loyalty toward God, and/or fear of God. Ethical wrongdoing is seen and experienced as *sin*, as rupture of personal or communal relationship with God. The normal feelings and experience of guilt for Judeo-Christian believers surely cannot be separated from beliefs, and ritual and devotional practices, having to do with God's judgment and forgiveness.

In all sin there is offense against a person (God), even when there is no offense against any other human person—for instance, if I have a vice which harms me but does not importantly harm any other human being. Therefore in the Judeo-Christian tradition reactions which are appropriate when one has offended another person are felt to be appropriate reactions to any ethical fault, regardless of whether another human being has been offended. I think this affects rather importantly the emotional connections of the word 'wrong' in Judeo-Christian discourse.

(4) When a Judeo-Christian believer is trying to decide, in an ethical way, whether it would be wrong for him to do a certain thing, he typically thinks of himself as trying to determine whether it would be against God's will for him to do it. His deliberations may turn on the

interpretation of certain religiously authoritative texts. They may be partly carried out in the form of prayer. It is quite possible, however, that his deliberations will take forms more familiar to the nonbeliever. Possibly his theology will encourage him to give some weight to his own intuitions and feelings about the matter, and those of other people. Such encouragement might be provided, for instance, by a doctrine of the leading of the Holy Spirit. Probably the believer will accept certain very general ethical principles as expressing commandments of God, and most of these may be principles which many nonbelievers would also accept (for instance, that it is always, or with very few exceptions, wrong to kill another human being). The believer's deliberation might consist entirely of reasoning from such general principles. But he would still regard it as an attempt to discover God's will on the matter.

(5) Typically, the Judeo-Christian believer is a nonnaturalist objectivist about ethical wrongness. When he says that something is (ethically) wrong, he means to be stating what he believes to be a fact of a certain sort—what I shall call a 'nonnatural objective fact'. Such a fact is objective in the sense that whether it obtains or not does not depend on whether any human being thinks it does. It is harder to give a satisfactory explanation of what I mean by 'nonnatural' here. Let us say that a nonnatural fact is one which does not consist simply in any fact or complex of facts which can be stated entirely in the languages of physics, chemistry, biology, and human psychology. That way of putting it obviously raises questions which it leaves unanswered, but I hope it may be clear enough for present purposes.

That ethical facts are objective and nonnatural has been believed by many people, including some famous philosophers—for instance, Plato and G. E. Moore. The term 'nonnaturalism' is sometimes used rather narrowly, to refer to a position held by Moore, and positions closely resembling it. Clearly, I am using 'nonnaturalist' in a broader sense here.

Given that the facts of wrongness asserted in Judeo-Christian ethics are nonnatural in the sense explained above, and that they accordingly do not consist entirely in facts of physics, chemistry, biology, and human psychology, the question arises, in what they do consist. According to the divine command theory (even the modified divine command theory), in so far as they are nonnatural and objective, they consist in facts about the will or commands of God. I think this is really the central point in a divine command theory of ethical wrongness. This is the point at which the divine command theory is distinguished from alternative theological theories of ethical wrongness, such as the theory that facts of ethical rightness and wrongness are objective, nonnatural facts about

ideas or essences subsisting eternally in God's understanding, not subject
to His will but guiding it.

The divine command account of the nonnatural fact-stating function
of Judeo-Christian ethical discourse has at least one advantage over its
competitors. It is clear, I think, that in stating that X is wrong a believer
normally commits himself to the view that X is contrary to the will or
commands of God. And the fact (if it is a fact) that X is contrary to the
will or commands of God is surely a nonnatural objective fact. But it is
not nearly so clear that in saying that X is wrong, the believer normally
commits himself to belief in any *other* nonnatural objective fact. (The
preceding sentence presupposes the rejection of the Moorean view that
the fact that X is wrong[3] is an objective nonnatual fact which cannot and
should not be analyzed in terms of other facts, natural or nonnatural.)

(6) The modified divine command theorist cannot consistently claim
that 'wrong' and 'contrary to God's commands' have exactly the same
meaning for him. For he admits that there is a logically possible situation
which he would describe by saying, 'God commands cruelty for its own
sake', but not by saying, 'It would be wrong not to practice cruelty for
its own sake'. If there were not at least some little difference between
the meanings with which he actually, normally uses the expressions
'wrong' and 'contrary to God's commands', there would be no reason
for them to differ in their applicability or inapplicability to the far-out
unthinkable case. We may now be in a position to improve somewhat
our understanding of what the modified divine command theorist can
suppose that difference in meaning to be, and of why he supposes that
the believer is unwilling to say that disobedience to a divine command
of cruelty for its own sake would be wrong.

We have seen that the expressions 'It is wrong' and 'It is contrary to
God's commands' or 'It is against the will of God' have virtually the
same uses in religious ethical discourse, and the same functions in the
religious ethical life. No doubt they differ slightly in the situations in
which they are most likely to be used and the emotional overtones they
are most apt to carry. But in all situations experienced or expected by
the believer as a believer they at least contextually imply each other,
and normally express the same or extremely similar emotional and
volitional attitudes.

There is also a difference in meaning, however, a difference which
is normally of no practical importance. All three of the following are
aspects of the normal use of 'it is wrong' in the life and conversation
of believers. (a) It is used to state what are believed to be facts about

---

[3] Moore took goodness and badness as primitive, rather than rightness and
wrongness; but that need not concern us here.

the will or commands of God. (b) It is used in formulating decisions a arguments about what to do (i.e., not just in deciding what one *ou* to do but in deciding *what to do*). (c) It expresses certain emotional and volitional attitudes toward the action under discussion. 'It is wrong' is commonly used to do all three of those things at once.

The same is true of 'It is contrary to God's commands' and 'It is against the will of God'. They are commonly used by believers to do the same three things, and to do them at once. But because of their grammatical form and their formal relationships with other straight-forwardly descriptive expressions about God, they are taken to be, first and last, descriptive expressions about God and His relation to whatever actions are under discussion. They can therefore be used to state what are supposed to be facts about God, even when one's emotional and decision-making attitude toward those supposed facts is quite contrary to the attitudes normally expressed by the words 'against the will of God'.

In the case of 'It is wrong', however, it is not clear that one of its functions, or one of the aspects of its normal use, is to be preferred in case of conflict with the others. I am not willing to say, 'It would be wrong not to do X', when both my own attitude and the attitude of most other people toward the doing of X under the indicated circum-stances is one of unqualified revulsion. On the other hand, neither am I willing to say, 'It would be wrong to do X', when I would merely be expressing my own personal revulsion (and perhaps that of other people as well) but nothing that I could regard as clothed in the majesty of a divine authority. The believer's concept of ethical wrongness therefore breaks down if one tries to apply it to the unthinkable case in which God commands cruelty for its own sake.

None of this seems to me inconsistent with the claim that part of what the believer normally means in saying 'X is wrong' is that X is con-trary to God's will or commands.

IV

The modified divine command theory clearly conceives of believers as valuing some things independently of their relation to God's commands. If the believer will not say that it would be wrong not to practice cruelty for its own sake if God commanded it, that is because he values kindness, and has a revulsion for cruelty, in a way that is at least to some extent independent of his belief that God commands kindness and forbids cruelty. This point may be made the basis of both philosophical and theological objections to the modified divine command theory, but I think the objections can be answered.

The philosophical objection is, roughly, that if there are some things I value independently of their relation to God's commands, then my value concepts cannot rightly be analyzed in terms of God's commands. According to the modified divine command theory, the acceptability of divine command ethics depends in part on the believer's independent positive valuation of the sorts of things that God is believed to command. But then, the philosophical critic objects, the believer must have a prior, nontheological conception of ethical right and wrong, in terms of which he judges God's commandments to be acceptable—and to admit that the believer has a prior, nontheological conception of ethical right and wrong is to abandon the divine command theory.

The weakness of this philosophical objection is that it fails to note the distinctions that can be drawn among various value concepts. From the fact that the believer values some things independently of his beliefs about God's commands, the objector concludes, illegitimately, that the believer must have a conception of ethical right and wrong that is independent of his beliefs about God's commands. This inference is illegitimate because there can be valuations which do not imply or presuppose a judgment of ethical right or wrong. For instance, I may simply like something, or want something, or feel a revulsion at something.

What the modified divine command theorist will hold, then, is that the believer values some things independently of their relation to God's commands, but that these valuations are not judgments of ethical right and wrong and do not of themselves imply judgments of ethical right and wrong. He will maintain, on the other hand, that such independent valuations are involved in, or even necessary for, judgments of ethical right and wrong which also involve beliefs about God's will or commands. The adherent of a divine command ethics will normally be able to give reasons for his adherence. Such reasons might include: 'Because I am grateful to God for His love'; 'Because I find it the most satisfying form of ethical life'; 'Because there's got to be an objective moral law if life isn't to fall to pieces, and I can't understand what it would be if not the will of God.'[4] As we have already noted, the modified divine command theorist also has reasons why he would not accept a divine command ethics in certain logically possible situations which he believes not to be actual. All of these reasons seem to me to involve valuations that are independent of divine command ethics. The person who has such reasons

---

[4] The mention of moral law in the last of these reasons may presuppose the ability to *mention* concepts of moral right and wrong, which may or may not be theological and which may or may not be concepts one uses oneself to make judgements of right and wrong. So far as I can see, it does not *presuppose* the *use* of such concepts to make judgments of right and wrong, or one's adoption of them for such use, which is the crucial point here.

wants certain things—happiness, certain satisfactions—for himself and others; he hates cruelty and loves kindness; he has perhaps a certain unique and 'numinous' awe of God. And these are not attitudes which he has simply because of his beliefs about God's commands.[5] They are not attitudes, however, which presuppose judgments of moral right and wrong.

It is sometimes objected to divine command theories of moral obligation, or of ethical rightness and wrongness, that one must have some reason for obeying God's commands or for adopting a divine command ethics, and that therefore a nontheological concept of moral obligation or of ethical rightness and wrongness must be presupposed, in order that one may judge that one ought to obey God's commands.[6] This objection is groundless. For one can certainly have reasons for doing something which do not involve believing one morally ought to do it or believing it would be ethically wrong not to do it.

I grant that in giving reasons for his attitudes toward God's commands the believer will probably use or presuppose concepts which, in the context, it is reasonable to count as nontheological value concepts (e.g., concepts of satisfactoriness and repulsiveness). Perhaps some of them might count as moral concepts. But all that the defender of a divine command theory of ethical wrongness has to maintain is that the concept of ethical wrongness which occurs in the ethical thought and discourse of believers is not one of the concepts which are used or presupposed in this way. Divine command theorists, including the modified divine command theorist, need not maintain that *all* value concepts, must be understood in terms of God's commands.

In fact some well-known philosophers have held forms of divine command theory which quite explicitly presuppose some nontheological value concepts. Locke, for instance, says in his *Essay*,

Good and evil . . . are nothing but pleasure or pain, or that which occasions or procures pleasure or pain to us. *Morally good and evil*, then, is only the conformity or disagreement of our voluntary actions to some law, whereby good or evil is drawn on us from the will and power of the law maker. . . . (*Essay*, II.xxviii.5)[7]

[5] The independence ascribed to these attitudes is not a *genetic* independence. It may be that the person would not have come to have some of them had it not been for his religious beliefs. The point is that he has come to hold them in such a way that his holding them does not now depend entirely on his beliefs about God's commands.

[6] I take A. C. Ewing to be offering an objection to this type on p. 112 of his book *Ethics* (London: English University Press, 1953).

[7] I quote from John Yolton's edition of *An Essay Concerning Human Understanding*, 2 vols. (London and New York: Everyman's Library, 1967).

Locke goes on to distinguish three laws, or types of law, by reference to which actions are commonly judged as to moral good and evil: '(1) The *divine* law. (2) The *civil* law. 3) The law of *opinion* or *reputation*, if I may so call it' (*Essay*, II.xxviii.7). Of these three Locke says that the third is 'the common *measure of virtue and vice*' (*Essay*, II.xxviii.11). In Locke's opinion the terms 'virtue' and 'vice' are particularly closely attached to the praise and blame of society. But the terms 'duty' and 'sin' are connected with the commandments of God. About the divine law Locke says,

This is the only true touchstone of *moral rectitude*; and by comparing them to this law, it is that men judge of the most considerable *moral good* or *evil* of their actions: that is, whether, as *duties or sins*, they are like to procure them happiness or misery from the hands of the ALMIGHTY. (*Essay*, II.xxviii.8).

The structure of Locke's analysis is clear enough. By 'good' and 'evil' we *mean* (nontheologically enough) pleasurable and painful. By 'morally good' and 'morally evil' we *mean* that the actions so described agree or disagree with some law under which the agent stands to be rewarded or punished. By 'duty' and 'sin', which denote the most important sort of moral good and evil, we *mean* (theologically now) actions which are apt to cause the agent good or evil (in the nontheological sense) because they agree or disagree with the law of God. I take it that the divine command theory advocated by Peter Geach,[8] and hinted at by Miss Anscombe,[9] is similar in structure, though not in all details, to Locke's.

The modified divine command theory that I have in mind does not rely as heavily as Locke's theory does on God's power to reward and punish, nor do I wish to assume Locke's analysis of 'good' and 'evil'. The point I want to make by discussing Locke here is just that there are many different value concepts and it is clearly possible to give one or more of them a theological analysis while giving others a nontheological analysis. And I do assume that the modified divine command theorist will give a nontheological analysis of some value concepts although he gives a theological analysis of the concept of ethical wrongness. For instance, he may give a nontheological analysis, perhaps a naturalistic one or a noncognitivist one, of the meaning of 'satisfactory' and repulsive', as he uses them in some contexts. He may even regard as *moral* concepts some value concepts of which he gives a nontheological analysis.

For it is not essential to a divine command theory of ethical wrongness

[8] In *God and the Soul* (London: Routledge, 1969), ch. 9. [Reading XI.]
[9] G. E. M. Anscombe, 'Modern Moral Philosophy', *Philosophy*, 33 (1958), pp. 1–19.

to maintain that all valuing, or all value concepts, or even all moral concepts, depend on beliefs about God's commands. What is essential to such a theory is to maintain that when a believer says something is (ethically) *wrong*, at least part of what he means is that the action in question is contrary to God's will or commands. Another way of putting the matter is this. What depends on beliefs about God and His will is: not all of the religious person's value concepts, nor in general his ability to value things, but only his ability to appraise actions (and possible actions) in terms of their relation to a superhuman, nonnaturally objective, law. Indeed, it is obvious that Judeo-Christian ethics presupposes concepts that have at least ethical overtones and that are not essentially theological but have their background in human social relations and political institutions—such as the concepts of promise, kindness, law, and command. What the specifically theological doctrines introduce into Judeo-Christian ethics, according to the divine command theory, is the belief in a law that is superior to all human laws.

This version of the divine command theory may seem *theologically* objectionable to some believers. One of the reasons, surely, why divine command theories of ethics have appealed to some theologians is that such theories seem especially congruous with the religious demand that God be the object of our highest allegiance. If our supreme commitment in life is to doing what is right just because it is right, and if what is right is right just because God wills or commands it, then surely our highest allegiance is to God. But the modified divine command theory seems not to have this advantage. For the modified divine command theorist is forced to admit, as we have seen, that he has reasons for his adherence to a divine command ethics, and that his having these reasons implies that there are some things which he values independently of his beliefs about God's commands. It is therefore not correct to say of him that he is committed to doing the will of God *just* because it is the will of God; he is committed to doing it partly because of other things which he values independently. Indeed it appears that there are certain logically possible situations in which his present attitudes would not commit him to obey God's commands (for instance, if God commanded cruelty for its own sake). This may even suggest that he values some things, not just independently of God's commands, but more than God's commands.

We have here a real problem in religious ethical motivation. The Judeo-Christian believer is supposed to make God the supreme focus of his loyalties; that is clear. One possible interpretation of this fact is the following. Obedience to whatever God may command is (or at least ought to be) the one thing that the believer values for its own sake and more than anything and everything else. Anything else that he values, he values (or ought to) only to a lesser degree and as a means to obedience to God. This conception of religious ethical motivation is obviously favorable to an *un*modified divine command theory of ethical wrongness.

But I think it is not a realistic conception. Loyalty to God, for instance, is very often explained, by believers themselves, as motivated by gratitude for benefits conferred. And I think it is clear in most cases that the gratitude presupposes that the benefits are valued, at least to some extent, independently of loyalty to God. Similarly, I do not think that most devout Judeo-Christian believers would say that it would be wrong to disobey God if He commanded cruelty for its own sake. And if I am right about that I think it shows that their positive valuation of (emotional/volitional pro-attitude toward) doing *whatever* God may command is not clearly greater than their independent negative valuation of cruelty.

In analyzing ethical motivation in general, as well as Judeo-Christian ethical motivation in particular, it is probably a mistake to suppose that there is (or can be expected to be) one only thing that is valued supremely and for its own sake, with nothing else being valued independently of it. The motivation for a person's ethical orientation in life is normally much more complex than that, and involves a plurality of emotional and volitional attitudes of different sorts which are at least partly independent of each other. At any rate, I think the modified divine command theorist is bound to say that that is true of his ethical motivation.

In what sense, then, can the modified divine command theorist maintain that God is the supreme focus of his loyalties? I suggest the following interpretation of the single-hearted loyalty to God which is demanded in Judeo-Christian religion. In this interpretation the crucial idea is *not* that some one thing is valued for its own sake and more than anything else, and nothing else valued independently of it. It is freely admitted that the religious person will have a plurality of motives for his ethical position, and that these will be at least partly independent of each other. It is admitted further that a desire to obey the commands of God (*whatever* they may be) may not be the strongest of these motives. What will be claimed is that certain beliefs about God enable the believer to integrate or focus his motives in a loyalty to God and His commands. Some of these beliefs are about what God commands or wills (contingently—that is, although He could logically have commanded or willed something else instead).

Some of the motives in question might be called egoistic; they include desires for satisfactions for oneself—which God is believed to have given or to be going to give. Other motives may be desires for satisfaction for other people; these may be called altruistic. Still other motives might not be desires for anyone's satisfaction, but might be valuations of certain kinds of action for their own sakes; these might be called idealistic. I do not think my argument depends heavily on this particular classification, but it seems plausible that all of these types, and perhaps others as well, might be distinguished among the motives for a religious person's ethical position. Obviously such motives might pull one in different directions, conflicting with one another. But in Judeo-Christian ethics beliefs about what God does in fact will (although He could have willed otherwise) are supposed to enable one to *fuse* these motives, so to speak, into one's devotion to God and His will, so that they all pull together. Doubtless the believer will still have some motives which conflict with his loyalty to God. But the religious ideal is that these should all be merely momentary desires and impulses, and kept under control. They ought not to be allowed to influence voluntary action. The deeper, more stable, and controlling desires, intentions, and psychic energies are supposed to be fused in devotion to God. As I interpret it, however, it need not be inconsistent with the Judeo-Christian ethical and religious ideal that this fusion of motives, this integration of moral energies, depends on belief in certain propositions which are taken to be contingent truths about God.

Lest it be though that I am proposing unprecedented theological positions, or simply altering Judeo-Christian religious beliefs to suit my theories, I will call to my aid on this point a theologian known for his insistence on the sovereignty of God. Karl Barth seems to me to hold a divine command theory of ethics. But when he raises the question of why we should obey God, he rejects with scorn the suggestion that God's *power* provides the basis for His claim on us. 'By deciding for God [man] has definitely decided not to be obedient to power as power.'[10] God's claim on us is based rather on His grace. 'God calls us and orders us and claims us by being gracious to us in Jesus Christ.'[11] I do not mean to suggest that Barth would agree with everything I have said about motivation, or that he offers a lucid account of a divine command theory. But he does agree with the position I have proposed on this point, that the believer's loyalty is not to be construed as a loyalty to God *as* all-powerful, nor to God *whatever* He might conceivably have willed. It is a loyalty to God *as* having a certain attitude toward us, a certain will for us, which God was free not to have, but to which in Barth's view, He has committed Himself irrevocably in Jesus Christ. The believer's devotion is not to merely possible commands of God as such, but to God's actual (and gracious) will.

---

[10] Karl Barth, *Church Dogmatics*, Vol. II, Pt. 2, trans. G. W. Bromiley and others (Edinburgh: T. & T. Clark, 1957), p. 553.   [11] Ibid., p. 560.

V

The ascription of moral qualities to God is commonly thought to cause problems for divine command theories of ethics. It is doubted that God, as an agent, can properly be called 'good' in the moral sense if He is not subject to a moral law that is not of His own making. For if He is morally good, mustn't He do what is right *because* it is right? And how can He do that, if what's right is right because He wills it? Or it may be charged that divine command theories trivialize the claim that God is good. If 'X is (morally) good' means roughly 'X does what God wills', then 'God is (morally) good' means only that God does what He wills—which is surely much less than people are normally taken to mean when they say that God is (morally) good. In this section I will suggest an answer to these objections.

Surely no analysis of Judeo-Christian ethical discourse can be regarded as adequate which does not provide for a sense in which the believer can seriously assert that God is good. Indeed an adequate analysis should provide a plausible account of what believers do in fact mean when they say, 'God is good'. I believe that a divine command theory of ethical (rightness and) wrongness can include such an account. I will try to indicate its chief features.

(1) In saying 'God is good' one is normally expressing a favorable emotional attitude toward God. I shall not try to determine whether or not this is part of the meaning of 'God is good'; but it is normally, perhaps almost always, at least one of the things one is doing if one says that God is good. If we were to try to be more precise about the type of favorable emotional attitude normally expressed by 'God is good', I suspect we would find that the attitude expressed is most commonly one of *gratitude.*

(2) This leads to a second point, which is that when God is called 'good' it is very often meant that He is *good to us*, or *good to* the speaker. 'Good' is sometimes virtually a synonym for 'kind'. And for the modified divine command theorist it is not a trivial truth that God is kind. In saying that God is good in the sense of 'kind', one presupposes, of course, that there are some things which the beneficiaries of God's goodness value. We need not discuss here whether the beneficiaries must value them independently of their beliefs about God's will. For the modified divine command theorist does admit that there are some things which believers value independently of their beliefs about God's commands. Nothing that the modified divine command theorist says about the meaning of ('right' and) 'wrong' implies that it is a trivial truth that God bestows on His creatures things that they value.

(3) I would not suggest that the descriptive force of 'good' as applied to God is exhausted by the notion of kindness. 'God is good' must be taken in many contexts as ascribing to God, rather generally, qualities of character which the believing speaker regards as virtues in human beings. Among such qualities might be faithfulness, ethical consistency, a forgiving dispostion, and, in general, various aspects of love, as well as kindness. Not that there is some definite list of qualities, the ascription of which to God is clearly implied by the claim that God is good. But saying that God is good normally commits one to the position that God has some important set of qualities which one regards as virtues in human beings.

(4) It will not be thought that God has *all* the qualities which are virtues in human beings. Some such qualities are logically inapplicable to a being such as God is supposed to be. For example, aside from certain complications arising from the doctrine of the incarnation, it would be logically inappropriate to speak of God as controlling His sexual desires. (He doesn't have any.) And given some widely held conceptions of God and His relation to the world, it would hardly make sense to speak of Him as *courageous*. For if He is impassible and has predetermined absolutely everything that happens, He has no risks to face and cannot endure (because He cannot suffer) pain or displeasure.[12]

Believers in God's goodness also typically think He lacks some human virtues which would *not* be logically inapplicable to a being like Him. A virtuous man, for instance, does not intentionally cause the death of other human beings, except under exceptional circumstances. But God has intentionally brought it about that all men die. There are agonizing forms of the problem of evil; but I think that for most Judeo-Christian believers (especially those who believe in life after death), this is not one of them. They believe that God's making men mortal and His commanding them not to kill each other, fit together in a larger pattern of harmonious purposes. How then can one distinguish between human virtues which God must have if He is good and human virtues which God may lack and still be good? This is an interesting and important question, but I will not attempt here to formulate a precise or adequate criterion for making the distinction. I fear it would require a lengthy digression from the issues with which we are principally concerned.

(5) If we accept a divine command theory of ethical rightness and

---

[12] The argument here is similar to one which is used for another purpose by Ninian Smart in 'Omnipotence, Evil, and Superman', *Philosophy*, 36 (1961), reprinted in Nelson Pike, ed., *God and Evil* (Englewood Cliffs, N. J.: Prentice-Hall, 1964), pp. 103–12.

I do not mean to endorse the doctrines of divine impassibility and theological determinism.

wrongness, I think we shall have to say that *dutifulness* is a human virtue which, like sexual chastity, is logically inapplicable to God. God cannot either do or fail to do His duty, since He does not have a duty—at least not in the most important sense in which human beings have a duty. For He is not subject to a moral law not of His own making. Dutifulness is one virtuous disposition which men can have that God cannot have. But there are other virtuous dispositions which God can have as well as men. Love, for instance. It hardly makes sense to say that God does what he does *because* it is right. But it does not follow that God cannot have any reason for doing what He does. It does not even follow that He cannot have reasons of a type on which it would be morally virtuous for a man to act. For example, He might do something because He knew it would make His creatures happier.

(6) The modified divine command theorist must deny that in calling God 'good' one presupposes a standard of moral rightness and wrongness superior to the will of God, by reference to which it is determined whether God's character is virtuous or not. And I think he can consistently deny that. He can say that morally virtuous and vicious qualities of character are those which agree and conflict, respectively, with God's commands, and that it is their agreement or disagreement with God's commands that makes them virtuous or vicious. But the believer normally thinks he has at least a general idea of what qualities of character are in fact virtuous and vicious (approved and disapproved by God). Having such an idea, he can apply the word 'good' descriptively to God, meaning that (with some exceptions, as I have noted) God has the qualities which the believer regards as virtues, such as faithfulness and kindness.

I will sum up by contrasting what the believer can mean when he says, 'Moses is good', with what he can mean when he says, 'God is good', according to the modified divine command theory. When the believer says, 'Moses is good', (a) he normally is expressing a favorable emotional attitude toward Moses—normally, though perhaps not always. (Sometimes a person's moral goodness displeases us.) (b) He normally implies that Moses possesses a large proportion of those qualities of character which are recognized in the religious-ethical community as virtues, and few if any of those which are regarded as vices. (c) He normally implies that the qualities of Moses' character on the basis of which he described Moses as good are qualities approved by God.

When the believer says, 'God is good', (a) he normally is expressing a favorable emotional attitude toward God—and I think exceptions on this point would be rarer than in the case of statements that a man is good. (b) He normally is ascribing to God certain qualities of character. He may mean primarily that God is kind or benevolent, that He is *good to* human beings or certain ones of them. Or he may mean that God possesses (with some exceptions) those qualities of character which are regarded as virtues in the religious-ethical community. (c) Whereas in saying, 'Moses is good', the believer was stating or implying that the qualities of character which he was ascribing to Moses conform to a standard of ethical rightness which is independent of the will of Moses, he is not stating or implying that the qualities of character which he ascribes to God conform to a standard of ethical rightness which is independent of the will of God.

VI

As I noted at the outset, the divine command theory of ethical wrongness, even in its modified form, has the consequence that believers and nonbelievers use the word 'wrong' with different meanings in ethical contexts, since it will hardly be thought that nonbelievers mean by 'wrong' what the theory says believers mean by it. This consequence gives rise to an objection. For the phenomena of common moral discourse between believers and nonbelievers suggest that they mean the same thing by 'wrong' in ethical contexts. In the present section I shall try to explain how the modified divine command theorist can account for the facts of common ethical discourse.

I will first indicate what I think the troublesome facts are. Judeo-Christian believers enter into ethical discussions with people whose religious or anti-religious beliefs they do not know. It seems to be possible to conduct quite a lot of ethical discourse, with apparent understanding, without knowing one's partner's views on religious issues. Believers also discuss ethical questions with persons who are known to them to be nonbelievers. They agree with such persons, disagree with them, and try to persuade them, about what acts are morally wrong. (Or at least it is normally *said*, by the participants and others, that they agree and disagree about such issues.) Believers ascribe, to people who are known not to believe in God, beliefs that certain acts are morally wrong. Yet surely believers do not suppose that nonbelievers, in calling acts wrong, mean that they are contrary to the will or commandments of God. Under these circumstances how can the believer really mean 'contrary to the will or commandments of God' when he says 'wrong'? If he agrees and disagrees with nonbelievers about what is wrong, if he ascribes to them beliefs that certain acts are wrong, must he not be using 'wrong' in a nontheological sense?

What I shall argue is that in some ordinary (and I fear imprecise) sense of 'mean', what believers and nonbelievers mean by 'wrong' in ethical contexts may well be partly the same and partly different. There are agreements between believers and nonbelievers which make common moral discourse between them possible. But these agreements do not show that the two groups mean exactly the same thing by 'wrong'. They do not show that 'contrary to God's will or commands' is not part of what believers mean by 'wrong'.

Let us consider first the agreements which make possible common moral discourse between believers and nonbelievers. (1) One important agreement, which is so obvious as to be easily overlooked, is that they use many of the same ethical terms—'wrong', 'right', 'ought', 'duty', and others. And they may utter many of the same ethical sentences, such as 'Racial discrimination is morally wrong'. In determining what people believe we rely very heavily on what they say (when they seem to be speaking sincerely)—and that means in large part, on the words that they use and the sentences they utter. If I know that somebody says with apparent sincerity, 'Racial discrimination is morally wrong', I will normally ascribe to him the belief that racial discrimination is morally wrong, even if I also know that he does not mean *exactly* the same thing as I do by 'racial discrimination' or 'morally wrong'. Of course if I know he means something *completely* different, I would not ascribe the belief to him without explicit qualification.

I would not claim that believers and nonbelievers use *all* the same ethical terms. 'Sin', law of God', and 'Christian', for instance, occur as ethical terms in the discourse of many believers, but would be much less likely to occur in the same way in nonbelievers' discourse.

(2) The shared ethical terms have the same basic grammatical status for believers as for nonbelievers, and at least many of the same logical connections with other expressions. Everyone agrees, for instance, in treating 'wrong' as an adjective and 'Racial discrimination is morally wrong' as a declarative sentence. '(All) racial discrimination is morally wrong' would be treated by all parties as expressing an A-type (universal affirmative) proposition, from which consequences can be drawn by syllogistic reasoning or the predicate calculus. All agree that if X is morally wrong, then it isn't morally right and refraining from X is morally obligatory. Such grammatical and formal agreements are important to common moral discourse.

(3) There is a great deal of agreement, among believers and non-believers, as to what types of action they call 'wrong' in an ethical sense and I think that that agreement is one of the things that make common moral discourse possible.[13] It is certainly not complete agreement.

[13] Cf. Ludwig Wittgenstein, *Philosophical Investigations*, 2nd ed. (Oxford: Blackwell, 1958), Pt. I, sec. 242: 'If language is to be a means of communication there must be agreement not only in definitions but also (queer as this may sound)

Obviously there is a lot of ethical disagreement in the world. Much of it cuts right across religious lines, but not all of it does. There are things which are typically called 'wrong' by members of some religious groups, and not by others. Nonetheless there are types of action which everyone or almost everyone would call morally wrong—such as torturing someone to death because he accidentally broke a small window in your house. Moreover any two people (including any one believer and one nonbeliever) are likely to find some actions they both call wrong that not everyone does. I imagine that most ethical discussion takes place among people whose area of agreement in what they call wrong is relatively large.

There is probably much less agreement about the most basic issues in moral theory than there is about many ethical issues of less generality. There is much more unanimity in what people (sincerely) say in answer to such questions as 'Was what Hitler did to the Jews wrong?' or 'Is it normally wrong to disobey the laws of one's country?' than in what they (sincerely) say in answer to such questions as 'Is it always right to do the act which will have the best results?' or 'Is pleasure the only thing that is good for its own sake?' The issue between adherents and nonadherents of divine command ethics is typical of basic issues in ethical and metaethical theory in this respect.

(4) The emotional and volitional attitudes normally expressed by the statement that something is 'wrong' are similar in believers and non-believers. They are not exactly the same; the attitudes typically expressed by the believer's statement that something is 'wrong' are importantly related to his religious practice and beliefs about God, and this doubtless makes them different in some ways from the attitudes expressed by non-believers uttering the same sentence. But the attitudes are certainly similar, and that is important for the possibility of common moral discourse.

(5) Perhaps even more important is the related fact that the social functions of a statement that something is (morally) 'wrong' are similar for believers and nonbelievers. To say that something somone else is known to have done is 'wrong' is commonly to attack him. If you say that something you are known to have done is 'wrong', you abandon certain types of defense. To say that a public policy is 'wrong' is normally to register oneself as opposed to it, and is sometimes a signal that one is willing to be supportive of common action to change it. These social functions of moral discourse are extremely important. It is perhaps not

in judgments.' In contemporary society I think it may well be the case that because there is not agreement in ethical definitions, common ethical discourse requires a measure of agreement in ethical judgements. (I do not mean to comment here more broadly on the truth or falsity of Wittgenstein's statement as a statement about the conditions of linguistic communication in general.)

surprising that we are inclined to say that two people agree with each other when they both utter the same sentence and thereby indicate their readiness to take the same side in a conflict.

Let us sum up these observations about the conditions which make common moral discourse between believers and nonbelievers possible. (1) They use many of the same ethical terms, such as 'wrong'. (2) They treat those terms as having the same basic grammatical and logical status, and many of the same logical connections with other expressions. (3) They agree to a large extent about what types of action are to be called 'wrong'. To call an action 'wrong' is, among other things, to classify it with certain other actions, and there is considerable agreement between believers and nonbelievers as to what actions those are. (4) The emotional and volitional attitudes which believers and nonbelievers normally express in saying that something is 'wrong' are similar, and (5) saying that something is 'wrong' has much the same social functions for believers and nonbelievers.

So far as I can see, none of this is inconsistent with the modified divine command theory of ethical wrongness. According to that theory there are several things which are true of the believer's use of 'wrong' which cannot plausibly be supposed to be true of the nonbeliever's. In saying, 'X is wrong', the believer commits himself (subjectively, at least, and publicly if he is known to be a believer) to the claim that X is contrary to God's will or commandments. The believer will not say that anything would be wrong, under any possible circumstances, if it were not contrary to God's will or commandments. In many contexts he uses the term 'wrong' interchangeably with 'against the will of God' or 'against the commandments of God'. The heart of the modified divine command theory, I have suggested, is the claim that when the believer says, 'X is wrong', one thing he means to be doing is stating a nonnatural objective fact about X, and the nonnatural objective fact he means to be stating is that X is contrary to the will or commandments of God. This claim may be true even though the uses of 'wrong' by believers and nonbelievers are similar in all five of the ways pointed out above.

Suppose these contentions of the modified divine command theory are correct. (I think they are very plausible as claims about the ethical discourse of at least some religious believers.) In that case believers and nonbelievers surely do not mean exactly the same thing by 'X is wrong' in ethical contexts. But neither is it plausible to suppose that they mean entirely different things, given the phenomena of common moral discourse. We must suppose, then, that their meaning is partly the same and partly different. 'Contrary to God's will or commands' must be taken as expressing only part of the meaning with which the believer uses 'wrong'. Some of the similarities between believers' and non-believers' use of 'wrong' must also be taken as expressing parts of the meaning with which the believer uses 'wrong'. This view of the matter agrees with the account of the modified divine command theory in Section III above, where I pointed out that the modified divine command theorist cannot mean exactly the same thing by 'wrong' that he means by 'contrary to God's commands'.

We have here a situation which commonly arises when some people hold, and others do not hold, a given theory about the nature of something which everyone talks about. The chemist, who believes that water is a compound of hydrogen and oxygen, and the man who knows nothing of chemistry, surely do not use the word 'water' in entirely different senses; but neither is it very plausible to suppose that they use it with exactly the same meaning. I am inclined to say that in some fairly ordinary sense of 'mean', a phenomenalist, and a philosopher who holds some conflicting theory about what it is for a physical object to exist, do not mean exactly the same thing by 'There is a bottle of milk in the refrigerator.' But they certainly do not mean entirely different things, and they can agree that there is a bottle of milk in the refrigerator.

VII

These remarks bring us face to face with some important issues in the general theory of analysis and meaning. What are the criteria for determining whether two utterers of the same expression mean exactly the same thing by it, or something partly different, or something entirely different? What is the relation between philosophical analyses, and philosophical theories about the natures of things, on the one hand, and the meanings of terms in ordinary discourse on the other hand? I have permitted myself the liberty of speaking as if these issues did not exist. But their existence is notorious, and I certainly cannot resolve them in this essay. Indeed, I do not have resolutions to offer.

In view of these uncertainties in the theory of meaning, it is worth noting that much of what the modified divine command theorist wants to say can be said without making claims about the *meaning* of ethical terms. He wants to say, for instance, that believers' claims that certain acts are wrong normally express certain attitudes toward those acts, whether or not that is part of their meaning; that an act is wrong if and only if it is contrary to God's will or commands (assuming God loves us); that nonetheless, if God commanded cruelty for its own sake, neither obedience nor disobedience would be ethically wrong or ethically permitted; that if an act is contrary to God's will or commands that is a nonnatural objective fact about it; and that that is the only nonnatural objective fact which obtains if and only if the act is wrong. These are among the most important claims of the modified divine command theory—perhaps they include the very most important. But in the form in which I have just stated them, they are not claims about the *meaning* of ethical terms.

I do not mean to reject the claims about the meanings of terms in religious ethical discourse which I have included in the modified divine command theory. In the absence of general solutions to general problems in the theory of meaning, we may perhaps say what seems to us intuitively plausible in particular cases. That is presumably what the modified divine command theorist is doing when he claims that 'contrary to the will or commands of God' is part of the meaning of '(ethically) wrong' for many Judeo-Christian believers. And I think it is fair to say that if we have found unresolved problems about meaning in the modified divine command theory, they are problems much more about what we mean in general by 'meaning' than about what Judeo-Christian believers mean by 'wrong'.[14]

[14] I am indebted to many who have read, or heard, and discussed versions of this essay, and particularly to Richard Brandt, William Frankena, John Reeder, and Stephen Stich, for helpful criticisms.

DIVINE COMMAND METAETHICS AS NECESSARY A POSTERIORI

ROBERT MERRIHEW ADAMS

III. THE SEPARATION OF NECESSITY AND NATURES FROM ANALYTICITY AND CONCEPTS

AN important group of recent papers (especially Donnellan, 1966 and 1972; Kripke, 1972; and Putnam, 1975:196-290)[1] has made a persuasive case for a view that there are necessary truths that are neither analytic nor knowable *a priori*. Among these are truths about the nature of many properties. And I am now inclined to believe that the truth about the nature of ethical wrongness is of this sort.

A case of individual identity or non-identity provides a first example of a truth that is necessary but empirical. In the Gospels according to Mark (2:14) and Luke (5:27-29) there is a story about a tax collector named "Levi", who left his business to follow Jesus. There is a tradition, supported by the relevant texts in Matthew (9:9 and 10:3) and by some important manuscripts of Mark (2:14), that this man was the Matthew who appears in the lists of the twelve apostles. This belief is naturally expressed by saying that Levi was Matthew, or that Levi and Matthew were the same man. But perhaps they were not; none of us really knows.

Suppose they were in fact two different men. That is a truth that is in principle knowable, but only empirically knowable. It is certainly not an analytic truth, which could be discovered by analyzing our concepts of Levi and Matthew. But there is a compelling argument for believing it to be a necessary truth if it is true at all. For suppose it a contingent truth. Then the actual world, w_1, would be one in which Matthew the apostle and Levi the tax collector are not identical, but a world, w_2, in which they would be identical would also be possible.

An extract from 'Divine Command Metaethics Modified Again', *Journal of Religious Ethics*, Vol. 7/1, Spring 1979, pp. 71-79. Reprinted by permission of the editor and the author.

[1] I have selected from these papers points that are relevant to my theory. I do not claim to give a comprehensive account of their aims and contents. I am also indebted here to David Kaplan and Bernard Kobes, for discussion and for the opportunity of reading unpublished papers of theirs.

Since identity is a transitive relation, however, and since Levi in w_1, is identical with Levi in w_2, and Levi in w_2 is identical with Matthew in w_2, and Matthew in w_2 with Matthew in w_1, it follows that Levi in w_1 is identical with Matthew in w_1. Thus the hypothesis that the non-identity of Matthew and Levi is contingent leads to a contradiction. This argument is not completely uncontroversial in its assumptions about trans-world identity, but it seems to me to be correct. A similar argument can be given for holding that if Levi and Matthew were in fact identical, that is a necessary truth, although it is not *a priori*.

It should be emphasized that "possible" is not being used in its *epistemic* sense here. Both worlds in which Matthew and Levi are identical and worlds in which they are distinct are epistemically possible: that is, either sort may be actual for all we know. But whichever sort is actual, the other sort lacks broadly logical possibility, or 'metaphysical possibility' as it is often called by those who hold the views I am exploring here.

Another interesting feature of this example is that there is a property which our understanding of the meaning of "Matthew" and "Levi" in this context tells us Matthew and Levi must have had if they (or he) existed, but which is a property that they (or he) possessed contingently. By "Matthew" we mean the individual who stands in a certain historical relation (not yet spelled out in a very detailed way by philosophers of language) to the use of "Matthew" (on certain occasions known to us) as a name of a man believed to have been one of the disciples of Jesus. It is epistemically possible that Matthew was named "Levi" and not "Matthew", or that he was not one of the twelve apostles but got counted as one by mistake. But no one who does not stand in an appropriate historical relation to the relevant uses of "Matthew" counts as Matthew; that is what is settled by the meaning with which we use "Matthew". Standing in this relation to these uses of "Matthew" is surely a contingent property of Matthew, however Matthew could have existed in a world in which he was never called "Matthew" during or after his life, or in a world which Jesus never had any disciples and the relevant use of "Matthew" never occurred.

Similar considerations apply to theories about the natures of pro-perties, or of kinds of things. Hilary Putnam uses the theory that the nature of water is to be H_2O as an example in arguing that such theories, if true, are commonly necessary truths but not *a priori* (see also Kripke, 1972:314–31). (As it happens, this example was given a somewhat dif-ferent treatment, hereby superseded, in Adams, 1973:107.)

Suppose a vessel from outer space landed, carrying a group of intelli-gent creatures that brought with them, and drank, a transparent, colorless, odorless, tasteless liquid that dissolved sugar and salt and other things that normally dissolve in water. Even if we non-chemists could not distinguish it from water, we might intelligibly (and prudently) ask whether this substance really is water. Our question would be answered, in the negative, by a laboratory analysis showing that the beverage from outer space was not H_2O but a different liquid whose long and complicated chemical formula may be abbreviated as XYZ (see Putnam, 1975:223).

Why is it right to say that this XYZ would not be water? I take it to be Putnam's view that it is not an analytic truth that water is H_2O. What is true analytically, by virtue of what every competent user of the word "water" must know about its meaning, is rather that if most of the stuff that we (our linguistic community) have been calling "water" is of a single nature, water is liquid that is of the same nature as *that*.

This view enables Putnam to maintain against Quine that substantial change and development in scientific theories is possible without change in meaning (although he agrees with Quine 'that meaning change and theory change cannot be sharply separated', and that *some* possible changes in scientific theory would change the meaning of crucial terms— see Putnam, 1975:255f.). 'Thus, the fact that an English speaker in 1750 might have called XYZ "water", while he or his successors would not have called XYZ water in 1800 or 1850 does not mean that the "meaning" of "water" changed for the average speaker in the interval' (Putnam, 1975:225). This claim is plausible. Had the visitors from outer space arrived with their clear, tasteless liquid in England in 1750, the English of that time might wisely have wondered whether the stuff was really water, even if it satisfied all the tests they yet knew for being water. And the correct answer to *their* question too would have been negative, if the liquid was XYZ and not H_2O.

Although it is not an *a priori* but an empirical truth that water is H_2O, Putnam thinks it is metaphysically necessary. Suppose there is a possible world, w_3, in which there is no H_2O but XYZ fills the ecological and cultural role that belongs to H_2O in the actual world. XYZ looks, tastes, etc. like H_2O, and is even called "water" by English speakers in w_3. In such a case, Putnam (1975:231) maintains, the XYZ in w_3 is *not* water, for in order to be water a liquid in *any* possible world must be the same liquid (must have the same nature, I would say) as the stuff that we actually call "water"—which is H_2O. We may say, on this view, that the property of being water *is* the property of being H_2O, so that nothing could have the one property without having the other, or lack one without lacking the other.

It should also be noted that on this view the property ascribed to water by the description that expresses the *concept* of water, or what every competent user of "water" knows, is not a property that belongs to water necessarily. The description is "liquid of the same nature as most of the stuff that we have been calling 'water'." But it is only contingent that water is called "water". Water could perfectly well have existed if no one had given it a name at all, or if the English had called it "yoof".

This view of the relation between the nature of water and the meaning of "water" seems to me plausible. And if we think it is correct, that will enhance the plausibility of an analogous treatment of the nature of right and wrong. But even if Putnam's claims about "water" are mistaken, we certainly *could* use an expression as he says we use "water"; and it would be worth considering whether "right" and "wrong" are used in something like that way.

IV. THE NATURE OF WRONGNESS AND THE MEANING OF "WRONG"

I do not think that every competent user of "wrong" in its ethical sense must know what the nature of wrongness is. The word is used—with the same meaning, I would now say—by people who have different views, or none at all, about the nature of wrongness. As I remarked in my earlier paper, 'There is probably much less agreement about the most basic issues in moral theory than there is about many ethical issues of less generality' (Adams, 1973:105). That people can use an expression to signify an ethical property, knowing it is a property they seek (or shun, as the case may be), but not knowing what its nature is, was realized by Plato when he characterized the good as

That which every soul pursues, doing everthing for the sake of it, divining that it is something, but perplexed and unable to grasp adequately what it is or to have such a stable belief as about other things (*Republic* 505D–E).

What every competent user of "wrong" must know about wrongness is, first of all, that wrongness is a property of actions (perhaps also of intentions and of various attitudes, but certainly of actions); and second, that people are generally opposed to actions they regard as wrong, and count wrongness as a reason (often a conclusive reason) for opposing an action. In addition I think the competent user must have some opinions about what actions have this property, and some fairly settled dispositions as to what he will count as reasons for and against regarding an action as wrong. There is an important measure of agreement among

competent users in these opinions and dispositions—not complete agreement, nor universal agreement on some points and disagreement on
others, but overlapping agreements of one person with another on some
points and with still others on other points. 'To call an action "wrong"
is, among other things, to classify it with certain other actions', as
having a common property, 'and there is considerable agreement . . .
as to what actions those are' (Adams, 1973:106). Torturing children for
fun is one of them, in virtually everyone's opinion.

Analysis of the concept or understanding with which the word 'wrong'
is used is not sufficient to determine what wrongness is. What it can tell
us about the nature of wrongness, I think, is that wrongness will be the
property of actions (if there is one) that best fills the role assigned to
wrongness by the concept. My theory is that contrariety to the commands of a loving God is that property; but we will come to that in
section V. Meanwhile I will try to say something about what is involved
in being the property that *best* fills the relevant role, though I do not
claim to be giving an adequate set of individually necessary and jointly
sufficient conditions.

(i) We normally speak of actions being right and wrong as of facts that
obtain objectively, independently of whether we think they do. "Wrong"
has the syntax of an ordinary predicate, and we worry that we may be
mistaken in our ethical judgments. This feature of ethical concepts gives
emotivism and prescriptivism in metaethics much of their initial implausi-
bility. If possible, therefore, the property to be identified with ethical
wrongness should be one that actions have or lack objectively.

(ii) The property that is wrongness should belong to those types of
action that are thought to be wrong—or at least it should belong to an
important central group of them. It would be unreasonable to expect a
theory of the nature of wrongness to yield results that agree perfectly
with pre-theoretical opinion. One of the purposes a metaethical theory
may serve is to give guidance in revising one's particular ethical opinions.
But there is a limit to how far those opinions may be revised without
changing the subject entirely; and we are bound to take it as a major
test of the acceptability of a theory of the nature of wrongness that it
should in some sense account for the wrongness of a major portion of
the types of action we have believed to be wrong.

(iii) Wrongness should be a property that not only belongs to the
most important types of action that are thought to be wrong, but also
plays a causal role (or a role as object of perception) in their coming to
be regarded as wrong. It should not be connected in a merely fortuitous
way with our classification of actions as wrong and not wrong.[2]

---

[2] Cf. Putnam (1975:290): 'I would apply a generally causal account of refer-

(iv) Understanding the nature of wrongness should give one more rather than less reason to oppose wrong actions as such. Even if it were discovered (as it surely will not be) that there is a certain sensory pleasure produced by all and only wrong actions, it would be absurd to say that wrongness *is* the property of producing that pleasure. For the property of producing such a pleasure, in itself, gives us no reason whatever to oppose an action that has the property.

(v) The best theory about the nature of wrongness should satisfy other intuitions about wrongness as far as possible. One intuition that is rather widely held and is relevant to theological metaethics is that rightness and wrongness are determined by a law or standard that has a sanctity that is greater than that of any merely human will or institution.

We are left, on this view, with a concept of wrongness that has both objective and subjective aspects. The best theory of the nature of wrongness, I think, will be one that identifies wrongness with some property that actions have or lack objectively. But we do not have a fully objective procedure for determining which theory of the nature of wrongness is the best, and therefore which property is wrongness.

For example, the property that is wrongness should belong to the most important types of action that are believed to be wrong. But the concept possessed by every competent user of "wrong" does not dictate exactly which types of action those are. A sufficiently eccentric classification of types of action as right or wrong would not fit the concept. But there is still room for much difference of opinion. In testing theories of the nature of wrongness by their implications about what types of action are wrong. I will be guided by my own classification of types of action as right and wrong, and by my own sense of which parts of the classification are most important.

Similarly, in considering whether identifying wrongness with a given property, P, makes wrongness more or less of a reason for opposing an action, I will decide partly on the basis of how P weighs with me. And in general I think that this much is right about prescriptivist intuitions in metaethics: to identify a property with ethical wrongness is in part to assign it a certain complex role in my life (and, for my part, in the life of society); in deciding to do that I will (quite reasonably) be influenced by what attracts and repels me personally. But it does not follow that the theory I should choose is not one that identifies wrongness with a property that actions would have or lack regardless of how I felt about them.

ence also to moral terms . . .' I do not know how similar the metaethical views at which Putnam hints are to those that are developed in section IV of the present paper.

V. A NEW DIVINE COMMAND THEORY

The account I have given of the concept of wrongness that every competent user of "wrong" must have is consistent with many different theories about the nature of wrongness—for example, with the view that wrongness is the property of failing to maximize human happiness, and with a Marxist theory that wrongness is the property of being contrary to the objective interests of the progressive class or classes. But given typical Christian beliefs about God, it seems to me most plausible to identify wrongness with the property of being contrary to the commands of a loving God. (i) This is a property that actions have or lack objectively, regardless of whether we think they do. (I assume the theory can be filled out with a satisfactory account of what love consists in here.) (ii) The property of being contrary to the commands of a loving God is certainly believed by Christians to belong to all and only wrong actions. (iii) It also plays a causal role in our classification of actions as wrong, in so far as God has created our moral faculties to reflect his commands. (iv) Because of what is believed about God's actions, purposes, character, and power, he inspires such devotion and/or fear that contrariness to his commands is seen as a supremely weighty reason for opposing an action. Indeed, (v) God's commands constitute a law or standard that seems to believers to have a sanctity that is not possessed by any merely human will or institution.

My new divine command theory of the nature of ethical wrongness, then, is that ethical wrongness *is* (i.e. is identical with) the property of being contrary to the commands of a loving God. I regard this as a metaphysically necessary, but not an analytic or *a priori* truth. Because it is not a conceptual analysis, this claim is not relative to a religious subcommunity of the larger linguistic community. It purports to be the correct theory of the nature of the ethical wrongness that *everybody* (or almost everybody) is talking about.

Further explanation is in order, first about the notion of a divine *command*, and second about the *necessity* that is claimed here. On the first point I can only indicate here the character of the explanation that is needed; for it amounts to nothing less than a theory of revelation. Theists sometimes speak of wrong action as action contrary to the 'will' of God, but that way of speaking ignores some important distinctions. One is the distinction between the absolute will of God (his 'good pleasure') and his revealed will. Any Christian theology will grant that God in his good pleasure sometimes decides, for reasons that may be mysterious to us, not to do everything he could to prevent a wrong action. According to some theologies nothing at all can happen contrary to

God's good pleasure. It is difficult, therefore, to suppose that all wrong actions are unqualifiedly contrary to God's will in the sense of his good pleasure. It is God's *revealed* will—not what he wants or plans to have happen, but what he has told us to do—that is thought to determine the rightness and wrongness of human actions. Roman Catholic theology has made a further distinction, within God's revealed will, between his commands, which it would be wrong not to follow, and 'counsels (of perfection)', which it would be better to follow but not wrong not to follow. It is best, therefore, in our metaethical theory, to say that wrongness is contrariety to God's *commands*; and commands must have been issued, promulgated, or somehow revealed.

The notion of the issuance of a divine command requires a theory of revelation for its adequate development. The first such theory that comes to mind may be a Biblical literalism that takes divine commands to be just what is written in the Bible as commanded by God. But there will also be Roman Catholic theories involving the *magisterium* of the Church, a Quaker theory about 'the inner light', theories about 'general revelation' through the moral feelings and intuitions of unbelievers as well as believers—and other theories as well. To develop these theories and choose among them is far too large a task for the present essay.

The thesis that wrongness is (identical with) contrariety to a loving God's commands must be *metaphysically necessary* if it is true. That is, it cannot be false in any possible world if it is true in the actual world. For if it were false in some possible world, then wrongness would be non-identical with contrariety to God's commands in the actual world as well, by the transitivity of identity, just Matthew and Levi must be non-identical in all worlds if they are non-identical in any.

This argument establishes the metaphysical necessity of property identities in general; and that leads me to identify wrongness with contrariety to the command of a *loving* God, rather than simply with contrariety to the commands of God. Most theists believe that both of those properties are in fact possessed by all and only wrong actions. But if wrongness is simply contrariety to the commands of God, it is necessarily so, which implies that it would be wrong to disobey God even if he were so unloving as to command the practice of cruelty for its own sake. That consequence is unacceptable. I am not prepared to adopt the negative attitude toward possible disobedience in that situation that would be involved in identifying wrongness simply with contrariety to God's commands. The loving character of the God who issues them seems to me therefore to be a metaethically relevant feature of divine commands. (I assume that in deciding what property is wrongness, and therefore would be wrongness in all possible worlds, we are to rely on our own actual moral feelings and convictions, rather than on those that we or others would have in other possible worlds.)

If it is necessary that ethical wrongness is contrariety to a loving God's commands, it follows that no actions would be ethically wrong if there were not a loving God. This consequence will seem (at least initially) implausible to many, but I will try to dispel as much as I can of the air of paradox. It should be emphasized, first of all, that my theory does not imply what would ordinarily be meant by saying that no actions *are* ethically wrong if there *is* no loving God. If there is no loving God, then the theological part of my theory is false; but the more general part presented in section IV, above, implies that in that case ethical wrongness is the property with which it is identified by the best remaining alternative theory.

Similarly, if there is in fact a loving God, and if ethical wrongness is the property of being contrary to the commands of a loving God, there is still, I suppose, a possible world, w_4, in which there would not be a loving God but there would be people to whom w_4 would seem much as the actual world seems to us, and who would use the world "wrong" much as we use it. We may say that they would associate it with the same *concept* as we do,[3] although the property it would signify in their mouths is not wrongness. The actions they call "wrong" would not be wrong—that is, they would not have the property that actually is wrongness (the property of being contrary to the commands of a loving God). But that is not to say that they would be mistaken whenever they predicated "is wrong" of an action. For "wrong" in their speech would signify the property (if any) that is assigned to it by the metaethical theory that would be the best in relation to an accurate knowledge of their situation in w_4. We can even say that they would believe, as we do, that cruelty is wrong, if by that we mean, not that the property they would ascribe to cruelty by calling it "wrong" is the same as the property that we so ascribe, but that the subjective psychological state that they would express by the ascription is that same that we express.

Readers who think that I have not sufficiently dispelled the air of paradox may wish to consider a slightly different divine command theory, according to which it is a contingent truth that contrariety to God's commands constitutes the nature of wrongness. Instead of saying that wrongness is the property that in the actual world best fills a certain role, we could say that wrongness is the property of having whatever property best fills that role in whatever possible world is in question.

[3] I follow Putnam in this use of "concept". I have avoided committing myself as to whether English speakers in *w4* would use "wrong" with the same *meaning* as we do. See Putnam. 1975:234.

On the latter view it would be reasonable to say that the property that best fills the role constitutes the nature of wrongness, but that the nature of wrongness may differ in different possible worlds. The theist could still hold that the nature of wrongness in the actual world is constituted by contrariety to the commands of God (or of a loving God—it does not make as much difference which we say, on this view, since the theist believes God is loving in the actual world anyway). But it might be constituted by other properties in some other possible worlds. This theory does not imply that no actions would be wrong if there were no loving God; and that may still seem to be an advantage. On the other hand I think there is also an air of paradox about the idea that wrongness may have different natures in different possible worlds; and if a loving God does issue commands, actual wrongness has a very different character from anything that could occur in a world without a loving God.

The difference between this alternative theory and the one I have endorsed should not be exaggerated. On both theories the nature of wrongness is actually constituted by contrariety to the commands of (a loving) God. And on both theories there may be other possible worlds in which other properties best fill the role by which contrariety to a loving God's commands is linked in the actual world to our concept of wrongness.

REFERENCES

ADAMS, ROBERT MERRIHEW
    1973 'A modified divine command theory of ethical wrongness'. pp. 318–47 in Gene Outka and John P. Reeder, Jr. (eds.), *Religion and Morality*, Garden City: Anchor. [Reading V in the present volume. Page references in the text are to this reprint.]
DONELLAN, KEITH
    1966 'Reference and definite descriptions'. *The Philosophical Review* 75:281–304.
    1972 'Proper names and identifying descriptions'. pp. 356–79 in Donald Davidson and Gilbert Harman (eds.), *The Semantics of Natural Languages.* Dordrecht and Boston: Reidel.
KRIPKE, SAUL A.
    1972 'Naming and necessity'. pp. 253–355 and 763–9 in Donald Davidson and Gilbert Harman (eds.), *The Semantics of Natural Languages.* Dordrecht and Boston: Reidel.

PUTNAM, HILARY
1975 *Mind, Language and Reality: Philosophical Papers, Volume 2.*
Cambridge: Cambridge University Press.
QUINE, WILLARD VAN ORMAN
1963 *From a Logical Point of View: 9 Logico-Philosophical Essays,*
second edition. New York and Evanston: Harper Torchbooks.
1966 *The Ways of Paradox and Other Essays.* New York: Random
House.

VII

DUTY AND THE WILL OF GOD[1]

R. G. SWINBURNE

FOR a theist, a man's duty is to conform to the announced will of God. Yet a theist who makes this claim about duty is faced with a traditional dilemma first stated in Plato's *Euthyphro*[2]—are actions which are obligatory, obligatory because God makes them so (e.g. by commanding men to do them), or does God urge us to do them because they are obligatory anyway? To take the first horn of this dilemma is to claim that God can of his free choice make any action obligatory or non-obligatory (or make it obligatory not to do some action). The critic claims that the theist cannot take this horn, for God cannot make bad actions good. Nowell-Smith writes that 'an omnipotent, omniscient, creator of the Universe ... might have evil intentions and might command me to do wrong; and if that were the case, though it would be imprudent to disobey, it would not be wrong.'[3] To take the second horn of the dilemma is to claim that actions are good or bad in themselves and remain so whatever choices God makes. This horn looks very uncomfortable for the theist for two reasons; it suggests two separate limitations to God's power, two ways in which he is not omnipotent. First it suggests that God is limited in that if he is to urge men to do what is obligatory he has to urge them to do what is obligatory independently of any action of his. This suggestion, Hugo Meynell points out, 'may well seem to the theist to be blasphemous. It appears to imply that there is some objective standard of goodness and badness, prior to God's will and commandment, to which God's will and commandment are morally obliged to conform. But it is of the essence of "God", as most people understand the meaning of the term, that, if he exists at all, the moral law is dependent on

From *Canadian Journal of Philosophy*, Vol. IV, No. 2, Dec. 1974, pp. 213–27. Reprinted by permission of the editor.

[1] I am most grateful to Mr. D. A. McNaughton and other colleagues at Keele and to Dr. C. J. F. Williams for their helpful criticisms of an earlier version of this paper.
[2] *Euthyphro*, 9e.
[3] P. H. Nowell-Smith, 'Morality: Religious and Secular', in *Rationalist Annual* (1961); republished in Ian T. Ramsey (ed.), *Christian Ethics and Contemporary Philosophy* (London, 1966), pp. 93–112; see p. 97.

his decrees and not *vice versa.*[4] The second reason why grasping the second horn looks uncomfortable for the theist is that, since he must surely hold that it is no accident that God chooses to do what is good and so urges us to do what it is obligatory to do rather than what it is obligatory not to do, it would seem that he must hold that God is in some way necessitated to will what (independently of his will) is good. That again might seem a considerable restriction on his omnipotence. The purpose of this paper is to show that this dilemma for theism can be resolved, that it poses no threat to the coherence of theism, given a plausible assumption of metaethics.

I begin with a few terminological points. I understand by God the unconstrained, omnipotent, omniscient creator and sustainer of the Universe. I make the assumption that he exists and attempt to show that *Euthyphro* dilemma does not reveal an inner incoherence in that assumption.

I understand by "omniscient" "knowing everything which it is logically possible to know" and to begin with I understand by "omnipotent" "able to do anything logically possible". There are well known difficulties about these definitions but to deal with them would need separate papers.[5] These difficulties do not however, with an exception to be discussed, affect the issues discussed in this paper. By God being unconstrained I mean that his choices are not determined or influenced even in part by causes (as opposed to reasons) over which he has no control. Our choices are obviously influenced in part by many factors, psychological and physiological, over which we have no control, factors which act on us as it were from without, e.g. desires for food or sex or rest. Yet on our normal understanding of God, no factors over which he has no control act from without on God. His freedom is unimpaired by

---

[4] Hugo Meynell, 'The Euthyphro Dilemma', *Proceedings of the Aristotelian Society*, Supplementary Volume (1972), pp. 223–34; see p. 224.

[5] I have attempted to provide a coherent account of the concept of omnipotence in my 'Omnipotence' (*American Philosophical Quarterly*, 10 (1973), 231–7). In his 'Omnipotence' (*Philosophy*, 48 (1973), 7–20) P. T. Geach claims (pp. 7 f.) that 'no graspable sense has ever been given to the sentence [*viz.*, "God can do everything", which he equates with "God is omnipotent"] that did not lead to self-contradiction or at least to conclusions manifestly untenable from a Christian point of view.' Geach sketches four accounts of omnipotence and brings objections against each of them. The objections to the first three accounts seem to tell against the coherence of the concept of omnipotence. I would claim in the cited article to have given an account of omnipotence immune from such objections. The objections to the fourth account seem to tell only against claiming that God is omnipotent. They suggest the need for modifying the claim that God is omnipotent in the way which I pursue in this paper. I must withdraw the claim of my earlier article to have given an account of omnipotence which allowed the theist to say that God is omnipotent, but continue to claim that I have given a coherent account of the concept of omnipotence such that it makes sense to say that there is an omnipotent being (although it is not coherent to say that that being is God).

sensual desire or nervous impulses. Although our normal understanding of God involves thinking of him as unconstrained, this is a characteristic seldom mentioned explicitly in definitions of God, perhaps because it is felt that omnipotence entails being unconstrained. Omnipotence does not however entail being unconstrained. A being strongly influenced by sensual desires to do one action rather than another might still be *able* to do the latter action. Unconstrainedness needs explicit mention in a definition of God. I shall later argue that omniscience limits the omnipotence of an unconstrained agent, and so "omnipotent" in the definition of God will come to be understood not as just above but instead as 'able to do anything logically possible for an unconstrained and omniscient agent to do'.

I do not distinguish between an act being obligatory, being right, being a duty, and being an act which ought to be done. Unless otherwise stated I equate an obligatory action with a good action, and I equate a bad action with a wrong action and an action which ought not to be done. In these uses of moral terms I am riding rather roughshod over some subtleties of ordinary usage, but these subtleties do not affect the substance of my argument, and I make these equations to conform my terminology to that of others who have written on the subject.

I use all these terms—"obligatory", "duty", "good", etc. in moral senses, unless otherwise stated. In talking of duty, I am talking not of legal duty, but of moral duty—and so on. I understand "moral duty", "moral goodness" in a sense in which these are overriding. This means for example that if to do A rather than B would be to do the morally good action, while to do B rather than A would be to do an action which is good merely in some other respect (e.g. it is more pleasurable or aesthetically more satisfying) then to do A rather than B would be to do the action which is overall the better action. I use other moral terms, "duty", "right", etc. with similar entailments. We can of course use "moral" in a different sense, in a sense in which it makes sense to say that a man thinks that religion or art are more important than morality. But I am using "moral" and moral terms in what is, I suspect, the more usual sense, in which necessarily whatever a man thinks most important constitutes his morality.[6] The man who says 'Better to serve God than to do my duty' is a less usual and more paradoxical character than the man who says 'My duty is to serve God rather than do what others tell me is my duty'.

I understand such moral terms as "right", "wrong" etc. in an objective sense, that is that sense in which actions are right or wrong quite

---

[6] For this distinction see Neil Cooper, 'Morality and Importance', in G. Wallace and A. D. M. Walker (eds.), *The Definition of Morality* (London, 1970).

independently of the agent's beliefs about whether or not he ought to do them. Brutus may have thought it right to kill Caesar, and for that reason we may judge him an honourable man who acted in accordance with the dictates of his conscience. In so far as this latter, that he followed his conscience, is the only criterion for the rightness of his action, you and I may agree that he did what he ought to have done. If we do say this, we are using "ought" in a subjective sense. We may however go on to discuss whether in fact, whatever Brutus' own view on the matter, he ought to have killed Caesar. You being a pacifist may say that he ought not to have done; I may say that he ought. Our disagreement is about whether he did what he ought to have done in an objective sense. It is in this sense that henceforward I will use the moral terms.

My assumption of metaethics is that expressions apparently attributing to things, goodness, obligatoriness etc. (e.g. 'capital punishment is always wrong') are statements which are true or false independently of human beliefs or attitudes towards those things; to call an action good is to attribute a property to it, not *merely* to express approval of it, commend it, or something similar. The status of ethical expressions is of course a very large philosophical issue on which it would be inappropriate to argue for a conclusion in an article devoted to another topic. Yet discussion of that topic is impossible without some view about the status of ethical expressions. In consequence I have to make an assumption about this and I shall make the one stated—that expressions apparently attributing to things goodness, obligatoriness, etc. are statements which are true or false independently of human beliefs or attitudes towards those things. I assume, in other words, that these are propositions of first-order ethics which have a truth-value, whether or not men recognize that truth-value, just as bodies are heavy or square or electrically charged whether or not men know this about them. The assumption does have a certain intrinsic plausibility. Torturing innocent children just for fun, one is inclined to say, is wicked whatever I or anyone else thinks about the matter—just as the Earth is a planet of the Sun, whether or not men recognize or approve this.

Given this assumption let us distinguish between contingent and necessary moral truths. A contingent moral truth is one which holds only because the world is as it is in some further contingent respect. A necessary moral truth is one which holds however the world is in contingent respects. Thus among contingent moral truths are such statements as 'I ought now to pay £10 to the bookshop' or 'I ought to give Smith a fail mark on his ethics paper'. These moral truths are contingent, because, although the cited actions are obligatory on me, they are obligatory only because of other contingent circumstances. Why I ought to pay the bookshop £10 is because I bought £10 of books from them and they have sent me a bill for the books. If such contingent circumstances did not hold, I would have no obligation to pay the bookshop £10. Contingent moral truths hold because the world is as it is in contingent respects. But that those moral truths hold under the contingent circumstances is itself a necessary moral truth. For if we state fully the contingent circumstances which make a contingent moral truth to hold, it cannot be a contingent matter that it does hold under those circumstances. Yet it is a moral truth that it does, and hence a necessary moral truth. It is a necessary moral truth that when I have bought £10 of books from the bookshop and they send me a bill for this, I ought to pay the bill. No doubt this moral truth holds because a much more general moral truth holds—that men ought to pay their debts—of which the specific truth is a consequence. Among the necessary moral truths one would expect to find general principles of conduct such as that one ought to care for one's children, not punish the innocent, not tell lies (together with whatever qualifications are needed). Nothing however for our purposes turns on which statements are necessary moral truths, or on the extent of the generality of those necessary moral truths. All that is important to see is that moral truths are either contingent or necessary in the stated senses; and that contingent moral truths hold because contingent circumstances are as they are and also because necessary moral truths hold.

My solution to the *Euthyphro* dilemma is in terms of this distinction. It is that the theist can happily take the first horn for actions which are contingently obligatory (i.e. for actions, the obligatoriness of which is a contingent moral truth), and the second horn for actions which are necessarily obligatory (i.e. for actions, the obligatoriness of which is a necessary moral truth). I proceed now to justify this solution.

To take the second horn for actions which are necessarily obligatory is to claim that their obligatoriness does not result from any free choice of God. Clearly that must be so. For a necessarily obligatory action is one which is obligatory however the world is in contingent respects, and a free choice of God is a contingent matter. This conclusion follows whatever the nature of those necessarily obligatory actions—it follows even if the only necessarily obligatory action were to do whatever God commands. That this was necessarily obligatory would be independent of the free choice of God. We have seen that if there is a contingent moral truth, then there is a necessary moral truth; from which it follows that if there is a contingently obligatory action, there is a necessarily obligatory action (*viz.* to do the former under the appropriate contingent circumstances). Hence if there are any obligatory actions at all (as we have been assuming), there is an obligatory action which is obligatory whatever the free choices of God. Does this mean that there cannot be an omnipotent God? We saw that grasping the second horn raised two separate difficulties for the theist in this respect. We must deal with each in turn.

First, there is the apparent limitation on God that if he is to urge men to do what is obligatory, he has to urge them to do what is obligatory independently of any action of his. Whether this is a limitation depends on whether the necessarily obligatory actions are obligatory from logical necessity or from some kind of factual necessity; that is whether the necessary moral truths that those actions are obligatory are analytic or synthetic. I understand "analytic" in a wide sense. I understand by a logically necessary or analytic statement a statement, the denial of which states nothing which it is coherent to suppose could be true. I understand by a synthetic statement a statement which is not analytic. If for any specified action which is obligatory (e.g. telling the truth) it is analytic that it is obligatory, then it is no restriction on God that if he is to urge men to do what is obligatory he must urge them to do those actions which of logical necessity are obligatory. In order to be omnipotent, as we have defined omnipotence, a being has only to be able to do the logically possible. We surely do not require that an omnipotent being be able to do the logically impossible for that requirement is not coherent. The traditional view that to be omnipotent a being does not have to be able to do the logically impossible seems correct.[7] The suggested restriction on God is no more a restriction than it is a restriction on God that if he is to keep Jones a bachelor he must keep him an unmarried man. If necessary moral truths are analytic, the first difficulty for the theist in grasping the second horn in respect of them disappears.

But if the necessity that if God is to urge men to do what is obligatory, he must urge them to do certain specifiable actions (e.g. truth telling) is a factual necessity, it does indeed involve a restriction on God's power. For it means that while it is coherent to suppose that God urge men to do what is obligatory without urging them to do these actions, there is nevertheless a natural necessity which prevents him from doing so. Yet the supposition that necessary moral truths are synthetic is indefensible, quite apart from any general difficulties in the idea of a synthetic necessary truth. Suppose that necessary moral truths are synthetic. Then take some necessary moral truth 'under circumstances C, A is obligatory'. This truth being synthetic, it is coherent to suppose that it does not hold. This could only be if there were a necessary moral

[7] St. Thomas Aquinas, *Summa Theologiae*, 1a.25.3. See my 'Omnipotence', *American Philosophical Quarterly*, 10 (1973), 231–7.

truth of the form 'under circumstances C^1, A is not obligatory' (where C^1 is a subset of C). This latter would be a synthetic truth, though a necessary one. So our universe is one where 'under circumstances C, A is obligatory' is a necessary moral truth, yet it is coherent to suppose that there be a universe where it is not, and instead 'under circumstances C^1, A is not obligatory' is a necessary moral truth. Now necessary moral truths hold whatever the world is like in contingent respects. So the latter universe could be exactly the same as ours in all contingent respects. So if necessary moral truths were synthetic, it would be coherent to suppose that there is a universe which differs from ours in the respect that under circumstances C^1, A was not obligatory, but in no contingent respect at all. Yet how could a world differ from ours solely in an ethical respect? What would it be like for a world to differ from our world solely in the respect that murder is not wrong in that world? What sense can be given to such a supposition? By the principle of supervenience[8] if one thing is good and another bad, they have to differ in some further respect, and if we understand by "further respect" "further contingent respect", it is hard to challenge that principle. I conclude that necessary moral truths are not synthetic. Hence they are analytic (in the stated sense) and so the first difficulty for a theist grasping the second horn for necessary moral truths disappears.

The second difficulty for a theist in grasping the second horn is that since presumably it is no accident that God chooses to do what is good, and so urges us to do what it is obligatory to do rather than what it is obligatory not to do, it would seem that he must be necessitated to choose to do what is, independently of his choice, good. I wish to show that if a being in unconstrained and omniscient, of logical necessity, he can choose only the good. This restriction on God is a restriction already imposed on his being omniscient and unconstrained. I shall however argue that it is one which makes him no less worthy of worship.

I begin with the point that actions, in the sense of things done intentionally, must have reasons, in the sense of reasons possessed by an agent for doing them. To do an action is to forward an end or goal, and the reason for doing the action is to forward the end. The doing of an action may be an end in itself or it may be the means to a further end. An action always has a reason, even if it is only the minimal reason that the agent wanted to do it. If a man says that he did something 'for no reason at all', the natural interpretation is that he did the action merely for the sake of doing it, not for any further reason. The suggestion that a man performed an action, that is did something intentionally, did something meaning to do it, without having a reason for doing it is incoherent. This

[8] See R. M. Hare, *The Language of Morals* (Oxford, 1952), pp. 80 et seq.

can be seen by the fact that a crucial test for whether some movement of my body was an action of mine or merely something that happened to my body (e.g. a reflex movement) is whether I can give a reason for having done it, that is whether I can answer the question 'Why did you do it?' If I cannot answer the question, that shows that the movement is not properly described as an action which I did. Now having a reason for an action consists in regarding some state of affairs as a good thing and the doing of the action as a means to forwarding that state, and hence itself a good thing. If my reason for going to London is to meet Jones, I must regard it as in some way a good thing that I should meet Jones, and so in some way a good thing that I go to London. If I regard it as in no way a good thing that I should meet Jones, if I regard my meeting Jones as an event which would serve no useful function at all, meeting Jones cannot be my reason for going to London. The point that to do an action I must (of logical necessity) see my performance of it as in some way a good thing is a very old one due to Aristotle, emphasised by Aquinas, and re-emphasised in our day by, among others, Stuart Hampshire.[9]

What however are we to make of the suggestion that a man might see doing A as a good thing in one way (e.g. by its giving sensual pleasure to himself), doing B (an action doing which is incompatible with doing A) as a good thing in another way (e.g. by its contributing to the life-long peace of mind of someone else), see doing B as overall a better thing than doing A, but nevertheless do A rather than B? When it is suggested that a case is of this sort, we may well suspect that it is not, that the agent did not really see doing B as overall a better thing than doing A. Yet we are sometimes prepared to allow that the situation is as suggested. We do seem to allow the possibility that a man might do an action which he regarded as a good thing only in some respect but on balance a bad thing. But although we allow this possibility, we do feel that some further explanation is called for. If a man really does accept that to do B would be to do what is on balance the better action, he has adequate reason for doing B but totally inadequate reason for doing A. Rational considerations point clearly in one direction, yet the agent goes in the other direction. Yet to say that someone recognizes that he has adequate reason for doing B rather than A is to say that in so far as no factors other than reasons influence what he does, he will do B rather than A. For although a man's belief or recognition that something is so does

---

[9] 'A man cannot be sincere in accepting the conclusion that some course of action is entirely mistaken, if he at the same time deliberately commits himself to this course of action' (Stuart Hampshire, *Freedom of the Individual* (London, 1965), p. 7.)

not necessarily affect his behaviour, it can only fail to do so if some special explanation can be provided of what prevented it from affecting behaviour. If a philosopher denies this, he is committed to the connection between a man's beliefs and what he does being a merely contingent one—which allows as a logical possibility that none of a man's beliefs might make any difference to his actions—which is absurd! So if you said that you recognized that overall it would be better for you to go home rather than to go to the cinema, and then you went to the cinema, we should have to suppose either that you were lying or had changed your mind, or that factors other than reasons influenced what you did. An explanation of your behaviour is needed, not only in terms of what you believed about the relative merits of the actions, in terms that is of reasons; but also in terms of other factors such as sensual desires and neurological impulses which led you to do what you did not have adequate reason for doing. If a man has strong sensual desires, it makes sense to suppose that he recognizes B as the better action but nevertheless intentionally does A. Such non-rational factors over which the agent does not have control explain 'weakness of will', a man acting 'against his better judgement'. But the suggestion that a man might see B as the better action, be subject to no non-rational forces 'pushing' him in the direction of doing A and nevertheless do A is incoherent.[10]

Moral considerations as we have understood them, are overriding. Why then does a man fail to do his duty? By my previous arguments either because he does not fully recognize his duty, or because he is influenced by forces not subject to his control. If the latter operate, the agent is in a situation of temptation, to which he may or may not yield.[11] Given all this, could God choose to do anything which was not morally good? Clearly not through ignorance, for he is omniscient. Both ordinary factual and moral truths are known to Him. While we have rather cloudy feelings that abortion and euthanasia are evils, he knows the truth about these matters (whatever it is!) with crystal clarity. God could not urge a man to murder his brother, through not knowing that murder was an

[10] The extreme position on this issue of R. M. Hare as represented in Chapter 5 of *Freedom and Reason* seems to be that necessarily if a man believes that B is the better action, he will do B unless it is psychologically impossible for him to do B. Many writers have opposed this position. Steven Lukes has pointed out that ordinarily we describe men as tempted and yielding to temptation when there is no *irresistable* temptation for them to yield to. Irving Thalberg points out that 'ought implies might not'. In Hare's account of moral action it would never be appropriate to blame a man for not living up to his principles. See the contributions of Hare, Lukes, Thalberg and others published in Geoffrey Mortimore (ed.), *Weakness of Will* (London, 1971).

[11] Nothing which I have written implies that the outcome of a struggle with temptation is predetermined.

evil. Nor could he choose to do something morally evil through being influenced by non-rational factors, through failing to resist temptation. By definition God is unconstrained and not subject to such factors. Of logical necessity a being unconstrained and omniscient does not choose the bad. This necessary restriction on God's omnipotence (to his not choosing to do an evil action) is a consequence of his being omniscient and unconstrained. The existence of this restriction means that we must understand the claim in our previous definition of God that he is omnipotent as saying that he is able to do anything logically possible for an unconstrained and omniscient agent to do.

God's omniscience (given that he is unconstrained) limits his omnipotence by limiting what he can set himself to do. If he chose to do an evil action he could do it. But being omniscient, he cannot choose to do it. This is because he will know that the action is an evil action, and so that he cannot by doing that action do an action which is better than any alternative (which is, by our previous argument, what every agent not influenced by non-rational forces seeks to do), and so he cannot do the action. It may at first seem surprising that knowledge can limit what we can set ourselves to do but a few mundane examples will easily show that it does. If I really know that I cannot jump to the moon, I cannot set myself or try to do it. No action of mine would properly be described as setting about jumping to the moon or trying to jump to the moon. I could only be said to be pretending to jump to the moon, or to be going through the motions which I would go through if I were trying to jump to the moon. If I really know that the bus has gone, I cannot try to catch it. My running to the bus-stop must be described in some other way.

My conclusion then is that God, being omniscient and unconstrained of logical necessity chooses only the good. Hence he will not urge us to do what it is obligatory not to do, but only what is obligatory to do.[12] Does this limitation on God's omnipotence make him less worthy of worship? Why should it? Being unconstrained hardly makes a being less worthy of worship. Although knowledge limits power of choice, by preventing us from trying to do what we cannot (e.g. change the past, or do good by murdering), quite clearly in general by allowing us to see what we can do and so allowing us to exercise our power effectively, it

---

[12] This general view that necessarily God can only will the good, and that necessarily his freedom is only a freedom to choose between equally good alternatives, is that of Aquinas. Thus: 'The will never aims at evil without some error existing in the reason, at least with respect to a particular object of choice. For, since the object of the will is the apprehended good, the will cannot aim at evil unless in some way it is proposed to it as a good; and this cannot take place without error. But in the divine knowledge there cannot be error. God's will cannot, therefore, tend towards evil' (*Summa Contra Gentiles*, 1.95.3; translated by Anton C. Pegis under the title, *On the truth of The Catholic Faith, Book I* (New York, 1955)).

allows us to use the power of choice which we have much more effectively. That a being's power cannot be exercised in self-defeating ways surely does not detract from his dignity.

So much for necessarily obligatory actions. What now of contingently obligatory actions? Given that necessary moral truths which, as we have seen, are analytic truths are as they are, what makes a contingently obligatory action A obligatory in some contingent circumstance C? What makes it my duty to pay the bookshop is that I have bought books from them and they have sent me a bill. But if there is a God who is creator and sustainer of the Universe, any contingent circumstances C are either brought about directly or indirectly by God or brought about by the free choice of some other agent (e.g. a man) kept in existence by God and allowed by him to exercise his choice. In the former case God by bringing about C makes A obligatory. In the latter case God by keeping some other agent in existence and allowing him to bring about C has permitted some other agent to make A obligatory. Either way God's action makes A obligatory (though in the latter case he permits some other agent to share in making A obligatory). Why it is wrong for me to stick pins into you is that you are so made that sticking pins into you hurts terribly, and so is wrong, and it is God who has made you thus—given that God exists as defined—and so has made it obligatory on me not to stick pins into you. This point is well made by Meynell when he writes that 'what is good or right in human action and dispositions depends ultimately on the divine will, if God exists; since in that case the whole context of human life within which moral terms have their application, and from which they derive their significance depends on it.'[13]

So then the conclusion follows that if it is a necessary truth that under circumstances C, A is obligatory, then God as the author of circumstances C is responsible for the contingent truth that A is obligatory. This holds whatever the form of necessary moral truths. It is however pertinent to ask whether the circumstances C which make A obligatory are always, sometimes, or never the issue of an explicit command by God. The command would presumably become known through some vehicle of Revelation, e.g. Mahommet or the Bible or the Church, telling us on behalf of God that the command had been issued. Yet while this question is relevant, it is important to note that whatever answer we give to it, the basic solution to the dilemma outlined in the previous part of the paper remains.

My answer to the new question is that sometimes the command of God would make actions obligatory which would not otherwise be

[13] Meynell, *op. cit.*, p. 232.

obligatory; and that always the command of God would make the strength of an obligation to do an action greater than it would otherwise be. Some actions however are obligatory whether or not God commands them; and so God cannot forbid them (since forbidding them would be evil, and it is not logically possible, as we have seen, for an omniscient and unconstrained being to do evil).

A powerful argument against this position is that we know perfectly well how to decide moral issues without bringing in the commands of God. Suppose we debate the rightness or wrongness of capital punishment. We know the kind of considerations which count for or against the wrongness of capital punishment as a penalty for murder. For is the consideration that if you find out that you have wrongly executed a man, you cannot remit any of his penalty or make amends. Against is the horror of murder and the need for an adequate punishment. Statistics of the deterrent effect of capital punishment or the lack of it are also relevant to one or other side of the controversy. We know how to settle the matter without bringing God in. Rightness or wrongness being established independently of God, his command cannot alter things.

This argument, though it seems initially powerful, is confused. Certainly we know how to decide moral issues if we ignore divine commands by supposing that there are none. But that does not mean that divine commands, if there are any, are irrelevant to moral issues, any more than the fact (if it is a fact) that we can show the wrongness of capital punishment, if we ignore any possible deterrent effect (i.e. suppose there to be none) means that deterrent effects if they exist, are irrelevant to its rightness or wrongness. Maybe divine commands, if they exist, are relevant, possibly decisively relevant—even though we can settle moral issues on the assumption that divine commands do not exist. I shall now proceed to argue that if God has issued commands, they do have moral relevance.

Their relevance, contrary to what Geach seems[14] to claim, is nothing to do with the power of God. Power does not give the right to command, even if it is infinite power and even if it is benevolent power.

There are at least two different considerations which make the commands of God, if there are any such, impose moral obligations which did not exist before. The first is that, by definition, he is our creator and sustainer. We depend for our existence at each instant on his will. Now many would hold that men have an obligation to please their benefactors. A man who makes no effort to please those who have done

---

[14] Peter Geach, *God and the Soul* (London, 1969), p. 127 [Reading XI]. For criticism of this see D. Z. Phillips, *Death and Immortality* (London, 1971), ch. 2.

much for him is generally felt to be behaving in an immoral way. A consequence of the general principle that men have an obligation to please their benefactors is that children have an obligation to please their parents, who brought them into the world and keep them alive, clothe, and feed them. The obligation to please parents would be fulfilled by conforming to the parents' wishes (which may be expressed by commands) e.g. that the child should do the shopping or the washing up, go to bed at a certain time or shut the door. There might be no special reason why the child ought or ought not to go to bed at the time in question other than that the parent has commanded it. But the parent's command makes what was otherwise not a duty a duty for the child. The child owes something to the parent in view of the parent's status. It is not that children have a duty to pay something back to the parent, but that because in an important respect the parent is the source of their being he is entitled to their consideration.

The moral views expressed in the last paragraph are by no means universal, but they are, I suspect, held by a considerable majority of the human race. A morality which did not think the worse of a man for making no effort to please those who had done him much good would seem a pretty poor morality. If the moral views of the last paragraph are correct then men are under a great obligation to obey the commands of God—a great obligation because, if theism is true, the dependence of the children of God on God is so much greater than the dependence of the children of men on men. We depend to a large extent on our parents for our initial existence and to some extent for our subsequent existence— they provide food, shelter etc. But we depend on other persons too for our subsequent existence—the police, our parents' employers, the state's welfare officers etc. And our parents are only able to bring us into existence and sustain us because of the operation of various natural laws (e.g. the laws of genetics, and embryology), the operation of which, is, on the theistic hypothesis, due to God. However our dependence on God, the author of Nature, is, if he exists, total. He gave to our parents the power and inclination to bring us into being, and to them and to others the power to keep us alive. He keeps operative natural laws, as a result of which we have food and drink and health. Our obligation to God must be correspondingly very much greater than to our parents.

The other consideration which makes the commands of God impose moral obligations which did not exist before is that God is the creator of the inanimate world and, not being known to have ceded ownership of it, is properly adjudged its owner. What greater claim could one have to property than having created it *ex nihilo* unaided? The owner of property has the right to tell those to whom he has loaned it what they are allowed to do with it. Consequently God has a right to lay down how that property, the inanimate world, shall be used and by whom. If God has made the Earth, he can say which of his children can use which part. The Bible is full of claims that God has given to persons various possessions (and thereby commanded other persons to leave them alone). Thus the Lord is said to have declared to Joshua that he gave to the Israelites the land of Canaan (*Joshua* 1.2ff.). The right of God to dispose of the material objects of the world as he wishes is affirmed by Aquinas: 'What is taken by God's command, who is the owner of the Universe, is not against the owner's will, and this is the essence of theft.'[15] It follows from this that it is logically impossible for God to command a man to steal—for whatever God commands a man to take thereby becomes that man's and so his taking it is not stealing.

Again the moral principle about property to which I have appealed would not be universally accepted, but, possibly with qualifications, it would, I believe, be very generally accepted, and for those who do accept it the conclusion about God follows directly. So appealing to widely accepted moral principles, I have argued that God's commands can impose obligations which did not exist before. By parity of argument the commands of God can add to the obligation to do an action which is obligatory anyway. An action of a child which is wrong anyway becomes wrong in a new way if the parent forbids it.

Scotus claimed[16] that although acts were often good or bad in themselves apart from considerations about God, God's commands made it obligatory to do them. The same point is certainly involved in what Miss Anscombe claims in her article 'Modern Moral Philosophy'[17] when she claims that the concept of obligation only has a sense within a law concept of ethics, that is within a concept of ethics in which to be obliged is to be commanded. My argument suggests that commands sometimes make acts right or wrong and make acts which are right or wrong anyway right or wrong in a new respect. We could well reserve the word "obligation" to refer to an act which it would be wrong not to do, and which is made thus by a command. I have not myself used "obligation" in this way, because I do not think that normally its use is restricted in this way. But there would be a point in so restricting its use in order to give a name to a certain kind of act which otherwise does not have one.

Still, there are surely limits to the obligations which a divine command could create. Exactly where they are to be put men will differ.

[15] *Summa Theologiae*, 1a.2ae.94.5., ad. 2, New Blackfriars ed., trans. Thomas Gilby, O.P., Vol. XXVIII (London, 1966).
[16] See F. Copleston, *A History of Philosophy*, Vol. II (London, 1950), p. 547.
[17] *Philosophy*, 33 (1958), 1–19.

There are certainly limits to the obligations which a parent's command can create, and to the obligations to obey the owner of property in respect of its use. If a parent commands a child to kill his neighbour, the command imposes no obligation. Nor does the command of an owner of vast estates not to use some of his unwanted corn to feed the starving. At least, most people would accept these moral judgments. Some might urge that God is so much more truly the author of our being and the owner of the land than are human parents and property owners that there are no limits to the obligations which would be produced by his commands.[18] But most would surely judge that even God could not remove my obligation to keep a solemn promise when the keeping of it would cause pain to no one, or my obligation not to torture the innocent. But if for some action A if God commanded us to do A, it would still be our duty not to do A, God would not command us to do A. For then commanding us to do A would be inciting us to do evil. Since to incite to evil is evil, God who necessarily wills the good would not incite to evil.

However, wherever we draw the line, whether God could by commanding impose any obligation or none, makes no difference to the main argument of this paper. Whether or to whatever extent God can impose obligations by issuing commands, he can certainly, if he exists as defined, impose them by producing the circumstances which create them. And even if his commands would not impose obligations which did not exist before, it remains the case that if God urged us to do something, necessarily the doing of it would not be evil. For God who necessarily does not will evil will not urge men to do evil. I conclude that given my metaethical assumption, whatever difficulties threaten the coherence of theism, the *Euthyphro* dilemma is not among them.

[18] As Ockham seems to have held. See F. Copleston, *A History of Philosophy* Vol. III (London, 1953), pp. 104 f.

VIII

GOD, MORALITY, AND PRUDENCE

BERNARD WILLIAMS

WE distinguished some time ago among views which seek to elicit a notion of a good man from considerations of human nature—those that set man in some transcendental framework and those that did not. Having just said something about the second sort, I shall now turn to look at an example of the first. In the course of doing this, it will be helpful to discuss a question which is important apart from the present issue—the relations of the moral and the prudential.

A leading feature of this sort of theory is that it seeks to provide, in terms of the transcendental framework, something that man is *for*: if he understands properly his role in the basic scheme of things, he will see that there are some particular sorts of ends which are properly his and which he ought to realize. One archetypal form of such a view is the belief that man was created by a God who also has certain expectations of him.

A central difficulty with this lies in the question of which properties of God are supposed to justify the claim that we ought to satisfy his expectations. If it is his power, or the mere fact that he created us, analogies with human kings or fathers (often employed in this connection) leave us with the recognition that there are many kings and fathers who ought not to be obeyed. If it is urged that God has infinite power and created everything, we point out that infinite kinghood or creatordom does not seem evidently more worthy of obedience but merely more difficult to disobey. If it is then said that in addition to these other properties God is good, the objection is forthcoming (as it was from Kant) that this already involves a recognition of what is admirable and valuable, a recognition of the kind which the appeal to God was supposed to underwrite.

Such arguments, which are very familiar, may be taken as attacking the idea that one might work out purely deductively and *a priori* the required life for man from a description of him as *created by God*. In that role, they seem to me successful. But such arguments tend to carry with them a larger ambition—to show that even if God's existence

From *Morality: An Introduction to Ethics* (1972), pp. 77–86. Reprinted by permission of Cambridge University Press.

were established, that fact could not in principle supply any acceptable or appropriate *motive* for moral conduct, of a kind which would otherwise be lacking. In this role, too, the arguments are very widely accepted, so that it is practically a philosopher's platitude that even if God did exist, that would not, to a clear-headed and moral thinker, make any difference to the situation of morality. The origins of this view go back to a famous discussion in Plato's *Euthyphro*, but in its modern form it owes most to Kant. It owes to him in particular a clear statement of the assumptions on which it rests—assumptions about the essential *purity* of moral motivation. These assumptions are pervasive in much moral thought, and their influence and importance goes a long way beyond the present issue of a religious morality. They are also very importantly mistaken.

The argument, in simplest form, goes something like this, Either one's motives for following the moral word of God are moral motives, or they are not. If they are, then one is already equipped with moral motivations, and the introduction of God adds nothing extra. But if they are not moral motives, then they will be motives of such a kind that they cannot appropriately motivate *morality* at all; in particular, they are likely to be motives of prudence, a possibility most crudely portrayed by certain evangelists (whether of belief or disbelief) in terms of hellfire. But nothing motivated by prudential considerations can be genuinely moral actions; genuinely moral action must be motivated by the consideration that it is morally right and by no other consideration at all. So, taking this all together, we reach the conclusion that any appeal to God in this connection either adds nothing at all, or it adds the wrong sort of thing.

Two questions are raised about morality and motivation by this sort of argument. First, whether there are really no relevant types of motivation except moral or prudential—that is to say, whether the distinction between moral and prudential is exhaustive. Second, whether a policy or outlook may not be moral, while being in some way at the same time prudential—that is to say, whether the distinction is exclusive. Let us take the second question first. Is it essential to morality to distinguish totally the moral and the prudential?

Here we need to make some distinctions. It is certainly true that it is essential to morality that a distinction is drawn *at some level* between the moral and the prudential. At the most primitive level, it is clear that any morality has to apply this distinction, or something like it, to actions and policies; it has to be able to distinguish actions and policies which are *selfish* and which minister to the gratification or safety of the agent at the expense of others, from those which take the interests of others into account. If some such distinction is not made, there are no moral considerations at all. It is clear that the religious morality we are discussing, however crudely put, can observe this distinction at the primitive level: it will, with respect to the secular world, approve policies and actions which take the interests of others into account and will disapprove selfish policies.

However, it may be thought that this level of drawing the distinction is, by itself, too primitive, and that we need to extend the distinction from merely classifying policies and intentional actions, to discriminating between motives. Thus one who gives money to charity merely to improve his reputation with the Rotary Club or to ease his own guilt, acts not more morally than if he had spent the money on his own pleasures. (The example illustrates why it was appropriate to speak of 'intentional action' and to distinguish this from the question of motive. The self-interested business man who writes a cheque to famine relief, does so intentionally, and his intention is that the money should go to famine relief: if famine is relieved by his action, this will not be, relative to his thoughts in so acting, an *accident*. The point is that his motive was not a concern for the relief of famine, but for his own reputation or comfort.)

If we say, as many would say, that the man who so acts acts no more morally than one who spends the money on himself, it will not follow that what he does is no better than what is done by the simply selfish man; for famine will be, hopefully, relieved, and this is better than that another combined cocktail cabinet and TV set should be bought. Nor, surely, can it follow that we merely approve of the act and do not in *any* sense approve of the agent; for we can say of him that he has intentionally done something which it is a good thing to have done, and this surely constitutes some sort of approval, if a limited sort, of him. The point, presumably, is that we do not *morally* approve of him. There is a very good point in saying this, but it must not be taken too far. For if we insist that to act morally is essentially to act from a moral motivation, we may well be tempted to add to that the innocuous-looking proposition that all that can matter from a moral point of view is that people should act morally, and then conclude (rightly, from those premises) that from the moral point of view any two situations of self-interested motivation are indistinguishable, and it must be impossible from the moral point of view to prefer one to the other. This is absurd. It is not perhaps logically absurd, but morally absurd—the Puritan moral absurdity that the only morally relevant property of the world is how much righteousness it contains. But since this is morally absurd (or, rather, since it is obviously not incoherent to regard it as morally absurd), it follows that something else *is* logically absurd: namely a view of morality

from which it follows that that is the only moral position which is coherently tenable.

What is, then, the point and content of saying that we do not *morally*
approve of the self-interested donor to charity, or that, though he does
a good thing, he does not act morally? With what motivations, first, are
we contrasting this man's motivation? Some, such as Kant and R. M.
Hare, have laid emphasis on the contrast with acting *from principle*;
roughly, doing it just because one thinks one ought to. Others, such as
Hume, have emphasized the contrast with doing something because one
cares disinterestedly about the situation which one's action is supposed
to alter or cares about the other people involved. Leaving aside the
notable differences between these two formulations, they do have something in common: that the man who has a moral motivation for doing
things of the non-self-regarding sort, has a disposition or general motive
for doing such things of that sort; whereas the self-interested man has
no such steady motive, for it will always only be luck if what benefits
others happens to coincide with what, by the limited criteria of simple
self-interest, happens to benefit him. This must surely, as Hume said,
have something to do with the *point* of selecting certain motives for
moral approbation: we are concerned to have people who have a general
tendency to be prepared to consider other people's interests on the same
footing as their own, and if necessary to put other people's interests first.

It is perhaps worth noting, in passing, that one of the (numerous) advantages of Hume's emphasis in this matter, with its stress on sympathy
and feeling for other people's situation, as opposed to the Kantian emphasis on acting from principle, is that it introduces a similarity between
the sorts of reasons one has for doing things for others, and the sorts of
reasons one has for doing them for oneself. Despite the mechanical
character of Hume's psychological system, it makes some sense of the
idea that to care about others' pain is an extension of caring about one's
own: the second is indeed a necessary condition of the first, and there
is certainly no problem (as there should not be) about why a man who
is concerned about others may not also be reasonably concerned about
himself. Under the Kantian emphasis, however, this suddenly emerges
as a problem, since to act with regard to one's own interests, in a straightforward way, is to act from a kind of motive which has nothing to do
with morality at all and is indeed alien to it. Since we are presumably
enjoined to maximize moral action, extremes of self-denial would seem
to follow, as derived, indeed, from the concept of morality itself. At
the best, doing what one simply wants to do will constitute unregulated
and probably guilty departures from the moral point of view. To cope
with this problem, the Kantian tradition produces a set of 'duties to

oneself', recognition of which licenses one to do for moral reasons some of the things one would be disposed to do anyway. This absurd apparatus is just the product of trying to adjust to some rather more reasonable view of human life the awkward consequences of holding three things—that morality is concerned above all with motivation, that moral motivation is motivation of principle, and that the moral point of view must be ubiquitous. To avoid these particular awkward consequences, it would be enough to abandon any one of these propositions; but there are good reasons for abandoning all of them.

To revert, after this diversion, to our religious moralist. We saw that he could quite easily draw a distinction, though a primitive one, between the moral and the prudential. I think that we can see now that he can even draw a more refined distinction, at the level of motivation. It was suggested that one (though perhaps not the only) point of distinguishing between moral and self-interested motivations was that of picking out general dispositions to do things of the non-self-interested sort. But dispositions of this sort, the man with even a crude religious morality will certainly admit. Indeed, perhaps what his God wants is that men should feel for the sufferings of each other and act in one another's interests because they so feel. So a lot of the time persons of this belief, if they did as God would like them to, would act from ordinary human motives which by most people (other than Kantians) would be regarded as themselves moral motives. If these fail, or temptation to selfish action is strong, then perhaps the crude believer's thoughts turn a while to hellfire, and this fortifies a disposition to do things of the non-self-interested sort (in the worldly sense of 'self-interest', that is). While his action is in this sense prudential, it is not prudential in that sense in which it is essential to the concept of morality that the prudential be contrasted with the moral. Indeed, there is a special reason why his actions, though prudential, are not selfish: namely there is presumably no effective way of aiming at salvation *at the expense of others*.

In fact, it is quite unrealistic to force onto our religious moralist (or anyone else) an exhaustive disjunction between the prudential and the moral. Leaving aside the more general operations of sympathy of which Hume wrote: what about someone who does something in the interests of another, and to his own disadvantage, because he loves that person; or, indeed, is in love with them; or admires them; or respects them; or because they are (after all) a member of the family? None of these reasons for acting have to be moral reasons, in any exigent or purified sense of that term; equally they are not prudential reasons. Nor, again, do they belong to the third class of motive moral philosophy has sometimes allowed, that of *inclination*, that is, doing something because you

feel like doing it. Clearly the list of examples could be extended indefi-
nitely to include vast numbers of the special relationships in which one
person can stand to another. It is a grotesque product of theory and
strenuous moralism to suppose that 'moral' and 'prudential' sufficiently
divide up the justifiable motives or reasons a man can have for doing
something: they leave out, in fact, almost everything. We do need something over and above these particular, or more specific, motivations, just
because they are particular and specific, and especially because the particular relationship I have to another person may be of a hostile character,
and there will in all probability be no other, more beneficient, particular
relationship in the offing to inhibit destructive conduct. So of course
we need, over and above, general motivations to control and regulate
these particular ones; and the most general thing that is over and above
is morality. But, happily for humanity, we do not have to leave it to
those general considerations to motivate everything of a desirable kind.
Some of our decent actions come not from that motive which Christians
misrepresent as our loving everybody, but just from our loving somebody.

The religious moralist, now, can see the general requirements as stem-
ming from a particular relation, that to God, and this relation can be
represented as one of love, or awe, or respect, or whatever words are
found appropriate for this baffling semantic task. And this relation he
will rightly resist being categorized as either moral or prudential in its
practical import. I think, however, that he may have to be careful about
saying that this is an attitude towards God which anyone who knows
what God is *ought* to have, for this might, in the way that Kant insisted
on, make morality prior to God again. He will have to say, rather, that
this is an attitude which anyone who knows what God is will inevitably
have; God is one whose word exacts an unquestioning acceptance. In
itself, this is still not enough, of course; compatibly with this much, God
could be an unfailing hypnotist. So the believer will proceed, as always,
by negation and analogy and say that it is not like that, but *more* like
a loving father, and so forth. I myself doubt whether at the end he will
produce any coherent account at all. But this is because of difficulties
in belief in God, not because of something in the nature of morality. I do
not think it right—and these arguments have been trying to show this—to
say, as many do, that even if God existed, this could give no special and
acceptable reason for subscribing to morality. If God existed, there might
well be special, and acceptable, reasons for subscribing to morality. The
trouble is that the attempt to formulate those reasons in better than the
crudest outline runs into the impossibility of thinking coherently about
God. The trouble with religious morality comes not from morality's being
inescapably pure, but from religion's being incurably unintelligible.

IX

MORALITY AND RELIGION RECONSIDERED[1]

BARUCH A. BRODY

THERE are many people who believe that, in one way or another, morality needs a religious backing. One of the many things that might be meant by this vague and ambiguous claim[2] is the following: there are certain moral truths that are true only because of the truth of certain religious truths. In particular, the truth of certain claims about the rightness (wrongness) of a given action is dependent upon the truth of certain religious claims to the effect that God wants us to do (refrain from doing) that action. This belief, in effect, bases certain parts of morality upon the will of God.

Philosophers have not commonly agreed with such claims. And there is an argument, whose ancestor is an argument in the *Euthyphro*,[3] that is supposed to show that such claims are false. It runs as follows: the proponents of the claim in question have reversed the order of things. Doing a given action *A* is not right (wrong) because God wants us to do (refrain from doing) *A*; rather, God wants us to do (refrain from doing) *A* because of some other reason which is the real reason why *A* is right (wrong) for us to do. For, if the situation were the way it is depicted by the proponents of the claim in question, we would have moral truths based upon the arbitrary desires of God as to what we should do (refrain from doing), and this is objectionable.

I would like to reexamine this issue and to show that the situation is far more complicated than philosophers normally imagine it to be.

From *Readings in the Philosophy of Religion: An Analytic Approach*, © 1974, pp. 592–603. Reprinted by permission of Prentice-Hall, Inc., Englewood Cliffs, New Jersey.

[1] I should like to thank David Rosenthal for his many insightful comments on an earlier version of this paper.

[2] Other things that might be meant are: (a) we know that certain moral truths are true because we know the truth of certain religious truths (perhaps, that God has revealed to us that the action is right), and (b) we have a reason to do what is right because of the truth of certain religious truths (perhaps, that God will reward us if we do). We will not discuss these claims in this paper.

[3] We leave aside, for this paper, the question as to exactly what was the argument in the *Euthyphro*. On that issue, see R. Sharvy's 'Euthyphro 9d–11b', *Nous* (1972) which influenced the way I constructed the argument to be considered below.

I should like to show (a) that the general argument suggested by the *Euthyphro* is not as persuasive as it is ordinarily thought to be, and (b) that it is even less persuasive when we see the religious claim applied to specific moral issues, and that this is so because the claims about the will of God can be supplemented by additional theological claims.

I

Let us begin by looking at the argument more carefully. We shall formulate it as follows:

(1) Let us suppose that it is the case that there is some action *A* that is right (wrong) only because God wants us to do (refrain from doing) it.

(2) There must be some reason for God's wanting us to do (refrain from doing) *A*, some reason that does not involve God's wanting us to do (refrain from doing) it.

(3) Therefore, that reason must also be a reason why *A* is right (wrong).

(4) So we have a contradiction, (1) is false, and either there are no actions that are right (wrong) because God wants us to do (refrain from doing) them or, if there are such actions, that is not the only reason why those actions are right (wrong).

What can be said by way of defense on (2)? The basic idea behind it seems to be the following: if God wanted us to do (refrain from doing) *A*, but he had no reason for that want that was independent of his act of wanting, then his act of wanting would be an arbitrary act, one that entails some imperfection in him. But God is a perfect being. Therefore, he must have some reason for wanting us to do (refrain from doing) *A*, some reason that is, of course independent of that want of his. Now it is not entirely clear that this argument is sound, for it is not clear that the performance by an agent of an arbitrary act (even an arbitrary act of willing) entails some imperfection in the agent.[4] But we shall let that issue pass for now and focus, for the moment, on the crucial step (3).

It is clear that step (3) must rest upon some principle like the following:[5]

(Trans.) If *p* because of *q* and *q* because of *r*, then *p* because of *r*.

---

[4] This is a claim that would certainly be denied by writers in the Calvinist tradition. Thus, Jonathan Edwards, writes as follows in connection with the question of salvation and damnation:

> It is meet that God should order all these things according to his own pleasure. By reason of his greatness and glory, by which he is infinitely above all, he is worthy to be sovereign, and that his pleasure should in all things take place. (*Jonathan Edwards* (Hill and Wang: 1935) p. 119).

[5] It could, of course, rest upon the weaker principle, that only held in cases where *q* was some agent's wanting something. But all of the points we will make are equally applicable to this weaker principle.

There are two things that should be noted about this principle. The first is that if we are to use it in our context we will have to take it as ranging over different types of cases in which we say 'because'. After all, there are significant differences between cases in which we make claims of the form '*A* is right (wrong) because God wants us to do (refrain from doing) *A*' and cases in which we make claims of the form 'God wants us to do (refrain from doing) *A* because *r*', for it is only in the latter type of case that we have the reason-for-wanting, 'because'. The second point is that there are real problems with this principle. While Joe may go home because his wife wants him to do so, and she may want him to do so because she wants to have it out with him, it may well not be the case that he goes home because she wants to have it out with him. So the principle is going to need some modifying, and it is not clear how one is to do this while still preserving the inference from (1) and (2) to (3).

Still, let us suppose that this can be done. Our argument faces the following further objection: God's wanting us to do (refrain from doing) *A* is not the whole of the reason why the action is right (wrong); the additional part of the reason is that he is our creator to whom we owe obedience. And when we take into account the full reason, the argument collapses. After all, the *Euthyphro* argument would then run as follows:

(1′) Let us suppose that there is some action *A* that is right (wrong) only because God wants us to do (refrain from doing) *A* and he is our creator to whom we owe obedience.

(2′) There must be some reason for God's wanting us to do (refrain from doing) *A*, some reason that does not involve God's wanting us to do (refrain from doing) *A*.

(3′) Therefore, that reason must also be a reason why *A* is right (wrong).

(4′) So we have a contradiction, (1′) is false, and either there are no actions that are right (wrong) because God, who is our creator and to whom we owe obedience, wants us to do (refrain from doing) them, or, if there are such actions, that is not the only reason why those actions are right (wrong).

And, even supposing that (Trans.) is true, (3′) would not follow from (1′) and (2′).

It is clear that the proponents of the *Euthyphro* argument have got to block this move. How might they do so? The most straightforward move is to deny the moral relevance of the fact that God is our creator, to claim that even if he is, we have no obligation to obey his wishes and that, therefore, the reason advanced in (1′) cannot be a reason why *A* is right (wrong).

Is this move acceptable? Consider, for a moment, our special obligation to obey the wishes of our parents.[6] Why do we have that obligation? Isn't it because they created us? And since this is so, we seem to have an obligation, in at least some cases, to follow their wishes. So, x's being our creator can be part of a reason for doing (refraining from doing) an action A if the other part is that that is x's wish. And if this is so in the case of our parents, why shouldn't it also be so in the case of God? How then can the defendents of the *Euthyphro* argument say that the fact that God created us cannot, together with some facts about his wishes, be a reason for doing (refraining from doing) some action A?

The proponents of the *Euthyphro* argument have a variety of ways, of differing plausibilities, of objecting to this defense of $(1')$. They might claim: (a) that we have no special obligations at all to our parents, (b) that it is no part of the special obligations that we have to our parents to do (refrain from doing) what they want us to do (refrain from doing); (c) that our special obligations to our parents are due to something that they do other than merely creating us, something that God does not do, so the whole question of our special obligations to our parents has nothing to do with the truth of $(1')$.[7]

But there is another move open to the proponents of the *Euthyphro* argument. Rather than attempting to object to $(1')$, they might construct the following alternative argument against it, one that has the additional merit of not depending upon (Trans.):

($1'$) Let us suppose that there is some action A that is right (wrong) only because God wants us to do (refrain from doing) A and he is our creator to whom we owe obedience.

($2'*$) There must be some reason for God's wanting us to do (refrain from doing) A, some reason that does not involve God's wanting us to do (refrain from doing) A, and some reason that is, by itself, a reason why A is right (wrong).

($4'$) So we have a contradiction, $(1')$ is false, and either there are no actions that are right (wrong) because God, who is our creator and to whom we owe obedience, wants us to do (refrain from doing) them, or, if there are such actions, that is not the only reason why those actions are right (wrong).

---

[6] This analogy between our obeying the will of God and the will of our parents is based upon the Talmudic discussion (in *Tractate Kedushin*, 30[b]) of the obligation to honor one's parents.

[7] Of the three moves, the third seems most plausible. But religious people might well respond to it as follows: let us grant that our special obligations to our parents are due to additional facts about the parent-child relationship (e.g., the way parents raise and sustain their children, etc.). God has those additional relations to all of his creations; and they therefore still have to him the special obligation of obedience.

The trouble with this move, of course, is that it rests upon the extremely strong assumption $(2'*)$, and even if, to avoid the problem with arbitrary acts of willing, we are prepared to grant $(2')$, there seems to be little reason to grant this stronger $(2'*)$ with its extra assumption about what are the types of reasons that God has for his acts of willing.

In short, then, the traditional argument that the rightness or wrongness of an action cannot depend upon the will of God rests upon some dubious premises, and things get worse when we add the idea that we have an obligation to follow God's wishes because he is our creator. There is, however, more to say about this issue, for there are reasons to suppose that some particular moral truths may depend in a special way upon the idea that God is the creator. We turn, therefore, to a consideration of these special cases.

II

Let us begin by considering a set of issues surrounding the idea of property rights. What is involved in one's owning a piece of property, in one's having a right to it? It seems to mean, in part, that while one may not use that property so as to infringe upon the rights of others, one may, if one wants, use it in such a way as to benefit while others lose. No doubt this distinction is unclear for there are cases in which it is difficult to say whether someone's rights have been infringed upon or whether he has simply lost out.[8] But the distinction is clear enough for our purposes.

How does one come to own a piece of property? One intuitively attractive picture runs as follows: if there is a physical object that belongs to no one, and if some person comes along and does something with it (mixes his labor with it), then the object in question belongs to that person.[9] He may then, in one way or another, transfer that property to someone else, who then has property rights in that object. Indeed, transference is now the most prevalent way of acquiring property. But all property rights are ultimately based, in this picture, upon these initial acts of acquisition through the mixing of one's labor with unowned objects. This picture certainly faces some familiar objections.[10] To begin with, what right does a person have to appropriate the ownerless piece of property for himself, thereby depriving all of us of the right to use it? And secondly, does the act of mixing his labor with it give him ownership rights over the initial, ownerless object or simply over the products

---

[8] Here is just one: let us suppose that I build a high wall at the back of my property, thereby depriving your yard of sunlight. There is no doubt that you have suffered a loss, but have I deprived you of any of your rights?

[9] See, for example, ch. 5 of Locke's *Second Treatise of Civil Government*.

[10] See, for example, ch. 3 of the First Memoir of Proudhon's *What is Property?*

(if any) of his interaction with it? But we shall leave aside these worries for now and suppose that something like this account is correct, for the question that we want to consider is whether or not it would have to be modified in light of any theological truths.

This picture clearly presupposes that, if there is such a thing as property owned by human beings, then there was, at least at one point in human history, such a thing as ownerless property, property that one could acquire if one mixed one's labor with it. But suppose that the universe was created by a personal God. Then, it might well be argued, he owns the whole universe, and there is not, and never has been, such a thing as ownerless property. Now suppose further that this creator allows men to use for their purposes the property that they mix their labor with, but he does so with the restriction that they must not use it in such a way as to cause a great loss to other people (even though the rights of these people are not infringed upon). That is to say, suppose that this creator allows people to take his property only if they follow certain of his wishes. Then, don't they have an obligation to do so, or, at least, an obligation to either return the property or to do so?[11] So, in short, if God, the creator, does wish us not to use the things of the world in certain ways, this will entail certain moral restrictions on property rights that might not be present otherwise.

Let us, at this point, introduce the idea of stewardship over property. We shall say that someone has stewardship over a piece of property just in case they own that piece of property subject to certain restrictions as to how they may use it and/or subject to certain requirements as to how they must use it, restrictions and/or requirements that were laid down by some previous owner of that piece of property. Now, what I have been arguing for is the idea that, if certain theological beliefs (that God created the universe but allows man to appropriate the property in it subject to certain restrictions and requirements that he lays down) are true, then men will have rights of stewardship, and not property rights, over the property that they possess. And if this is so, then there will be moral truths (about restrictions and requirements that property-possessors must follow)[12] that might not be true if these theological beliefs

---

[11] If the individual was aware of what these wishes are before he takes the property then it would seem that he has the obligation to follow them. But if he was not, and if they turn out to be strange and/or arbitrary, then perhaps he only has the weaker obligation, and then only from that time at which he becomes aware of what the wishes are.

[12] It goes without saying that what exactly these restrictions are will vary from one theological system to another. The cases that are of the most interest for current discussions of property rights have to do, of course, with those systems in which the restrictions require one, in effect, at least to take into account the interests of other people and not merely their rights.

were false. So we have here a set of moral claims whose truth or falsehood might depend upon the truth or falsehood of certain theological claims.

The question that we must now consider is whether or not the *Euthyphro* argument, even if sound in general, could be used against the claim we are now considering. How would it run in this context? Presumably, it would run as follows:

(1″) Let us suppose that there are certain restrictions on property rights and that they exist only because God, from whom we get our stewardship over the earth, has imposed them.

(2″) There must be some reason why God has imposed these restrictions, a reason that does not involve his wanting us to follow them.

(3″) Therefore, that reason must also be a reason why we should follow those restrictions.

(4″) So we have a contradiction, (1″) is false, and either there are no such restrictions or there is some additional reason as to why they exist.

As we saw in the last section, when we considered (1′)-(4′), even if we grant (2″) and (Trans.), (3″) doesn't follow from (1″) and (2″). Now even if we grant what we are reluctant to grant in the last section, viz., that (1′) is objectionable because the mere fact that someone created us gives us no moral reason for following his wishes, we would still have no reason for independently objecting to (1″). For if we have mere stewardship over the property we possess, then surely we do have an obligation to follow the wishes of him from whom we got our stewardship, and if God did create the world, then it certainly looks as though our property possession is a property stewardship gotten ultimately from God.

This point can also be put as follows. Neither (3′) nor (3″) follows from the previous steps in their respective arguments, even if we grant the truth of (Trans.), because the reasons they provide for the moral claims in question involve some other theological facts besides God's willing certain things. Now the defenders of the *Euthyphro* argument may try to attack (1″) on independent grounds, but it is difficult to see the grounds that they would have. So it looks then as though certain theological claims are relevant to certain moral truths having to do with the existence and extent of rights over property.

To be sure, the defenders of the *Euthyphro* argument might, in desperation, trot out the following argument:

(1″) Let us suppose that there are certain restrictions on property rights and that they exist only because God, from whom we get our stewardship over the earth, has imposed them.

(2″*) There must be some reason why God has imposed these restrictions, a reason that does not involve his wanting us to follow them, and one that is, by itself, a reason why we should follow these restrictions.

(4″) So we have a contradiction. (1″) is false, and either there are no such restrictions or there is some additional reason as to why they exist.

But like step (2′*) of the previous section, step (2″*) has little to recommend it. Even if a perfect God has to have reasons for wanting us to behave in certain ways, and, a fortiori, for imposing restrictions on our behavior, it is unclear why they must meet the very strong final requirement laid down by (2″*).

III

In the previous section, we have discussed the implications of the theological idea that God, the creator, owns the universe for the issue of property rights. It is sometimes felt that this idea also has implications for the moral issue of the permissibility of suicide.[13] We will, in this section, explore that possibility.

The liberal argument for the permissibility of suicide is stated very clearly early on in the *Phaedo*:

. . . sometimes and for some people death is better than life. And it probably seems strange to you that it should not be right for those to whom death would be an advantage to benefit themselves, but that they should have to await the services of someone else. (62A).

It will do no good, of course, to object that the person might have some extremely important obligations that he would leave unfulfilled if he committed suicide, and this is why it is wrong for him to do so, because we could easily confine the discussions to cases in which he has no such obligations or to cases in which he could arrange for the executors of his estate to fulfill them. And moreover, such an argument would really only show that one should not be remiss in fulfilling one's obligations, it would not really show that there was something particularly wrong with the way the person who committed suicide did that.

Plato himself does not accept this argument for suicide (although he does think one can accede in being condemned to death), and he is opposed to suicide on the grounds that we are the possessions of the gods. His argument runs as follows:

If one of your possessions were to destroy itself without intimation from you that you wanted it to die, wouldn't you be angry with it and punish

---

[13] R. F. Holland, in 'Suicide' in Rachels's *Moral Problems* (Harper and Row: 1971) discusses other ways in which the moral issues surrounding suicide are intertwined with theological questions.

it, if you had any means of doing so . . . so if you look at it this way, I suppose it is not unreasonable to say that we must not put an end to ourselves until God sends more compulsions like the one we are facing now. (62C)

Leaving aside the peculiarity of the idea that one ought, if one can, to punish those who succeed in destroying themselves—as opposed to the more reasonable idea that one ought to punish those who merely try,—the idea that Plato is advancing is that the gods' property rights extend to us, and that we therefore have no right to destroy ourselves unless they give their permission.[14]

There are cases in which many religious people want to allow that suicide is permissible. One such case[15] is that of the person who commits suicide rather than face being compelled to do some very evil act. Thus, in a great many religious traditions, it would even be thought to be a meritorious act to commit suicide rather than face being tortured into committing acts of apostasy. Another such case is that of the person who commits suicide rather than reveal under torture secrets that would lead to the destruction of many innocent people. Can these exceptions be reconciled with the argument against suicide that we have been considering? It seems to me that they can. After all, the crucial objection to our destroying ourselves is that we have no right to do so without the permission of our owner, God, and the religious person might well add the additional claim that God has (perhaps in a revelation) already given his permission in these cases.

Obviously, the *Euthyphro* argument cannot be raised against the claim that we are considering. After all, the crucial first premise[16] would be the claim that

(1''') Let us suppose that we cannot take our own lives only because we are the property of God, who created us, and he does not want us to destroy this piece of his property.

Then even if we add

(2''') There must be some reason why he doesn't want us to do so, some reason that does not involve this want of his.

we will not, even assuming (Trans.), get the crucial

[14] Plato here is assuming the overly strong thesis that we never have a right to destroy someone else's property without their permission. Whether and how he could get a weaker thesis that would still leave the argument intact is something that cannot be considered here.

[15] For a discussion of such cases, see the opinion of Rabenu Tam mentioned in the Tosafot glosses to *Talmud, Tractate Avodat Zarah*, 18a.

[16] Notice that the obligation to listen to the wishes of the property owner is stronger here than in the previous case. Even if his wishes are strange and/or arbitrary, that does not give us a right to disregard them and destroy the property.

($3'''$) Therefore, that reason must also be a reason why we should not take our own lives.

We can, no doubt, consider using

($2'''$*) There must be some reason why he doesn't want us to do so, some reason that does not involve this want of his, and which is, by itself, a reason why we should not take our own lives.

instead of ($2'''$), but it is no more plausible than ($2'$*) and ($2''$*). Nor can we easily object to ($1'''$) in the way that we did to ($1'$). Even if we have no obligation to listen to the wishes of him who has created us, just because he has created us, we do have an obligation not to destroy someone else's property, and, if God created us then perhaps we are God's property.

Having said this, we can now see that more is at stake here than a mere prohibition of suicide. For if we are the property of God, then perhaps we just have an obligation to do whatever he says, and then perhaps we can return to our initial general claims about morality and consider the possible claim that

($1'$#) Actions are right (wrong) for us to do just in case and only because God, who has created us and owns us and whom we therefore have an obligation to follow, wants us to do (refrain from doing) them.

So a great deal hinges on this point.

Despite all that we have seen, it is unclear that this argument against suicide (and, a fortiori, the more general claim just considered) will do. In the case of property rights, the crucial idea was that God, who created the world, owns all property, and this claim seemed a coherent one. But here, in ($1'''$), the crucial idea is that God, because he created us, owns us. And perhaps one can object directly to ($1'''$) that it is incoherent. Does it make sense, after all, to talk of an all-just being owning or possessing a human being? Isn't doing that an unjust act, one that cannot meaningfully be ascribed to an all-just being?

It is difficult to assess this objection. There is no doubt that the objection to the institution of slavery is exactly that we think it unjust for one human being to own another human being, to have another human being as his possession. But is it unjust for God, who is vastly superior to us and is our creator, to possess human beings? To put this question another way, is slavery unjust because it is wrong for one human being to possess another (in which case, both the argument against suicide and the general claim, with their supposition that we are the possessions of God, can stand) or because it is wrong that a human being be a possession, a piece of property (in which case, both collapse on the grounds of incoherence)? Religious people have, very often, opted for the former alternative,[17] and as it is difficult to see an argument to disprove their contentions, we have, probably, to conclude that theological claims might make a difference to the truth or falsity of moral claims concerning suicide, and perhaps to a great many other issues as well.

IV

There is still one final issue about which it is often claimed that theological beliefs about the will of a God who created the world are relevant to the truth of moral beliefs about that issue. This is the moral issue raised by vegetarians. At least some vegetarians argue as follows: we normally suppose that it is wrong, except in certain very special cases, to take the life of an innocent human being. But we normally have no objections to taking the life of members of many other species to obtain from their bodies food, clothing, etc. Let us call these normal moral views the conventional consciousness. Now, argues the vegetarian, it is difficult to defend the conventional consciousness. What characteristics are possessed by all human beings, but by no members of any other species, and are such as to justify such a sharp moral distinction as the one drawn by the conventional consciousness?

I think that no one would deny that there is a gradation of development between different species, and most would concede that this gives rise to a gradation of rights. While few would object to killing a mosquito if it is being a minor nuisance, many would object to killing a dog on the same grounds. The interesting point, says the vegetarian, is that when we get to the case of human beings, the conventional consciousness accords to them many rights (including the strong right to life) even though there is not a sufficiently dramatic biological difference between these species to justify such a sharp moral difference. Therefore, concludes the vegetarian, we should reject the conventional consciousness and accord more of these rights (especially the right to life) to members of more species of animals.

This vegetarian argument draws further support from the fact that the intuitions embedded in the conventional consciousness are about species. After all, there are a variety of extreme cases (newly born infants, severely retarded individuals, people who are near death) in which many of the subtler features of human beings are not present but in which the conventional consciousness accords to the people in question far more rights than those normally accorded to animals. This makes it far more

---

[17] This is evidenced in the Talmudic idea (*Kedushin*, 22[b]) that it is wrong for man to sell himself into slavery because God would object on the grounds that 'they are my slaves, and not the slaves of slaves'.

difficult to believe that there are some characteristics (a) possessed by all human beings, (b) not possessed by all animals, and (c) which justify the moral distinctions drawn by the conventional consciousness. So, the vegetarian concludes, we must reject the conventional consciousness.

There is a religious response to this vegetarian argument which runs as follows: when God created the world, he intended that man should use certain other species for food, clothing, etc. God did not, of course, give man complete freedom to do what he wants with these creatures. They are not for example, to be treated cruelly. But, because that was God's intention, man can, and should use these creatures to provide him with food, clothing, etc. This view is embodied in the following Talmudic story:[18]

A calf was being taken to the slaughter, when it broke away, hid his head under Rabbi's skirts, and lowed in terror. *Go, said he, for this wast thou created.* (B. Metzia, 85a)

It is pretty clear, once more, that the *Euthyphro* argument will not do against the claim we are considering. It is

(1'''') Man can take the lives of animals so that he can obtain from their bodies food, clothing, etc., only because God, who created the world and owns everything in it, intended that he do so.

and even if we grant

(2'''') There is some reason why he intended things that way, some reason that does not involve that intention.

and (Trans.), we do not get the crucial

(3'''') This must also be a reason why it is permissible for us to take the lives of animals for the sake of obtaining food, clothing, etc.

The crucial objection to this claim has to do with the coherency of (1''''). Let us suppose that we are not troubled by the religious claims discussed in the previous section; let us suppose that we find nothing objectionable with the idea that God owns us. Then, presumably, even if we are impressed with the vegetarian argument, we will find nothing objectionable with the idea that God owns animals as well. But we may still find (1'''') objectionable. For it, in effect, supposes that God's property rights extend so far as to allow the life of the piece of property in question to be taken by others, indeed, to so order things that this is done. And is this compatible with the idea of an all-just being? After all, even enlightened systems of slavery did not allow the slave-owner to

---

[18] To be sure, Rabbi is punished for his answer, but only, as the text makes clear, because he fails to show compassion, not because his answer is unacceptable.

take (or to have taken) the life of his slave. Does God's majesty really mean then that he can do even this?

We are straining here with the limits of the idea that everything is God's property because he is the creator of everything. When we applied the idea to inanimate objects, we saw that it could have important implications for the question of property rights. If we didn't object to applying it to human beings, we saw that it could (at least) have important applications for the question of the permissibility of suicide. If we are now prepared to take it to further extremes, it could serve as a response to the vegetarian's argument about animals and their right to life.

V

In a way, this essay can be seen as a gloss on the Psalmist's remarks that 'the earth and all that fill it belong to God.' We have tried to show that this idea may have important moral implications, and that it would therefore be wrong to suppose that there are no moral claims whose truth or falsehood may depend upon the truth or falsehood of theological claims. But it is, of course, clear that this is not the only theological belief that may have moral consequences. On other occasions, we shall look at other such theological beliefs.

X

THEISM AND MORALITY

ROBERT YOUNG

IN this paper I propose to give close attention to two recent discussions of the relation between theism and morality. It will be helpful first to sketch some of the considerations that have emerged from the many discussions of the relation between theism and morality and which form the background to the two recent contributions I shall discuss.

I

In the *Euthyphro* Plato raises the issue of whether certain codes, principles and actions are morally right or wrong *only because God commands* them or of whether, alternatively, they are reflections of God's knowledge that these codes, principles, actions really are morally right or wrong (in which case it would seem that they would be right or wrong independently of God). Euthyphro defines a holy or pious action as an action loved by the gods. Socrates tries to get Euthyphro to adopt the alternative view that the gods love certain actions because they are holy. In other words, he claims that the moral value of actions is independent of, and the cause of, the attitude of the gods to it.[1]

Of the various possible issues which people may have in mind when they speak of the relation between theism and morality, the issue discussed in the *Euthyphro* is the most significant philosophically. The others tend to centre around largely factual matters like: (i) Are certain of Yahweh's putative actions and commands in accordance with moral norms?—for instance, where he intervenes on behalf of Israel when she is not guiltless; in his savagery in the prosecution of war; in urging the theft of Egyptian property at the time of the escape from Egypt. (ii) Does acceptance of religious beliefs require concomitantly the acceptance of certain moral beliefs?

In general when the issue raised in the *Euthyphro* has been discussed

From *Canadian Journal of Philosophy*, Vol. VII, No. 2, 1977, pp. 341–51. Reprinted by permission of the editor.

[1] Throughout I shall presume the truth of an objectivist metaethic because the problems to be discussed only get any real grip when this presumption is made, a presumption which historically has been common to the most significant discussions of these problems.

by philosophers it has been concluded that Socrates was correct in defending the position he did. Doing a particular action, it has been argued, cannot be right *only because* God commands that it be right, since it is, first of all, perfectly conceivable that God could (according to Socrates and his supporters) have commanded that certain actions which are, in truth, wrong be right, but that this fact alone could surely not make the wrong action be right. Had God, for instance, willed that rape be morally right (or if God did will that Egyptian property be *stolen* by the fleeing followers of Moses—is expropriation of exploited wages theft?) his merely commanding it could surely not make it so. Since moral rightness is not (on an objectivist ethic) an arbitrary matter, if God is to command that some act be right, he cannot do so for no other reason than that he wants to, because this *would* render moral truth arbitrary.

Secondly, it has been argued that 'right' of 'ought' has a *meaning* which is independent of obeying God. For instance, William Frankena (in 'Is Morality Logically Dependent on Religion?' [Reading I in the present volume]) in G. Outka and J. Reeder (eds.), *Religion and Morality* (New York, 1973)) argues in the following way to show there is no logical dependence of morality upon a Christian, or other theistic, view. He contends that it is to muddy the waters to define religion so broadly that all ultimate views or concerns about the universe—theistic, humanistic and atheistic—effectively fall under it. Yet if one doesn't, then it makes sense to talk about entailments which flow out from some basic view of man which is not, however, theistic or Christian. To preclude such a possibility seems to be question-begging in favour of a logical dependence of morality on Christian, or other theistic, views.

There are two points which critics might make here to try to nullify Frankena's contention. First, it might be urged that Frankena's point is only about *meaning* and does not show that God's commands are not the *criterion* for moral rightness. If we waive any qualms occasioned by the introduction of the controversial meaning/criterion distinction the objector's point can be conceded. But it must be added that the initial point made above and much of my subsequent argument are directed specifically against claims about the criterion for moral rightness. Secondly, it has to be acknowledged that a theist might argue that while it *makes sense* to speak of entailments flowing out from some non-theistic view of man, it is only those which flow out of a theistic one that are *valid* (or, alternatively, supportable). And, of course, this may be so but, until we know whether it *is* God's commands that make actions and so on morally right, we cannot assess such a contention—the claims stand or fall together.

Against this background it may be wondered just why theists do object to the idea that such moral principles or codes as are supposed to be revealed by God are based upon his recognition of the independent rightness and wrongness of the actions referred to in the principles or codes. Basically it is, I suspect, because this would seem to entail that such codes or principles are not *essentially* theistic ones but merely ones supported by theists. Why this should be disturbing has not, I believe, ever convincingly been made out, though I would hazard that the heart of the worry is supposed to be that the attitude towards God's commands (displayed in accepting such a conclusion) is deficient. It may be clearer why believers wish to avoid subscribing to the alternative idea that such codes or principles merely reflect arbitrary commands on God's part as to how people should behave. This alternative must be rejected because the postulation of such arbitrary commands introduces an unreasoning, and hence imperfect, element into the conception of God.

II

There are believers who, faced with these alternatives and finding neither acceptable, have tried to chart a third position which does not sever conceptually all connections between theism and morality. Two very recent papers by contemporary philosophers have attempted to show that God's commands are not arbitrary, that they are indeed reason-based, and yet that actions are right or wrong only because God has commanded that people do, or refrain from doing, them. Each is worth close study because the thesis common to them is not only arrestingly controversial but subtly argued for.

Baruch Brody in 'Morality and Religion Reconsidered' [Reading IX in the present volume] in his anthology *Readings in the Philosophy of Religion* (Englewood Cliffs, N.J., 1974) argues that once we take account of the fact that God is the creator and therefore has special rights *vis-à-vis* the world and everything in it, including human beings, then we can see why certain actions which would not otherwise be right or wrong are right or wrong just because God has willed that things be so in his creation. Brody's argument may best be taken in stages.

In the first stage he seeks to undermine the objection that his contentions rest on the mistaken assumption that there is moral relevance in the fact that God is our creator. He attempts to do this by drawing attention to the special obligations he claims we have to obey the wishes of our parents[2] and arguing that these special obligations provide an

[2] There are interesting connections here with remarks by B. Williams in *Morality* (Harmondsworth, 1973), ch. 8; [Reading VIII in the present volume.] R. Swinburne gives his backing to much the same point in 'Duty and the Will of God', *Canadian Journal of Philosophy*, 4 (1974), pp. 213–27 (especially pp. 224 f.). [Reading VII.]

appropriate analogy for our obligations to our creator. One form of counter-argument to Brody here would be as follows: our special obligations to our parents are due to additional facts about the parent-child relationship (e.g. the way parents raise and sustain their children and so on). To this Brody replies that God also has these additional relations to all of his creatures, and, therefore, his creatures still have special obligations of obedience to him.

Brody also tries to anticipate a possible counter-argument which goes as follows:

(1) Let us suppose that there is some action, A, that is right (wrong) only because God wants us to do (refrain from doing) A and he is our creator to whom we owe obedience;

(2) There must be some reason for God's wanting us to do (refrain from doing) A, some reason that does not involve God's wanting us to do (refrain from doing) A, and some reason that is, by itself, a reason why A is right (wrong);

(3) So we have a contradiction, (1) is false, and *either* there are no actions that are right (wrong) because God, who is our creator and to whom we owe obedience, wants us to do (refrain from doing) them, *or*, if there are such actions, that is not the only reason why those actions are right (wrong).

Brody's objection is that (2) is extremely strong and that there is little reason to grant such a strong assumption which specifies the types of reason that God has for his acts of willing. It is, of course, only to be thought of as being extremely strong by those who deny that there could be any other right-making considerations than God's commands. There is no pressure on those who do not accept such a view to share Brody's intuitions about the strength of premise (2). So there seems to be no decisive barrier to someone's contending that even if there are special obligations owed to God because he is our creator, these could not be such as to require our doing any action which was not judged on independent grounds to be morally right. As with the case of our parents, to which Brody appeals, if our genuine, special obligations to them were to come into conflict with a particular more stringent moral obligation, if we fulfilled our filial obligations this would not be to act morally rightly.

In the second stage of his argument, Brody considers three issues where he thinks theological beliefs are relevant to moral truths. First he considers the idea that if certain theological beliefs (e.g. that God created the universe but allows man to appropriate the property in it subject to certain restrictions and requirements that he lays down) are true, then men will have rights of stewardship, but not property rights, over the property they possess. And if this be so then there will be moral truths (about restrictions and requirements that property-possessors must follow) that might not be true if these theological beliefs were false. For if we have mere stewardship over the property we possess, then surely, urges Brody, we do have an obligation to follow the wishes of him from whom we got our stewardship, and if God did create the world, then it certainly looks (according to Brody) as though our possession of property is a property stewardship ultimately from God. The second issue Brody focusses on is the obligation we have not to suicide (except where God expressly permits this). He urges that we do have an obligation not to destroy without his permission someone else's property, and, if God created us, then being God's property we should not destroy ourselves except with his permission. Thirdly, if God owns all the animals in the world this may provide the basis, says Brody, for responding to the vegetarian's argument against the killing of animals for food, clothing etc., since God may have given express permission for their use for such purposes by others of his creatures.

It is worth remarking one rather odd consequence of this account, namely that moral truth assumes a special sort of conditional status. The moral truths will be such *if* God exists and is our creator. (I am tempted to add 'and only if' here, but Brody may not wish to deny that there could be a possible world in which God does not exist but yet these moral truths remain moral truths—for reasons not depending on God's determining will. Even so he does often talk as if he is committed to a form of the logical equivalence thesis.)

Much more importantly, though, anyone subscribing to a position like Brody's has to hold that even if a perfect God has reasons for wanting us to behave in certain ways, and, *a fortiori*, for imposing restrictions on our behaviour, that such reasons need not be independent of his merely wanting us to follow his restrictions. Perhaps Brody is right that it would be difficult to show that such a claim is unsupportable. Nevertheless, I remain unconvinced and want now to indicate why.

There do seem to be occasions where one would morally be justified in using some property, which one was stewarding, for purposes other than those decreed by the owner of the property. For example, where one could use the property to alleviate some serious human distress while not depriving the rightful owner of a significantly disproportionate share of his overall property holdings, so to act would surely be morally proper.

As for Brody's second example, it is instructive to notice that he appeals to the principle that we have an obligation not to destroy someone else's property which, as he states his position, seems to be a principle true *independently of whether we are God's property*. Now it may be that Brody wishes only to claim that there are *some* moral obligations whose basis is in theological truths, though *not* that *all* moral obligations are grounded in such considerations (see p. 141 above). If so then it would be necessary to consider a further point which he himself raises, namely the propriety of speaking of God possessing human beings. He suggests that there are two alternative reasons why one might object to such possession or enslavement. One could hold *either* that slavery is unjust because it is wrong for one human being to possess another (from which nothing would follow about the morality of a vastly superior being's having property rights over and hence possessing human beings), *or* that it is unjust because it is wrong that a human being be a possession, a piece of property (from which it would follow that even a vastly superior being like God morally could not claim property rights over human beings). Brody contends that religious believers have very often opted for the former alternative and that it is difficult to see how to disprove their contentions.

But whichever of these claims about injustice is accepted, one could ask 'Is the matter referred to unjust *because* God has decreed that it is?' The answer seems to be the same for either—'no'—and the reason is that it is certain features about what promotes human well-being which reveal the injustice of slavery and these would hold independently of God's being our creator. Furthermore, it does strike me as a dubious claim that theists as such should opt for the former of Brody's alternative possibilities. This for the reason that in e.g. the Judaeo-Christian tradition believers are said to be *sons and daughters* of God, not to stand in a relationship to him of master to slave or owner to chattel. Such believers, who would seem to be prime candidates for those accepting a theologically based morality, would not have the reason for espousing such a morality which is defended by Brody. Thirdly, if we take seriously Brody's reliance on the *absence* of strong reasons for rejecting his constructions of a theologically based morality (e.g. against suicide), it would seem that it would be entirely *optional* to view morality as theologically based. That is, it would be permissible but not obligatory to do so. This seems to be a highly restricted thesis. Indeed, the thesis thus construed would preclude our deriving most of the moral principles needed for an adequate moral conceptual scheme. Finally, it does appear that there could be circumstances under which suicide would at least be morally permissible even though God had not expressly revealed that such circumstances were morally proper ones within which suicide would not violate his property rights. And presumably such cases would be morally permissible because of considerations quite independent of

God's determining, or even of his permissive, will. This, at the very least, would force the abandonment of any claim that a theologically based moral obligation was absolute. These third and fourth points do seem to rob the divine command theory of its natural interest.

Brody himself raises *one* serious worry about his third example, vegetarianism. His argument, as he acknowledges (p. 151, above), supposes that God's property rights extend so far as to allow the life of the piece of property in question to be taken by others. Even enlightened systems of slavery, as he points out, did not allow the slave-owner to take (or to have taken) the life of his slave. The trouble is that, having raised this objection, he fails to consider the further question of whether killing a sentient creature which was the property of another could ever be morally permissible even though the owner had not consented. Again, there surely are cases where, irrespective of considerations of God's will, this appears to be so.[3] (If this claim be thought question-begging against Brody, I could only say that I do not know how either side could hope to advance discussion of the issue any further because the counter-charge could equally well be brought against Brody.)

III

The 'modified divine command theory' of ethical rightness and wrongness espoused by Robert Merrihew Adams ('A Modified Divine Command Theory of Ethical Wrongness', [Reading V in the present volume] in Outka and Reeder (eds.), *op. cit.*) is a rather more subtle theory than Brody's, but I shall argue that it, too, is not finally acceptable.

Adams's starting point is that it is not logically impossible for God to command cruelty for its own sake. The central points of his thesis as he develops it are as follows: believers' claims that certain acts are wrong normally express certain attitudes toward those acts, whether or not that is part of the meaning of the claims;[4] that an act is wrong if, and only if, it is contrary to God's will or commands (assuming God loves us); that nonetheless, if God commanded cruelty for its own sake, neither

---

[3] By focussing just on the notion of 'private property' (and, indeed, in taking it to be justifiable) Brody significantly narrows the range of questions about the obligatoriness of vegetarianism. He effectively sidesteps what may plausibly be regarded as more urgent questions about the justice of our treatment of non-humans as well as the possibility that meat-eating should be ruled out or reduced for consequentialist reasons.

[4] Adams's discussion of whether believers' claims are claims about the *meaning* of ethical terms is very good (see especially section VI). Even so, as he points out, his remarks on the meaning of such terms as believers use, are readily detachable from the rest of his theory. (Because the believer shares a common moral discourse with unbelievers, 'wrong' cannot just simply mean 'contrary to God's will or commands'. But this, as Adams recognizes, is a general difficulty that applies to much else than merely moral discourse.)

obedience nor disobedience would be ethically wrong or ethically permitted; that if an act is contrary to God's will or commands that this is a non-natural objective fact about it; and that that is the only non-natural objective fact which obtains, if, and only if, the act is wrong.

Adams's theory is legitimately a (modified) divine command theory because ethical facts are facts about the will and commands of God (hence their non-natural status). The crux of his theory is that since a modified divine command theorist *values* some things independently of God's commands (though not his conception of *ethical* right and wrong), such valuations will be necessary for, and be involved in, a divine command theorist's valuation of God and his commands. Where a favorable valuation of God seems to be precluded (because the believer considers God has commanded an unloving action) the believer's concept of right and wrong would collapse. I quote from Adams (pp. 94–5, above):

... the modified divine command theorist also has reasons why he would not accept a divine command ethics in certain logically possible situations which he believes not to be actual. All of these reasons seem to me to involve valuations that are independent of divine command ethics. The person who has such reasons wants certain things—happiness, certain satisfactions—for himself and others; he hates cruelty and loves kindness; he has perhaps a certain unique and 'numinous' awe of God. And these are not attitudes which he has simply because of his beliefs about God's commands. They are not attitudes, however, which presuppose judgments of moral right and wrong.

One difficulty with this seems to be that if these *values* are, as Adams claims, not being *used* in the believer's concept of ethical wrongness, appeal could be made to them to override a moral judgment. Now Adams does claim to be explicating only the understanding of morality of one Judaeo-Christian believer (namely, himself). But it is also clear that he considers his explication catches the view of a wide cross-section of Judaeo-Christian believers. Typically, I would have thought, such believers share the conviction common among meta-ethical objectivists that moral values normally ought to be overriding. In certain circumstances it may be thought proper so to act that other values (e.g. prudential ones or aesthetic ones) are given precedence over moral values where the moral considerations are regarded as inconsequential. But it is usual to hold that *ceteris paribus* moral values ought to be overriding, unless their relative unimportance in the situation may be assumed. It seems pertinent to ask just what kind of values Adams takes his 'independent valuations' to be, given the possibility that they may be used to override moral judgments (even those believed to be commanded by God). Adams claims (p. 98, above) that

. . . (the believer's) positive valuation of (emotional/volitional pro-attitude toward) doing *whatever* God may command is not clearly greater than (his) independent negative valuation of cruelty.

Here a moral judgment is overridden by an independent value-judgment about the badness[5] of cruelty for its own sake. The suggestion seems to be, furthermore, that these 'valuations' are 'emotional/volitional pro-attitudes'. Underlying these pro-attitudes there presumably must be a reason why it is these rather than other pro-attitudes which the believer has. Adams does not seem to think the apparent irrationality of his valuations is important except in bringing to the surface problems of religious ethical motivation. But it surely is of consequence *why* he values kindness and the like. Perhaps (like Bishop Butler) he thinks we are just so constituted as to value kindness and be averse to cruelty. But if this is so we should, first, have been informed of this, and, second, have been given some reason for believing that the God who presumably constituted us thus would wish subsequently to command us to act against our inalienable preferences. This is, of course, purely a speculative remark. But it is, I think, worth repeating that Adams does owe us an account of why we do have the independent values he says we have.

As far as God's 'valuations' are concerned, Adams suggests (p. 102, above) that:

It hardly makes sense to say that God does what He does *because* it is right. But it does not follow that God cannot have any reason for doing what He does. It does not even follow that He cannot have reasons of a type on which it would be morally virtuous for a man to act. For example, He might do something because He knew it would make His creatures happier.

There are two points worth considering here. To begin with, it just does make perfectly good sense to talk of God doing what he does because it is right. This holds even if we share Adams's view that truths about God's loving nature are only contingent truths. Adams's failure to do more than assert that a counter-position to his own 'hardly makes sense' is a serious flaw. Secondly, if God's reasons for doing what He does are not ones based on the moral rightness (and hence, other things being equal, the preferability) of certain courses of action, it would be helpful if we had some idea of what His motivations could possibly be. Adams's suggestion that it might be tied up with e.g. making his creatures happier seems to betray a misunderstanding of the point of morality. For many, including Judaeo-Christians, promoting the well-being of humans (and perhaps all sentient creatures) *is* the whole point, or a large part of the point, of having moral principles at all.

[5] It must be the 'badness' not the 'wrongness' to which Adams appeals.

The final criticism I want to make concerns Adams's suggestion that the believer's moral concepts would break down if God commanded cruelty for its own sake. One would have though that on Adams's theory a believer's judgments about the moral nature of God would be formed because of the obvious coincidence of God's actions with his commands (these latter being the measure of moral rightness). The proper response then for someone like Adams to God's commanding cruelty for its own sake (presuming that the evidence for the command actually having been given is incontrovertible) would be either that God had temporarily forsaken his other qualities (omniscience, etc.) or that he (the believer) had previously had a mistaken conception of the morally right as excluding cruelty for its own sake. The former presumably Adams would find unacceptable, yet it is hard to see how conceptual break-down could be confined to the believer's *moral* concepts. For given that the believer would, on Adams's construction, be forced to back his own independent valuations over and against the pro-cruelty pronouncement of a (contingently) wholly good but also all-knowing, etc., being, the believer would seem to be forced into a position where he gambles that his own independent valuations are more reliable than the deliberations of an all-knowing God[6] viewing things *sub specie aeternitatis*. A believer forced into such a position, and not regarding himself as duty-bound to endorse God's pronouncement, would surely end up having to jettison some others of his beliefs about God (whether or not the beliefs were about attributes supposed only to be contingently true of God).

The upshot of my consideration of the views of Brody and Adams is that their attempts to occupy the middle ground represent no gain for the Judaeo-Christian theist. The believer who accepts that God knows perfectly what is morally right and wrong (though not because it is his willing or commanding that makes actions morally right and wrong) does not appear to lose anything of theological consequence. Where there is evidence that God has willed something, it should be possible to establish the moral rightness of what he has willed by attending to those features which are right-making for actions. That God has willed such an action would provide a reason for doing it, but the reason would not have force independent of the pre-existing moral rightness of the action. There seems, then, to be theological *gain* in being free of the difficulties I have claimed beset even the most subtle versions of divine command theories. Furthermore, there seems to me to be no theological *loss* in

---

[6] Even though I do not think his own position can be sustained, R. Swinburne does draw attention to the importance of God's omniscient nature in determining what God morally can will. See 'Duty and the Will of God', *op. cit.*, pp. 128 f., above.

endorsing the Socratic position on the relation between moral truth and the divine will. God's stature as wholly good is in no way diminished and the overridingness of moral truth is not called into question.[7]

[7] I am grateful to John Kleinig, Bruce Langtry and Paul Helm for their vigorous but much appreciated criticism of a draft of this essay. I have continued to go my own way on some matters.

XI

THE MORAL LAW AND THE LAW OF GOD

PETER GEACH

IN modern ethical treatises we find hardly any mention of God; and the idea that if there really is a God, his commandments might be morally relevant is wont to be dismissed by a short and simple argument that is generally regarded as irrefutable. 'If what God commands *is not* right, then the fact of his commanding it is no moral reason for obedience, though it may in that case be dangerous to disobey. And if what God commands *is* right, even so it is not God's commanding it that makes it right; on the contrary, God as a moral being would command only what was right apart from his commanding it. So God has no essential place in the foundations of morals.'

The use of this argument is not confined to a recent or narrowly local school of philosophers; it was used by the British Idealists when they dominated British philosophy, and, as we shall see, it was used much earlier than that. Nor is its use confined to people who do not believe in God; on one occasion when I attacked the argument, my chief opponents were not atheists but professing Christians. This is not surprising; for the argument was used by Christians of an earlier generation, the Cambridge Platonists, as a stick to beat that dreadful man Hobbes with. (I shall have more to say about Hobbes later on.) And they in turn got the argument from Plato's *Euthyphro*.

Let me summarize that dialogue. Euthyphro and Socrates are discussing the trial in which Euthyphro is to appear as prosecutor of his own father. Euthyphro's father had tied up a peasant who killed another peasant in a drunken brawl, notified the authorities, thrown the prisoner into a ditch, and put the matter out of his mind; meanwhile the prisoner died of hunger and cold. Euthyphro (Mr. Right-mind, as Bunyan might have called him) feared lest the gods might punish him if he sat at meat with a man who had done such a deed, unless he set matters right by prosecuting the offender. He must have known that this would be an ineffectual gesture; the old-fashioned Homeric idea that Zeus will punish men for callous insolence to the poor was not going to impress the Athenian court.

From *God and the Soul* (1969), pp. 117–29. Reprinted by permission of Routledge & Kegan Paul Ltd.

Socrates (that is, I presume, Plato) finds it outrageous that a man prosecutes his own father over the death of a no-good peasant (he reiterates this term '*thēs*' to rub it in how little the man's death mattered) and he tries to dissuade Euthyphro by tricky arguments, in a style much admired and imitated by modern moral philosophers. Euthyphro is easily tied in knots by asking him whether pious deeds are pious because they please the gods, or please the gods because they are pious deeds; whether men ever disagree except about moral matters, for which there is no decision procedure like arithmetical calculation or physical measurements; and so on. But Mr. Right-mind is not convinced; again and again he cuts himself loose from these dialectical knots with the assertion that it doesn't matter who was the murderer and what relation he was to the prosecutor and whether the victim was a peasant, but only whether a man was foully done to death in a way that all the gods must hate. The dialogue ends with Euthyphro telling Socrates he has no more time for discussion and going off on his legal business.

Was this, as the received view represents, a victory for Socrates? Or was it a victory for simple piety over sophistical tricks? Euthyphro admittedly had one weak point: he believed in many gods who were sometimes at variance with one another and so might command different things. But this is irrelevant for our purposes; for Euthyphro's unswerving fidelity to the divine law would be no less objectionable to modern moral philosophers if he had believed in one God. The main issue is whether a man's moral code ought to be influenced in this way by beliefs about Divine commands.

In the first place, I want to reject a view—which some Christians have at least approached—that all our appraisals of good and bad logically depend on knowledge of God. To get a clear and indisputable example I shall take a bad sort of act. For there is a logical asymmetry between good and bad acts: an act is good only if everything about it is good, but may be bad if *anything* about it is bad; so it might be risky to say we knew an act to be good *sans phrase*, rather than to have some good features. But there is no such risk in saying that we know certain kind of act to be bad. Lying, for example, is bad, and we all know this; giving a man the lie is a deadly insult the world over.

If a philosopher says he doubts whether there is anything objectionable in the practice of lying, he is not to be heard. Perhaps he is not sincere in what he says; perhaps his understanding is debauched by wickedness; perhaps, as often happens to philosophers, he has been deluded by a fallacious argument into denying what he really knows to be the case. Anyhow, it does not lie in his mouth to say that here I am abandoning argument for abuse; there is something logically incongruous to use Newman's phrase, if we take the word of a Professor of Lying that he does not lie. Let me emphasize that I am not saying a sane and honest man must think one should *never* lie; but I say that, even if he thinks lying is sometimes a necessary evil, a sane and honest man must think it an evil.

Now it is logically impossible that our knowledge that lying is bad should depend on revelation. For obviously a revelation from a deity whose 'goodness' did not include any objection to lying would be worthless; and indeed, so far from getting our knowledge that lying is bad from revelation, we may use this knowledge to test alleged revelations. Xenophanes rejected traditional Greek religious beliefs because the gods were represented as liars and cheats; and (if Browning could be trusted) it would be a fatal objection to the claims of the Druses' Messiah Hakim that he commanded his followers to lie about their religion under persecution. It is not that it would be too dreadful to believe in mendacious deities; a revelation destroys its own credibility if it is admitted to come from deities or from a prophet who may lie. We know lying to be bad before needing to examine any alleged revelation. Sir Arnold Lunn has jeered at unbelievers for esteeming truthfulness apart from any supernatural hopes or fears, and has quoted with approval a remark of Belloc that one can't be loyal to an abstraction like truth; a pagan Greek would have retorted that Lunn and Belloc were *akolastoi*, incorrigibly wicked, if they could not see directly the badness of lying.

The knowledge of God is thus *not* prerequisite to our having *any* moral knowledge. I shall argue however that we do need it in order to see that we must not do evil that good may come, and that this principle actually follows from a certain conception of God. If I can make this out, the sophistry from which I started will have been completely refuted; for accepting or rejecting this principle makes an enormous difference to one's moral code.

I must first clear up an ambiguity in the phrase 'doing evil that good may come'. We cannot ask whether e.g. Caesar's death was a good or bad *thing to happen*; there are *various* titles under which it may be called good or bad. One might very well say e.g. that a violent death was a bad *thing to happen to a living organism* but a good *thing to happen to a man who claimed divine worship*, and this would again leave it open whether doing Caesar to death was a good or bad *thing to do* for Brutus and the rest. Now when I speak of 'not doing evil that good may come', what I mean is that certain sorts of act are such *bad things to do* that they must never be done to secure any good or avoid any evil. For A to kill a man or cut off his arm is not necessarily a *bad thing to do*, though it is necessarily bad that such a thing should happen to a living organism.

Only by a fallacy of equivocation can people argue that if you accept the principle of not doing evil that good may come, then you must be against capital punishment and surgical operations.

Suppose that A and B are agreed that adultery is a bad sort of behaviour, but that A accepts the principle of not doing evil that good may come, whereas B rejects it. Then in A's moral deliberations adultery is simply out: as Aristotle said, there can be no deliberating when and how and with whom to commit it (EN 1107a16). For B, on the other hand, the *prima facie* objection to adultery is defeasible, and in some circumstances he may decide: Here and now adultery is the best thing. Similarly, Sir David Ross holds that the objection to punishing the innocent, viz. that then we are not 'respecting the rights of those who have respected the rights of others', is only a *prima facie* objection; in the general interest it may have to be overruled, 'that the whole nation perish not'—a Scripture quotation that we may hope Sir David made without remembering who was speciously justifying whose judicial murder.

It is psychologically possible to hold the principle of not doing evil that good may come independently of any belief in Divine commandments: I have already cited the example of Aristotle on adultery. We have to see whether this is also logically consistent.

We must first settle what sort of answer is relevant if a man asks 'Why shouldn't I commit adultery?'; only then can we see what reason against, if any, is decisive. One obviously relevant sort of reply to a question 'Why shouldn't I?' is an appeal to something the questioner wants, and cannot get if he does so-and-so. I maintain that only such a reply is relevant and rational. In post-Kantian moral theory another sort of reply has been offered as relevant—an appeal not to an agent's Inclinations but to his Sense of Duty. Now indeed you can so train a man that 'You *must* not', said in a peculiar manner, strikes him as a sufficient answer to 'Why shouldn't I?'; he may feel a peculiar awe at hearing this from others, or even on saying it himself; it may even be part of the training to make him think he *must* not ask why he *must* not. (Cf. Lewis Carroll's juvenile poem 'My Fairy'.) The result of such training is what people like Sir David Ross call 'apprehending obligation'. When I speak of the Sense of Duty (in capitals) I shall always be referring to this notion.

Now, as we know, a totalitarian regime can make a man 'apprehend' all sorts of things as his 'obligations', if Providence does not specially protect him. But on the Sense of Duty theory a man so trained is admirable if he does what he thinks he *must* do, regardless of the nature and quality of his acts; for is he not acting from the highest of motives, the Sense of Duty? If a young Nazi machine-guns a column of refugees till he bleeds to death, instead of retiring for medical treatment, is not his Sense of Duty something to fill us with awe?

To myself, it seems clear that although '*You mustn't*' said in this peculiar way may psychologically work as a final answer to 'Why shouldn't I?', it is no rational answer at all. This Sense of Duty, as Bradley said (*Appearance and Reality*, c. 25) 'is empty self-will and self-assurance, which swollen with private sentiment or chance desire, wears the mask of goodness. And hence that which professes itself moral would be the same as mere badness, if it did not differ, even for the worse, by the addition of hypocrisy. We may note here that our country, the chosen home of Moral Philosophy, has the reputation abroad of being the chief home of hypocrisy and cant.'

Let us forget about the Sense of Duty, for I think it can be shown that an action's being a good or bad thing for a human being to do is of itself a fact calculated to touch an agent's inclinations. I shall here appropriate the powerful arguments, in the spirit of Aristotle, recently developed by Mrs. Philippa Foot. Moral virtues, she argues, are habits of action and avoidance; and they are such as a man cannot rationally choose to go without, any more than he can rationally choose to be blind, paralytic, or stupid; to choose to lack a virtue would be to choose a maimed life, ill-adapted to this difficult and dangerous world. But if you opt for virtue, you opt for being the sort of man who *needs* to act virtuously (just as if you choose to take up smoking you opt to be the kind of man who *needs* to smoke); moreover, you cannot decide at the outset to act virtuously only when it is not too awkward or dangerous or unpleasant—that is deciding not to have the habit of virtue at all. If, for example, you opt for courage, you may perish through facing danger a coward would have shirked; but our world is such that it is not even safe not to be brave—as Horace said, death pursues after cowards too. And if you opt for chastity, then you opt to become the sort of person who *needs* to be chaste; and then for you, as Aristotle said, there can be no deliberating when and with whom to commit adultery; adultery is out.

But somebody might very well admit that not only is there something bad about certain acts, but also it is desirable to become the sort of person who needs to act in the contrary way; and yet *not* admit that such acts are to be avoided in all circumstances and at any price. To be sure, a virtuous person cannot be ready in advance to do such acts; and if he does do them they will damage his virtuous habits and perhaps irreparably wreck his hard-won integrity of soul. But at this point someone may protest 'Are you the only person to be considered? Suppose the price of your precious integrity is a most fearful disaster! Haven't you got a hand to burn for your country (or mankind) and your friends?'.

This sort of appeal has not, I think, been adequately answered on Aristotelian lines, either by Aristotle or by Mrs. Foot.

It is just at this point, I think, that the law of God becomes relevant. I shall not argue as to the truth of the theological propositions I shall use in the following discussion; my aim in this essay is to show that *if* a man accepts them he may rationally have quite a different code from someone who does not. And the propositions I shall use all belong to natural theology; in Hobbes's language, I am considering only 'the Kingdom of God by Nature'.

If God and Man are voluntary agents, it is reasonable to believe that God will not only direct men to his own ends willy-nilly like the irrational creatures, but will govern them by command and counsel. The question is then whether God has given laws to man which forbid whole classes of actions, as human laws do. There appear strong reasons for doubting whether God's commands could be like this.

Laws have to be framed in broad general terms because the foresight of legislation is limited, and because the laws would be unmanageably complicated if the legislators even tried to bring in all the contingencies they could themselves forsee; nor can there be somebody always at every man's elbow to give him commands suiting the particular contingency. But God is subject to none of these human limitations; so is it not a grossly anthropomorphic view of God to imagine him legislating in general terms because hard cases make bad law?

It is not a question, I reply, of God's knowledge and power, but of man's. Man's reason can readily discern that certain practices, like lying, infanticide, and adultery, are generally undesirable, even to the point that it is generally desirable that men should not *think* of resorting to them. But what man is competent judge in his own cause, to make exception in a particular case? Even apart from bias, our knowledge of the present relevant circumstances is grossly fallible; still more, our foresight of the future. Some men, like Dr. Buchman's disciples, have claimed to have Divine guidance in all conjunctures of life; but such claims are open to doubt, and certainly most men are not thus favoured. So unless the rational knowledge that these practices are *generally undesirable* is itself a promulgation of the Divine law *absolutely forbidding* such practices, God has left most men without any promulgation of commands to them on these matters at all; which, on the theological premises I am assuming, is absurd.

The rational recognition that a practice is generally undesirable and that it is best for people on the whole not even to think of resorting to it is thus *in fact* a promulgation to a man of the Divine law forbidding the practice, even if he does not realise that this is a promulgation of the Divine law, even if he does not believe there is a God.

This is not a paradox. You have had a city's parking regulation pro-mulgated to you by a No Parking notice, even if you are under the illusion that you may ignore the notice and think it has been put up by a neighbour who dislikes cars. And similarly anyone who can see the general objectionableness of lying and adultery has had God's law against such actions promulgated to him, even if he does not recognize it as God's law.

This means that the Divine law is in some instances promulgated to all men of sound understanding. No man can sincerely plead ignorance that lying, for example, is generally objectionable. I am *not* saying that a sane and honest man must see that lying is *absolutely excluded*; but he must have some knowledge of the *general objectionableness* of lying, and this is in fact a promulgation to him of the Divine law against lying. And he can advance from this knowledge to recognition of the Divine law as such, by a purely rational process.

To make this point clearer, let us consider a modern ethical philoso-pher who says 'I do on the whole object to lying, but this is just a prac-tical attitude I take up—it is quite wrong to call it "knowledge"'. I do *not* say of him what I should of a man who professed to have no special objection to lying: that he is just a vicious fellow, or a fool talking at random, who deserves no answer. What I do say is that his very protest shows that he does possess that sort of knowledge which is in fact God's promulgation of a law to him. His erroneous philosophy will not allow him to call it knowledge; but that does not prevent it from *being* know-ledge—philosophers in fact know many things that their own theories would preclude them from knowing. And since he has this knowledge, he has had God's law against lying promulgated to him, even if he does not believe in God.

Thus, whatever a man may think, his rational knowledge that it is a bad way of life for a man to be a liar or an adulterer is in fact a pro-mulgation to him of the Divine law; and he is able to infer that it is such a promulgation if he rightly considers the matter. As Hobbes said:

These dictates of reason men use to call by the name of laws, but im-properly: for they are but conclusions or theorems concerning what con-duceth to the conservation and defence of themselves: whereas law, properly, is the word of him that by right hath command over others. But yet if we consider the same theorems as delivered in the word of God that by right commandeth over all things, then are they properly called laws.

There is a current malicious interpretation of Hobbes on which 'the word of God' would mean whatever the sovereign chooses to decree to be canonical Scripture. High-minded people are prepared to talk about

Hobbes with reckless disregard of the truth: the late Lord Lindsay, in his Preface to the Everyman *Leviathan*, perpetrated a serious garbling of Hobbes' text, giving the false text an air of authenticity by the use of antique spelling.[1] But what Hobbes himself says elsewhere is: 'God declareth his word by the dictates of natural reason.' As an historical footnote I add that a very similar line of reasoning is to be found in Berkeley's youthful sermon on Passive Obedience. The debt Berkeley owes to Hobbes is quite obvious: but no doubt a clergyman could hardly cite such an authority explicitly without destroying the edifying effect of his discourse.

But what if somebody asks 'Why should I obey God's Law?' This is really an insane question. For Prometheus to defy Zeus made sense because Zeus had not made Prometheus and had only limited power over him. A defiance of an Almighty God is insane: it is like trying to cheat a man to whom your whole business is mortgaged and who you know is well aware of your attempts to cheat him, or again, as the prophet said, it is as if a stick tried to beat, or an axe to cut, the very hand that was wielding it. Nebuchadnezzar had it forced on his attention that only by God's favour did his wits hold together from one end of a blasphemous sentence to another—and so he saw that there was nothing for him but to bless and glorify the King of Heaven, who is able to abase those who walk in pride. To quote Hobbes again 'God is King, though the nations be angry: and he that sitteth upon the cherubim, though the earth be moved. Whether men will or no they must be subject always to the divine power. By denying the existence or providence of God, men may shake off their ease, but not their yoke.'

This reasoning will not convince everybody; people may still *say* that it makes sense, given that there is a God, to defy him; but this is so only because, as Prichard said, you can no more make a man think than you can make a horse drink. A moral philosopher once said to me: 'I don't think I am morally obliged to obey God unless God is good: and surely it is a synthetic proposition that God is good.' I naturally asked him how he understood the proposition that God is good; he replied 'Well, I have no considered view how it should be analysed; but provisionally I'd say it meant something like this: God is the sort of God whom I'd choose to be God if it were up to me to make the choice.' I fear he has never understood why I found the answer funny.

I shall be told by such philosophers that since I am saying not: It is your supreme moral duty to obey God, but simply: It is insane to set

---

[1] Page xvi of Everyman edition. Lindsay's garbling confounds Law and Right of Nature; which Hobbes emphatically distinguishes in the very passage (c. 14 *ad init.*) that Lindsay claims to be quoting!

about defying an Almighty God, my attitude is plain power worship. But since this is worship of the Supreme Power, it is as such wholly different from, and does not carry with it, a cringing attitude towards earthly powers. An earthly potentate does not compete with God, even unsuccessfully: he may threaten all manner of afflictions, but only from God's hands can any affliction actually come upon us. If we fully realize this, we shall have such fear of God as destroys all earthly fear: 'I will show you whom you shall fear', said Jesus Christ to his disciples.

'But now you are letting your view of the facts distort your values.' I am not sure whether this piece of claptrap is meant as moral reprobation or as a logical objection; either way, there is nothing in it. Civilized men know that sexual intercourse is liable to result in child-bearing; they naturally have quite different sexual morals, one way or another, from savages who do not know this. And they are logically justified in evaluating sexual intercourse differently; for they have a different view of what sort of act it is. Now for those who believe in Almighty God, a man's every act is an act either of obeying or of ignoring or of defying that God; so naturally and logically they have quite different standards from unbelievers—they take a different view as to what people are in fact doing.

'But suppose circumstances are such that observance of one Divine law, say the law against lying, involves breach of some other absolute Divine prohibition?'—If God is rational, he does not command the impossible; if God governs all events by his providence, he can see to it that circumstances in which a man is inculpably faced by a choice between forbidden acts do not occur. Of course such circumstances (with the clause 'and there is no way out' written into their description) are consistently describable; but God's providence could ensure that they do not in fact arise. Contrary to what unbelievers often say, belief in the existence of God does make a difference to what one expects to happen.

Let us then return to our friend Euthyphro. Euthyphro regarded his father's act of leaving a poor man to die forgotten in a ditch as not just *prima facie* objectionable, but as something *forbidden* by the gods who live for ever; and he was horribly afraid for himself if he went on living with the offender as if nothing had happened. He did well to be afraid, the fear of God is the beginning of wisdom. To be sure, it is not all of wisdom.

The fear of God of which I have spoken is such fear as restrains even the wish to disobey him; not merely servile fear, which restrains the outward act, but leaves behind the wish 'If only I could do it and get away with it!' And, as is proper in a paper of this kind, I have confined myself to what Hobbes called the Kingdom of God by Nature. It is no part of our merely natural knowledge of God that we can boldly call

God our Father and serve him in filial love: we are his children, if we are, purely by his free gift of the Spirit of adoption, and not by birthright: and the fear of God for his power irresistible is at least the *beginning* of wisdom—without it there is only pitiable folly. I agree, indeed, with Hobbes that gratitude for God's benefits would not be a sufficient ground for *unreserved* obedience if it were severed from fear of God's irresistible power.

That fear is an ultimate suasion. We cannot balance against our obedience to God some good to be gained, or evil to be avoided, by disobedience. For such good or evil could in fact come to us only in the order of God's Providence; we cannot secure good or avoid evil, either for ourselves or for others, in God's despite and by disobedience. And neither reason nor revelation warrants the idea that God is at all likely to be lenient with those who presumptuously disobey his law because of the way they have worked out the respective consequence of obedience and disobedience. Eleazar the scribe (2 Maccabees 6), with only Sheol to look forward to when he died, chose rather to go there by martyrdom—*praemitti se velle in infernum*—than to break God's law. 'Yet should I not escape the hand of the Almighty, neither alive nor dead.'

The wicked can for the moment use God's creation in defiance of God's commandments. But this is a sort of miracle or mystery; as St. Paul said, God has made the creature subject to vanity against its will. It is reasonable to expect, if the world's whole *raison d'être* is to effect God's good pleasure, that the very natural agents and operations of the world should be such as to frustrate and enrage and torment those who set their wills against God's. If things are not at present like this, that is only a gratuitous mercy, on whose continuance the sinner has no reason to count. 'The world shall fight with him against the unwise. . . . Yea, a mighty wind shall stand up against them, and like a storm shall blow them away.'

XII

GOD AND OUGHT

DEWI Z. PHILLIPS

WHY should I obey God's commands? Many philosophers suggest that I should do so only if I have judged that *this* command of God's is good or that *all* God's commands are good. In other words, an acceptance of God's commands must depend on my moral judgment. I want to deny this. I am not denying that one can understand certain moralities without understanding religion or that God is sometimes the object of moral judgment. What I am denying is that the relation between God and what I ought to do is *necessarily* parasitic on moral judgment. On the contrary, for believers, 'good' means 'whatever God wills'.

But is it not obvious that what I have just said cannot be the case? If 'good' means 'whatever God wills', the question 'Is what God wills good?' ought to be redundant. Clearly, the question is perfectly meaningful. Must we not admit then that *we* are the ones to decide whether what God wills is good or not? I do not think so. Often in the theses of philosophers who argue in this way, 'good' is a blanket term under which all its complexities and variations slumber unnoticed. I want to suggest that that such arguments cannot account for moral situations with which we are all perfectly familiar, and that this failure to account for moral situations applies equally to religious phenomena. Let us examine these two shortcomings.

We are often asked in philosophical discussions on morality and religion to distinguish between descriptive statements and evaluative statements. One cannot argue from a descriptive statement about God to the assertion of an obligation to God. Because God is our Father it does not follow that his name should be hallowed. To think otherwise, these philosophers would have us believe, is to confuse the moral and the non-moral; to attempt to derive an 'ought' from an 'is'. But if the Heavenly Father has fared so ill at their hands, would the earthly fathers fare any better? The problem of the nature of the connection between the matter-of-fact status of being a father and the obligations children have to their parents has been treated by A. I. Melden in *Rights and*

From *Christian Ethics and Contemporary Philosophy*, edited by I. T. Ramsey, 1966, pp. 133–9. Copyright © SCM Press Ltd. 1966. Reprinted by permission of SCM Press Ltd. and Macmillan Publishing Co., Inc.

Right Conduct (Blackwell 1959). Readers will no doubt recognize many of his arguments in the following remarks.

Melden stresses the need to take account of the institution of the family in any explanation of parental rights and the obligations of children to their parents. The only weakness of an otherwise illuminating analysis is what I take to be an over-emphasis on what Melden calls 'the role' of the father. He concentrates too much on what the father does, and too little on who he is, namely the father of his children. But then Melden speaks sometimes as if this distinction is non-existent; as if what a father is can be explained in terms of what he does. This is especially the case when he talks of the father as forfeiting his rights. The child says to his father, 'You have never been a father to me.' If one fails to play the role of father, one sacrifices one's rights as a father. It must be admitted that there are occasions when we should say that a man is no longer fit to be a father, and we would not blame the child for disowning him. ('He drove my mother to her grave.') The trouble with Melden's way of talking, however, is that it makes it look as if being a father is a role that *anyone* can play. He points out, for instance, that the child may come to regard someone other than his natural father as his 'father'. But there is a difference between a natural father and a 'father' nevertheless. It is the ignoring of the connection between fatherhood and nature which constitutes and important gap in Melden's account. So many problems concerning the child-parent relationship cannot be understood unless this connection is recognized. So many of the obligations I have to my father do not depend on whether he has done things for me or even on whether he loves me. It is certainly not a case of tit-for-tat. ('If my father hits me, why shouldn't I hit him back?') I do not want to deny that imperfections in the father may lead to his being rejected by the child. On the other hand, many people would say that the rejection of the father is an imperfection in the child; that the child who loves his father only as long as he is a good father has an imperfect love of his father. ('You should not leave your father destitute in his old age.'–'But he never went out of his way to help me.'–'That doesn't matter.'–'He never tried to understand me.'–'That's not the point.'–'What is the point then?'–'That he is your father.')

'Because he *is* your father': what does this mean? Surely it refers to the fact that this is the man who begat you; this is the man to whom you owe your existence. There is only *one* such man. The sadness of those who never knew their fathers cannot normally be explained in terms of what the father has done. Neither can the restless desire to find a lost father one has never known be explained in this way. These sentiments together with the situations discussed above cannot be understood unless one takes into account, not simply what the father does for his children, but who the father is, namely, the man to whom the children owe their existence.[1] (Is not this the root of the analogy with 'God the Father'—One to whom I owe my existence?)

No doubt I shall be accused by some philosophers of having moved my argument from descriptive to evaluative statements. Evaluative statements are said to depend on my preferences or pro-attitudes. But one cannot understand my obligations to my father in terms of my decision that to obey my father is good. When did I *decide* that I have obligations to my father? Surely, the most natural explanation of my considerate conduct is, 'Because he is my father.' Melden is correct when he says that my father's rights and my obligations to him cannot be understood in isolation from the institution of the family in which these rights and obligations flourish. The distinction between descriptive and evaluative statements in this context is confused and misleading. Outside the institution of the family the fact that this is the man who begat me would not have the moral significance that it has within the family. As Melden points out, the embryological facts about a male parent do not yield the concept 'father' at all. We appreciate the force of a reminder of our obligations when someone says, 'Remember, he is your father.' He does not have to add, 'And you ought to give special consideration to your father,' since to understand what is meant by calling someone your father is to understand that one has certain obligations towards him.

It seems, then, that the status of being a father entails certain rights which the children of the father have obligations to satisfy. It is possible to argue from 'He is my father' to 'I ought not to leave him destitute' for example, since the understanding of the latter statement is involved in the understanding of the former. But here the dissenting philosophers could ask, If 'He is my father' means 'I ought to give him special consideration' why is it that I can come to a moral decision on a given occasion not to satisfy my father's rights? But the fact that I decide sometimes not to satisfy my father's rights does not imply that my father only has rights when I decide to satisfy them! Melden exposes the confusion between my actions which meet obligations and obligatory actions. I can meet my obligations to my father in a variety of ways. Melden calls these actions 'obligation-meeting' actions. But obligation-meeting actions are not always obligatory. Rights compete for satisfaction. Sometimes I decide that I ought not to give moral satisfaction to my father's rights. If obligation-meeting actions were always obligatory, Melden points out, many familiar moral situations would be distorted

[1] The distortions which result from ignoring this aspect of fatherhood were pointed out to me in discussion by Mr Rush Rhees.

or unintelligible. For example, it would be moral depravity to waive one's rights, whereas in fact we often praise people for doing so. Again, moral perplexity over competing rights would not be a practical problem but a logical absurdity. The question, 'What ought I to do?' does not make the right any less a right, for what one is questioning is not the right, but whether the right is a sufficient reason for action favourable to it in a given situation. The fact that we must decide sometimes what our duty is does not imply that there are no competing rights; it is these rights which make the decision difficult. Otherwise, what is moral tragedy, where, whatever one does, one is going to hurt someone?

Although Melden seems to contrast his account of moral rights with a religious account of morality, I see no reason why the lesson he teaches in moral philosophy cannot be applied to the philosophy of religion.

To understand what it means to call someone a father is to understand why his children act towards him in certain distinctive ways. To understand what it means to believe in God is to understand why God must be obeyed. Certain actions can only be understood in the light of the child-parent relationship. For example, the fact that I do not hit a man who has hit me is given new significance if I tell you that the man who hit me is my father. Other actions cannot be understood unless one understands that they are responses to God's will, as for example, the sacrifice of financial betterment in the vocation to the ministry. As in morality, in religion too, there are reminders of duty in face of laxity: 'Remember the Lord your God.' The prophets said this time and time again to the Children of Israel. There was no need for them to add, 'You ought to obey God.' They *knew* that because they knew *him*.

But what of the so-called trump card in the argument? If 'good' means 'the commands of God', the question, 'Is the will of God good?' ought to be redundant. But why should the question be redundant? God's will does not cease to mean what it does simply because it is questioned. We saw that moral rights compete for satisfaction, but here, the competition is not between rights *within* the same moral community, but between the claims of morality and religion as such. The believer who is not troubled by doubts and to whom life has been kind, does not ask, 'Is what God wills good?' When the question is asked, morality has invaded the realm of religion and the fight is on. The struggle begins simply because the will of God is questioned. It is important to notice, however, that the fight is not confined to one camp. If belief has doubts, so has unbelief: if morality invades religion, religion invades morality. For example, the believer may begin to doubt the goodness of God because of the death of a loved one. On the other hand, the unbeliever may, through the moral experience of his own inadequacy as a person, begin to wonder whether there is something important after all in the idea of divine forgiveness and salvation. The fact that the will of God is questioned does not destroy the internal connection between the will of God and what one ought to do, since when someone is torn between morality and religion what decides the issue is to be found not, as many philosophers think, in an independent moral judgment,[2] but in the nature of the decision; that is, in the relevant moral or religious considerations which win the day.

The religious concept of duty cannot be understood if it is treated as a moral concept. When the believer talks of doing his duty, what he refers to is doing the will of God. In making a decision, what is important for the believer is that it should be in accordance with the will of God. To a Christian, to do one's duty *is* to do the will of God. There is indeed no difficulty in envisaging the 'ethical' as the obstacle to 'duty' in this context. For example, a man may, because of what he takes to be his moral obligations towards his family, refuse to give up his job in response to what he believes is God's call to enter the ministry. The Christian would then say with Kierkegaard, 'Here there can be no question of ethics in the sense of morality. . . . Ordinarily speaking, a temptation is something which tries to stop a man from doing his duty, but in this case it is ethics itself which tries to prevent him from doing God's will. But what then is duty? Duty is quite simply the expression of the will of God' (*Fear and Trembling*, O.U.P. 1939, pp. 84-5).

At this point, I must warn the reader that despite my remarks hitherto, I am not arguing for a sharp separation between religious discourse and moral discourse. I cannot accept the account offered by some theologians which makes religion appear to be a technical language, cut off, alien and foreign to the language spoken by everyone else in the community. This picture is false and misleading. It cannot account even for religious phenomena such as the traffic between unbelief and belief. But more important is the fact that it fails to see the importance of calling religion a language or a way of life. Such accounts make religion look like a technique. But a technique in itself could never be a language nor a way of life. Religious doctrines, worship, ritual, etc., would not have the importance they do were they not connected with practices other than those which are specifically religious. When a man prays to God for forgiveness, for example, his prayer would be worthless did it not arise from problems in his relationship with other people. These problems can be appreciated by the religious and the non-religious alike.

[2] What would this *independent* judgment be?

Because of such connections between religious and non-religious activity it is possible to convey the meaning of religious language to someone unfamiliar with it, even if all one achieves is to stop him from talking nonsense. But one hopes for more than that. By the use of analogies, contrasts and comparisons with which we can journey so far, but must then discard in favour of others, one hopes to convey something of the meaning and force of religious language. It is not my purpose here to discuss which analogies can best be employed for this task. What I do want to stress is that despite the existence of connections between religious and non-religious discourse, the criteria of sense and nonsense in the former are to be found *within* religion. It is this religious meaning which the analogies, contrasts and comparisons try to explain. Just as Melden insists on the basic role to be played by the institution of the family in an explanation of the moral concepts he is dealing with, so I am insisting on a reference to the institution of religion whenever one wants to understand what religious people are saying.

One can be faced with conflicting obligations. Some of these may be obligations to God. Unlike morality, which recognizes that sometimes it is not wrong to decide against one's obligations to one's father, religion recognizes no circumstances in which one is justified in deciding against one's obligations to God. This is because in rejecting God's will, one is not rejecting *one* claim among many within an institution such as the family; one is rejecting the foundation of an institution. To reject God's claim is not to reject one of many competing claims in a way of life; it is to reject a way of life as such.

Many philosophers think that moral judgment is necessarily prior to religious assent. Nothing could be further from the truth, for as Camus says, 'When man submits God to moral judgment, he kills him in his own heart.'

NOTES ON THE CONTRIBUTORS

WILLIAM K. FRANKENA has recently retired from being Professor of Philosophy at the University of Michigan, Ann Arbor.

JAMES RACHELS is Professor of Philosophy at the University of Alabama.

PHILIP L. QUINN is Professor of Philosophy at Brown University.

NELSON PIKE is Professor of Philosophy at the University of California, Irvine.

ROBERT MERRIHEW ADAMS is Professor of Philosophy at the University of California, Los Angeles.

R. G. SWINBURNE is Professor of Philosophy at the University of Keele.

BERNARD WILLIAMS is Provost of King's College, Cambridge.

BARUCH A. BRODY is Professor of Philosophy at Rice University.

ROBERT YOUNG is Senior Lecturer in Philosophy at La Trobe University.

PETER GEACH is Professor of Logic at the University of Leeds.

DEWI Z. PHILLIPS is Professor of Philosophy at the University College of Swansea.

BIBLIOGRAPHY

I. SOME CLASSIC SOURCES

PLATO, *Euthyphro*.

AUGUSTINE, *City of God*, i. 20, 25, xvi, 32.

— *On the Trinity*, xiii. 10.

ANSELM, *de Veritate* (trans. Hopkins and Richardson in *Truth, Freedom and Evil* (New York, 1967), pp. 91 ff.).

— *Cur Deus Homo?*, i. 12.

— *Proslogion*, xi.

AQUINAS, *Summa Theologiae*, Ia 19; Ia, IIae, 91, 93, 94.

— *Summa Contra Gentiles* I, 95.

DUNS SCOTUS, *The Oxford Commentary on the Four Books of the Sentences*, Book II, Dist. xxxvii (trans. J. J. Walsh in *Philosophy in the Middle Ages*, ed. Hyman and Walsh (Indianapolis, 1973), pp. 601 ff.).

WILLIAM OF OCKHAM, *Philosophical Writings*, ed. P. Boehner, ch. XI (Edinburgh, 1957).

THOMAS BRADWARDINE, *De Causa Dei* (ed. Sir Henry Savile, 1618), i. 21.

MARTIN LUTHER, *The Bondage of the Will*, trans. J. I. Packer and O. R. Johnston (London, 1957), ch. V. 6.

JOHN CALVIN, *Institutes of the Christian Religion*, III. xxiii. 2.

RENE DESCARTES, *Sixth Reply to the Meditations*.

THOMAS HOBBES, *Leviathan*, Part II, ch. 31.

RALPH CUDWORTH, *A Treatise Concerning Eternal and Immutable Morality*, Book I, chs. 1–3.

RICHARD PRICE, *A Review of the Principal Questions in Morals*, ch. 5.

I. KANT, *Religion Within the Bounds of Reason Alone* (trans. T. M. Greene and H. H. Hudson, New York, 1960).

S. KIERKEGAARD, *Fear and Trembling* (trans. with an introduction and notes by W. Lowrie, Princeton U. P., 1945).

II. RECENT BOOKS AND COLLECTIONS OF ARTICLES

W. W. BARTLEY III, *Morality and Religion* (London, 1971).

A. FLEW, *God and Philosophy* (London, 1966), ch. 5.

A. C. GARNETT, *Religion and the Moral Life* (New York, 1955).

R. W. HEPBURN, *Christianity and Paradox* (London, 1958), ch. 8.

A. KENNY, *The God of the Philosophers* (Oxford 1979), Ch. 9.

H. D. LEWIS, *Morals and the New Theology* (London, 1947).

— *Morals and Revelation* (London, 1951).

W. G. MACLAGAN, *The Theological Frontier of Ethics* (London, 1961).

K. NIELSEN, *Ethics Without God* (London, 1973).

P. L. QUINN, *Divine Commands and Moral Requirements* (Oxford, 1978).

R. SWINBURNE, *The Coherence of Theism* (Oxford, 1977), Ch. 11.

I. T. RAMSEY (ed.), *Christian Ethics and Contemporary Philosophy* (London, 1966).

G. OUTKA and J. P. REEDER (eds.), *Religion and Morality* (Garden City, N. Y., 1973).

III. ARTICLES

R. M. ADAMS, 'Must God Create the Best?', *Philosophical Review*, 1972.
— 'Autonomy and Theological Ethics', *Religious Studies*, 1979.
— 'Moral Arguments for Theistic Belief', in *Rationality and Religious Belief*, ed.
    C. F. Delaney (Notre Dame, Indiana, 1979).
G. E. M. ANSCOMBE, 'Modern Moral Philosophy', *Philosophy*, 1958; reprinted in
    W. D. Hudson (ed.), *The Is/Ought Question* (London, 1969) and *Ethics*,
    ed. Judith J. Thomson and Gerald Dworkin (New York, 1968).
P. BROWN, 'Religious Morality', *Mind*, 1963.
— 'God and the Good', *Religious Studies*, 1966.
K. CAMPBELL, 'Patterson Brown on God and Evil', *Mind*, 1965.
R. CHISHOLM, 'Supererogation and Offence: a conceptual scheme for ethics',
    Ratio, 1963.
S. R. CLARK, 'God, Good and Evil, *Proceedings of the Aristotelian Society*,
    1967-7.
J. P. CROSSLEY, 'Theological Ethics and the Naturalistic Fallacy', *Journal of
    Religious Ethics*, Spring 1978.
J. DONNELLY, 'Conscience and Religious Morality', *Religious Studies*, 1973.
C. DORE, 'God, "Soul-making" and Apparently Useless Suffering', *American
    Philosophical Quarterly*, 1970.
— 'Ethical Supernaturalism and the Problem of Evil', *Religious Studies*, 1973.
D. EMMET, 'On "Doing what is right" and "Doing the Will of God"', *Religious
    Studies*, 1967.
D. D. EVANS, 'Does Religious Faith Conflict with Moral Freedom?', in Outka
    and Reeder (eds.), *Religion and Morality* (1973).
J. FEINBERG, 'Supererogation and Rules', *Ethics*, 1960-1.
A. G. N. FLEW, 'The "Religious Morality" of Mr. Patterson Brown', *Mind*, 1965.
R. M. HARE, 'Can I be blamed for Obeying Orders?', in his *Applications in Moral
    Philosophy* (1972).
S. KANE, 'The Concept of Divine Goodness and the Problem of Evil', *Religious
    Studies*, 1975.
E. D. KLEMKE, 'On the alleged inseparability of Religion and Morality', *Religious
    Studies*, 1975.
J. R. LUCAS, 'Childlike Morality', in his *Freedom and Grace* (London, 1976).
A. MACINTYRE, 'Atheism and Morals', in Alasdair Macintyre and Paul Ricoeur,
    The Religious Significance of Atheism (New York, 1969).
D. M. MACKINNON, 'The Euthyphro Dilemma', *Proceedings of the Aristotelian
    Society*, Supplementary volume, 1972.
T. C. MAYBERRY, 'God and Moral Authority', *The Monist*, 1970.
H. MEYNELL, 'The Euthyphro Dilemma', *Proceedings of the Aristotelian Society*,
    Supplementary volume, 1972.
K. NIELSEN, 'Some Remarks on the Independence of Morality from Religion',
    Mind, 1961.
P. H. NOWELL-SMITH, 'Morality: Religious and Secular', *Rationalist Annual*,
    1961, reprinted in I. T. Ramsey (ed.), *Christian Ethics and Contemporary
    Philosophy* (1966).   .
R. A. OAKES, 'Reply to Professor Rachels', *Religious Studies*, 1972.
T. PENELHUM, 'Divine Goodness and the Problem of Evil', *Religious Studies*,
    1966.

184   BIBLIOGRAPHY

D. Z. PHILLIPS, 'Moral and Religious Conceptions of Duty: An Analysis', *Mind*, 1964.

J. P. REEDER, 'Patterson Brown on God's Will as the Criterion of Morality', *Religious Studies*, 1969.

D. A. REES, 'The Ethics of Divine Commands', *Proceedings of the Aristotelian Society*, 1956–7.

P. REMNANT, 'God and the Moral Law', *Canadian Journal of Theology*, 1958.

J. L. STOUT, 'Meta-ethics and the Death of Meaning', *Journal of Religious Ethics*, 1978.

J. O. URMSON, 'Saints and Heroes', in *Essays in Moral Philosophy*, ed. A. I. Melden (Seattle, 1958).

INDEX OF NAMES